FUN WITH THE FAMILY ™

in KENTUCKY

HUNDREDS OF IDEAS
FOR DAY TRIPS WITH THE KIDS

TERESA DAY

The Globe Pequot Press

GUILFORD, CONNECTICUT

DEC 04

To Michael, Anthony, and Esta . . . intrepid travelers, all.

3 3187 00212 5694

Fun with the Family is a trademark of The Globe Pequot Press.

Text design by Nancy Freeborn
Maps by M. A. Dubé © The Globe Pequot Press

ISBN 0-7627-2287-8

Manufactured in the United States of America
First Edition/First Printing

Contents

KENTUCKY

N

LOUISVILLE

Henderson • 60
HUDSON PARKWAY
Morganfield
109
41A
41
WESTERN
KENTUCKY
60
Marion
641

Owensboro
54
81
231
GREEN RIVER PARKWAY
85
431
62

NORT
CENTR
Elizabethtown•
62
54
Leitchfield•
259
Mammoth
Cave
70
31W

WESTERN KENTUCKY PARKWAY

Paducah
60
24
Wickliffe
62
45
80
PURCHASE PARKWAY
Clinton•
51
45
•Hickman

Dawson
Springs
•Princeton

62
Lake Barkley

62
24
68

Mayfield
641
94
Murray•

109
Hopkinsville•
41
Fort Campbell•

62
PENNYRILE PARKWAY
431
Fairview Russellville
68
79
•Guthrie

231
•Bowling Green Glasgow
31E
South Union
31W 65
231

S
C

31W
62

31
S
CH
65

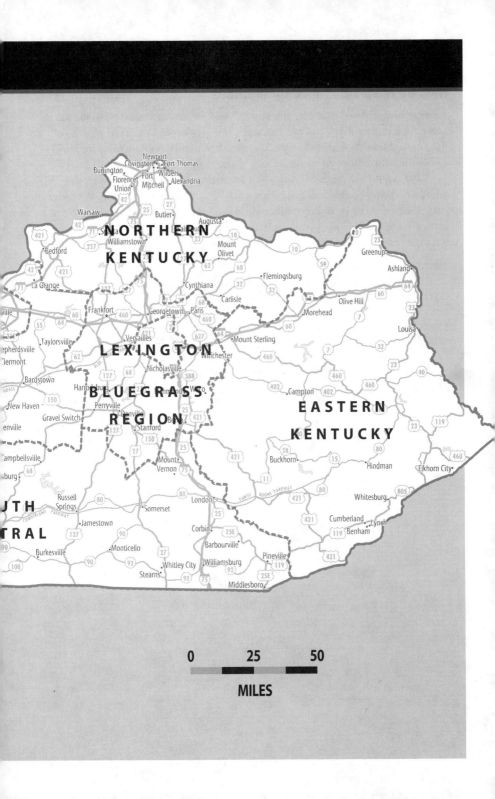

Help Us Keep This Guide Up to Date

Every effort has been made by the authors and editors to make this guide as accurate and useful as possible. However, many changes can occur after a guide is published—establishments close, phone numbers change, hiking trails are rerouted, facilities come under new management, etc.

We would love to hear from you concerning your experiences with this guide and how you feel it could be improved and be kept up to date. While we may not be able to respond to all comments and suggestions, we'll take them to heart and we'll make certain to share them with the author. Please send your comments and suggestions to the following address:

The Globe Pequot Press
Reader Response/Editorial Department
P.O. Box 480
Guilford, CT 06437

Or you may e-mail us at: editorial@globe-pequot.com

Thanks for your input, and happy travels!

Acknowledgments

Special thanks to Laura Crawford for helping prepare this information. Thanks also to the many friends and colleagues who shared their experiences and suggestions.

Introduction

Kentucky is a wonderful playground for families. With beautiful scenery and abundant recreation areas, a history full of fascinating events and characters, rich cultural traditions, friendly people, and dozens (probably hundreds) of amazing, quirky, and just plain strange attractions, Kentucky can provide your family with enough fun and discovery to last several generations. This book points out some of them, from places my children and I have returned to time and time again to others that I just learned about in the course of doing research.

One of the very best things the state offers families is an excellent system of state parks. If you want to get away, even for a day, you just can't go wrong with a state park. Kentucky has seventeen "resort parks"—one-stop vacation spots with lodging, food, recreation, and special activities—plus thirty-three other "recreational parks" and historic sites, all with many free and affordable activities. When my children were very young, sometimes we'd just drive to a park and visit the playground or feed the ducks, and it would be a great day.

This book divides the state into eight areas, two of them cities—there's enough to do in Louisville and Lexington alone for many day trips. Because ideas of "fun" vary widely, I've tried to include a variety of attractions—outdoor, historic, cultural, and recreational. Age appropriateness, too, varies from child to child. I've indicated general guidelines, but the best guideline is your knowledge of your children's interests and abilities.

Price ranges are based on the following guide:

Rates for Lodging

$	up to $50
$$	$51 to $75
$$$	$76 to $99
$$$$	$100 and up

Rates for Restaurants

$	most entrees under $10
$$	most $10 to $15
$$$	most $15 to $20
$$$$	most over $20

Rates for Attractions

$	up to $5 per person
$$	$6 to $10 per person
$$$	$10 to $20 per person
$$$$	over $21 per person

State and local travel departments are great sources for information, and I urge you to use them in planning your trips and while on the road. The local visitor center is usually our first stop. We ask a lot of questions and take an armload of brochures. In addition to the local tourism bureaus mentioned in each chapter, you can get information from the state tourism department by calling (800) 225-8747 or visiting www.kentuckytourism.com.

For state park information, call (800) 255-PARK, or visit www. kystateparks.com. Keep in mind that state park campgrounds do not take reservations—sites go on a first-come, first-served basis. Lodges and cottages, on the other hand, can be booked up to three years in advance, and sometimes are. That doesn't mean you can't get reservations. Cottages usually go first, but you can often reserve a lodge room a few weeks from your visit. As you might expect, summer and fall weekends fill up first.

My family has had a lot of fun in Kentucky. I hope this guide will help you and your family have a good time here, too.

The prices and rates listed in this guidebook were confirmed at press time. We recommend, however, that you call establishments to obtain current information before traveling.

Attractions Key

The following is a key to the icons found throughout the text.

 Swimming

 Animal Viewing

 Boating / Boat Tour

 Food

 Historic Site

 Lodging

 Hiking / Walking

 Camping

 Fishing

 Museums

 Biking

 Performing Arts

 Amusement Park

 Sports / Athletic

 Horseback Riding

 Picnicking

 Skiing / Winter Sports

 Playground

 Park

 Shopping

 Plants / Gardens / Nature Trails

 Farms

Louisville

Louisville is a good kid-size city—big enough to have a lot to see and do, but not so big that it seems intimidating. People are friendly, and there's an optimistic outlook—it seems like there's always something "new" in the works. In recent years, the new project in Louisville has been exciting redevelopment along the riverfront, which has added a new waterfront park, baseball stadium, and state-of-the-art skateboarding park.

Louisville sits along the Ohio River. The city was founded in 1778, when George Rogers Clark arrived with a group of settlers. Clark planned to use the location as a base for his "Northwest Campaign" against the British, but some of the settlers stayed behind. Today Louisville is Kentucky's largest metropolitan area, with about a million residents. Distinctive neighborhoods, great parks, and a comfortable pace make it a good place to live (I know; I grew up here). Those same qualities make it a good place to visit.

Another asset for visiting families is the diverse mix of attractions. There's a little bit of a lot of different things going on in Louisville, so whether your interest is sports, the arts, outdoor activities, history, horses, or just taking in the scenery, Louisville can fill the bill.

To help you in getting around, keep in mind that Interstates I-64 east-west, I-71 north-south, and I-65 north-south pass through Louisville. I-264 (Watterson Expressway) loops through the city from east to west (with exits to most major thoroughfares), and I-265 (Gene Snyder Freeway) connects the southwestern and northeastern parts of Jefferson County. There are one-way streets in the downtown area, so if you haven't been here before, expect to spend some time circling the block to get where you really want to go. If you get lost, just remember that friendly part: Louisvillians will be happy to give you directions.

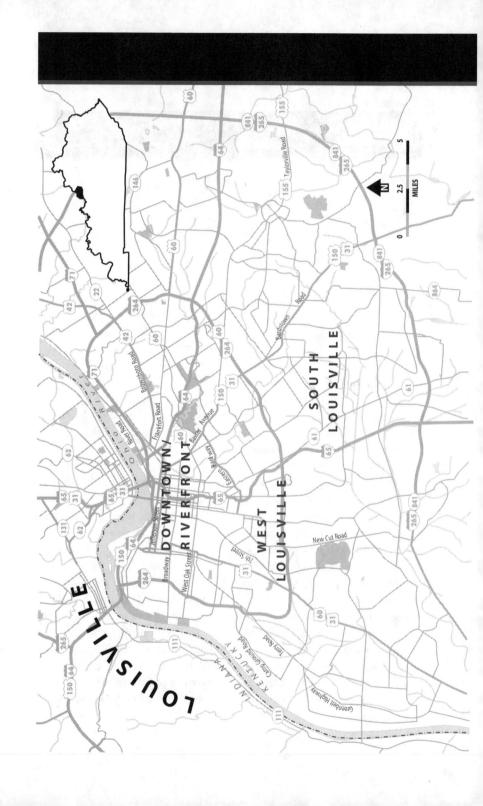

Teresa's Top Ten Picks for Louisville

1. Louisville Zoological Gardens, (502) 459–2181
2. Louisville Science Center, (502) 561–6100
3. The Speed Art Museum and Art Sparks, (502) 634–2700
4. Stage One Children's Theatre, (502) 584–7777
5. Riverside, The Farnsley-Moremen Landing, (502) 935–6809
6. Waterfront Park, (502) 574–3768
7. Gheens Science Hall and Rauch Planetarium, (502) 852–6664
8. Louisville Slugger Museum, (502) 588–7228
9. Cherokee Park, (502) 456–8100
10. Louisville Bats Baseball, (502) 212–BATS

Downtown/Riverfront

WATERFRONT PARK (all ages)
129 East River Road, Louisville 40202; (502) 574–3768, www.louisvillewater front.com. **Free**.

A fifty-five-acre recreation and event area with playgrounds (including separate ones for toddlers), scenic pools and fountains, and 2 miles of bikeways and walking paths, Waterfront Park can be a place to relax before or after seeing other downtown attractions, or a destination in itself. On a typical weekend you might find an antique Corvette show in the parking lot, a benefit concert for children with disabilities on the "Great Lawn," and a bevy of kite fliers and Frisbee players in between. Waterfront Park's current facilities are the first phase of a development plan scheduled to be completed in 2005. Phase 2, under way, includes additional children's play areas, a water play area, a plaza with an informal cafe, an amphitheater, docks for pleasure boaters, a community rowing school and center, and additional walking paths. In the final phase, an abandoned bridge will be converted into a walkway across the Ohio River.

BIKE LOUISVILLE (all ages)

Festival Plaza area, adjacent to Waterfront Park; (502) 589–BIKE. Hours vary seasonally; summer hours are Tuesday through Sunday from 11:00 A.M. to 9:30 P.M. $$–$$$

If you go to Waterfront Park, you will undoubtedly see people riding around jauntily in four-wheeled, foot-pedaled vehicles. Be prepared for someone in your crew to plead, "Can we ride one of those, puh-leese?" If you say yes, you can rent one from the folks at Bike Louisville. They operate out of a little kiosk near Joe's Crab Shack and offer the afore-mentioned "quadcycles," plus tandems, mountain bikes, kids' bikes, and beach cruisers. Expect some sticker shock (up to $24 per hour for the largest quad) and sore thighs. It's harder to pedal than you think, especially if you're the only one who can reach the pedals. Yet, if gigan-tic smiles and whoops of glee are any measure, most riders seem to find the trip worth the expenditure of cash and muscle.

RIVERWALK (all ages)

6½-mile paved bike and walking path connecting Waterfront Park to Shawnee and Chickasaw Parks in western Louisville. **Free.**

Best for hardy groups, this urban hike/bikeway offers views of river barges and bridges, a somewhat eerie passage beneath I-64, a scenic overlook of the McAlpin Lock & Dam, and jaunts through inner-city neighborhoods before you arrive at the tree-lined paths of Shawnee Park.

LOUISVILLE BATS BASEBALL (all ages)

401 East Main Street, Louisville 40202; (502) 212–BATS, www.batsbaseball. com. Season opens early April and runs through early September. Weekday games at 7:15 P.M., Saturday games at 6:15 P.M., and Sunday games at 1:15 P.M. $, children under 2 **Free.** *Parking ($) available next to the stadium.*

The Louisville Bats, a Cincinnati Reds affiliate team, take on other AAA competitors in Louisville Slugger Field, the new 13,000-seat sta-dium near the riverfront. There's not a bad seat in the house—especially if you're a youngster. You're close to the action, so bring your glove. In addition to watching the game, kids can ride the merry-go-round, hang out at the jungle gyms, get their faces painted, and be entertained by an assortment of costumed characters including Jake the Diamond Dog, Birdzerk, and Buddy Bat. Picnic areas abound, whether you bring your own snacks or buy hot dogs, sodas, and pizza slices on site. If someone on your home team is celebrating a birthday, call ahead to get his or her name on the Jumbotron screen. The playing surface, by the way, is Ken-tucky bluegrass.

EXTREME SPORTS PARK (all ages)

Witherspoon and Clay Streets, Louisville 40202, near Louisville Slugger Field; www.louky.org/skatepark/. Open daily 24 hours. 𝐅𝐫𝐞𝐞. *No rentals available. No rest rooms.*

If you want to convince your kids that you're still cool, lead an expedition to Extreme Sports Park (just don't call it "gnarly" or you'll blow it). Louisville's state-of-the-art "X-park" opened in April 2002 with over 40,000 square feet of bowls, pipes, ramps, and rails, and is already drawing rave reviews from extreme bikers, bladers, and skateboarders around the country. Areas are color-coded by difficulty level, but for most of us, just watching these stunts will be extreme enough. A second phase of construction will include an indoor arena and rest room facilities.

Mɔre for Sports Fans University of Louisville football
games are played at Cardinal Stadium, a 42,000-seat stadium near the campus in South Louisville. **The U of L basketball** team (coached by Rick Pitino, former University of Kentucky and Boston Celtics coach) plays at Freedom Hall at the Kentucky Fair and Exposition Center. For ticket info about both, call (502) 852–5863.

 STAGE ONE CHILDREN'S THEATRE (ages 4 and up)

501 West Main Street, Louisville 40202; (502) 584–7777, www.stageone.org. The season runs fall through spring. Performances are Saturdays at 2:00 and 5:00 P.M. and Sundays at 2:00 P.M. at the Kentucky Center for the Arts, 5 Riverfront Plaza. $$$

Louisville's oldest theater company caters to the youngest patrons. Stage One, a professional company, brings adventure yarns, classic fairy tales, fantasy stories, and thought-provoking contemporary dramas to life onstage. Plays are geared to a variety of age groups, from participatory drama for ages four to seven to plays for young teens that deal with complex moral and ethical issues. A recent season included *The Legend of Sleepy Hollow, Dr. Seuss' Green Eggs and Ham, Hansel and Gretel, Jemima Boone,* and *Dream,* a drama about Dr. Martin Luther King Jr. High quality and highly entertaining, Stage One is an excellent place to introduce your children to live theater.

KENTUCKY CENTER FOR THE ARTS (all ages)

5 Riverfront Plaza (Fifth and Main Streets), Louisville 40202; (502) 562–0100 for show schedule, (502) 562–0198 for tour reservations; www.kca.org. Performance tickets: $$$–$$$$; tours $.

At the heart of Louisville's performing arts scene since its star-studded opening in 1983, the Center for the Arts is host to performances ranging from touring Broadway shows to concerts and speeches. A tour of the center's three performing halls and some behind-the-scenes areas can be scheduled in advance (call at least a week before you want to visit) and is geared to the age group of participants. You can check out the fascinating contemporary sculptures found inside and outdoors anytime, free.

ACTORS THEATRE OF LOUISVILLE (ages 6 and up)

316 West Main Street, Louisville 40202; (502) 584–1265 or (800) 4ATL–TIX, www.actorstheatre.org. $$$–$$$$

Most of the productions by this nationally acclaimed theater company are geared to adult audiences, with a few notable exceptions. Older children may enjoy ATL's spine-tingling version of *Dracula* performed throughout the month of October. Even five- and six-year-olds will enjoy the annual production of Charles Dickens's *A Christmas Carol*. For these two holiday productions, order tickets well in advance since many performances sell out. Also, ATL's Apprentice Company usually gives a couple of **Free** children's theater performances in late July and early August. You must pick up tickets at

Amazing Kentucky Fact Superstar actor Tom Cruise, originally Thomas Cruise Mapother IV, went to high school at St. Xavier High School in Louisville.

the box office or order them by mail. Call or visit the Web site for performance dates.

LOUISVILLE ORCHESTRA (ages 3 and up)

300 West Main Street, Louisville 40202; (502) 587–8681, www.louisville orchestra.org. Dates and location depend upon concert series. $$–$$$$

In addition to its venerable Masterworks series for general audiences, which is performed at the Kentucky Center for the Arts, Louisville's excellent orchestra offers special performance series for young music lovers. There are several Saturday OrKIDStra performances

between Septem-
ber and May at
the Brown The-
atre. In July, the
orchestra per-
forms its
ROARchestra

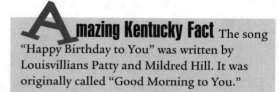

series at the Louisville Zoo. These concerts combine music with lively activities; past performances have featured everything from whistling to a petting zoo. Older children might also enjoy the Nightlites perfor- mances, which feature light classical music and are performed at The Louisville Palace theater on Fourth Avenue.

BELVEDERE/RIVERFRONT PLAZA (all ages)

Riverfront between Fourth and Sixth Streets. Free.

This eight-acre plaza is a good place to view the river. You'll see motorboats, huge barges, and a giant clock across the river in southern Indiana. The clock at the Colgate-Palmolive Plant is the second largest in the world. The Belvedere often is the site of concerts and special events.

BELLE OF LOUISVILLE/SPIRIT OF JEFFERSON (all ages)

401 West River Road (end of Fourth Street), Louisville 40202; (502) 574–2355, www.belleoflouisville.com. $$$, children $$.

A bevy of river cruise types and times are offered aboard the *Belle,* an authentic 1914 sternwheeler with whimsical calliope, and the newer *Spirit,* built in 1962 to look like a vintage riverboat. Most sightseeing cruises last a couple of hours and include a narrated presentation about Louisville history and river lore. The *Belle of Louisville* operates from Mem- orial Day until the end of October. While the *Belle* has some indoor seat- ing, keep in mind that the old gal does not have any air-conditioning, and a two-hour cruise on a steamy steamboat might be difficult for young children. The more updated *Spirit of Jefferson* cruises year-round. Both boats have onboard concessions and rest rooms.

LOUISVILLE SCIENCE CENTER AND IMAX THEATRE (all ages)

727 West Main Street, Louisville 40202; (502) 561–6100 or (800) 591– 2203, www.louisvillescience.org. Open year-round Monday to Thursday from 9:00 A.M. to 5:00 P.M., Friday and Saturday from 9:30 A.M. to 9:00 P.M., Sunday from 9:00 A.M. to 6:00 P.M. $$, check into the museum/IMAX combo ticket.

Here's more than 40,000 square feet of science and natural history exploration and fun, housed in a beautiful old cast-iron-front nineteenth-century warehouse building. Permanent exhibits include the highly interactive "The World Within Us," which lets children see how they will look in thirty years, exercise with a skeleton, and explore body systems at work, and "The World We Create," which challenges youngsters to build and invent. There's also a space gallery with a replica of an Apollo space capsule, bubble activities, Kentucky's largest indoor climbing wall, and the action-packed IMAX Theatre. If your children are under seven, be sure to reserve a forty-five-minute session in Kidzone (no additional charge, but ticket required). Kidzone is the playroom of your dreams—a huge water play area, dramatic and dress-up play areas, and creative building areas—with no way for your child to escape. (Your kids will love it too.) Don't be late for your session, though, or you may find yourself looking through a locked door with a very sad child. When it's time to break for lunch, head to the museum's Galaxy Bistro, which offers a good mix of kid food and grown-up fare.

A Little Too Much Adventure

Older children and adults love the IMAX film experience for its big, loud, "in your face" action. But before you take younger children, consider whether it might all seem a little too real for comfort. A friend took her nearly three-year-old son to see an IMAX film about elephants, thinking he would love it because he was obsessed with elephants. But when the huge beasts came thundering forward on the screen he was terrified — and at five, he still refuses to go to movies of any kind.

KENTUCKY ART AND CRAFT GALLERY & GIFT SHOP (ages 8 and up)

609 West Main Street, Louisville 40202; (502) 589–0102. Open Monday to Saturday from 10:00 A.M. to 4:00 P.M. Free.

If you like handmade crafts, your kids can tag along with you to this nice gallery. The permanent and changing displays showcase works by contemporary Kentucky artists and craftspeople. There's everything from quilts and baskets to ceramics, but youngsters will like the whimsical folk art best.

LOUISVILLE SLUGGER MUSEUM (all ages)

800 West Main Street, Louisville 40202; (502) 588–7228, www.sluggermuseum. org. Open Monday to Saturday from 9:00 A.M. to 5:00 P.M., Sunday from noon to 5:00 P.M. (April through November). $$, children 5 and under **Free**.

Any youngster who watches or plays baseball has heard of Louisville Slugger bats, and here's a chance to see how they're made. By the way, although the company started in Louisville in 1884, for a while "Louisville" Sluggers were actually made in southern Indiana. In the 1990s, the Hillerich & Bradsby company came back to Louisville in a BIG way. How big? Well, there's a 120-foot-tall, 68,000-pound bat leaning against the building that houses this combination museum/manufacturing facility. Plus there's a giant baseball glove holding a ball carved out of a fifteen-ton piece of limestone. Inside, exhibits honor the game's big stars and big plays. The ninety-minute tour begins with a moving film, *The Heart of the Game,* and includes visiting the "Ballfield," where you can sit in a dugout and step up to a virtual plate to get a sense of what it feels like to have a ball heading your way at 90 miles per hour. There are also recordings of the calls of actual famous plays, and bats used by big leaguers such as Babe Ruth and Hank Aaron are on display. A walk through a white ash "forest" leads to the bat-making factory. Go during the week to see it all: There's no bat production on Sundays and holidays or on Saturdays from December to March. At the start of the tour, you can order a miniature bat with your child's (or your) name engraved on it; it will be waiting for you at the end of the tour.

GLASSWORKS (ages 6 and up)

815 West Market Street, Louisville 40202; (502) 584–4510. Open Monday to Saturday from 11:00 A.M. to 4:00 P.M., from 9:30 A.M. in the summer. Tours begin every half hour. $$ adults, $ students.

Learn how three kinds of glass are made at this beautiful combination gallery and workshop. The one-hour tour begins with a short video, *Transformed by Light,* then takes you through the three departments—the Frameworks area, where glass is melted and sculpted; the Architectural Glass area, where stained glass is made; and the Hot Shop, where glass is hand blown. If you aren't too nervous at the thought of your children in a confined location with lots of fragile, expensive glass, take a few minutes to visit the gift shop.

Urban Bird-Watching While downtown, be sure to look for "The Flock of Finns," a public art display featuring the work of Louisville folk artist Marvin Finn. Known for his colorful painted birds, this octogenarian artist created twenty-eight metal birds ranging from 3 to 9 feet tall. The flock can be found roosting at various changing locations in the city. Get a sneak peak at www.flockoffinns.org. **Free**.

FALLS OF THE OHIO INTERPRETIVE CENTER AND PARK (all ages)

201 West Riverside Drive, Clarksville, Indiana, 47129; (812) 280–9970 (if calling from Louisville, area code not needed), www.fallsoftheohio.org. Open year-round, Monday to Saturday from 9:00 A.M. to 5:00 P.M., Sunday from 1:00 to 5:00 P.M. $. Take the Second Street Bridge from downtown Louisville.

Yes, technically, this attraction is in Indiana, but it would be a shame to be this close and not take advantage of the opportunity to go back in time 360 million years. Back then, the Louisville area was at the bottom of an inland sea; when the water receded, it left behind the fossils of hundreds of different plants and animals. This is, in fact, the world's largest exposed fossil bed from the Devonian period. The best time to visit is August through October, when the river is at its lowest level. The Interpretive Center offers a stirring laser disc presentation and an eclectic assortment of exhibits related to the history of the Falls of the Ohio, most notably a life-size diorama depicting area inhabitants through the ages (with the main attraction being a 20-foot mammoth skeleton replica). There's also a Lewis and Clark exhibit and hands-on activities such as building a bridge with Styrofoam blocks and making fossil rubbings.

Trolley Hoppin' The Toonerville II Trolley is a fun and **Free** way to get around downtown Louisville. Trolleys run from the riverfront to Broadway approximately every twelve minutes, starting at 7:30 A.M. Monday to Friday and 9:30 A.M. Saturday, with stops at major hotels and other attractions (call 502–585–1234 for route information). These reproduction trolley buses honor Louisville's historic trolley system and are named for the comic strip trolley made famous in the early 1900s by Louisvillian Fontaine Fox Jr.

CATHEDRAL OF THE ASSUMPTION (ages 7 and up)
*429 West Muhammad Ali Boulevard, Louisville 40202; (502) 583–3100,
www.cathedral-heritage.org. Open Monday to Saturday from 10:30 A.M. to 4:30
P.M.* **Free**.

Children and adults will be in awe looking at the 8,000 24-karat
gold-leaf stars on the ceiling, the ornate columns, and vaulted ceilings of
this beautiful Catholic cathedral, one of the oldest in the United States
in continuous use. But the Cathedral of the Assumption offers much
more than a
history lesson
in church
architecture. It
has become a
vibrant center
celebrating

Amazing Kentucky Fact Only New
York City has more cast-iron storefronts than
Louisville's Main Street.

spirituality and interfaith understanding. Visit the Spiritual Art Gallery,
which exhibits art from diverse spiritual perspectives across cultures, and
the Inspiration Gift Shop, where you're as likely to find a Buddha statue
as a crucifix. Or attend one of the many concerts or lectures offered.

Coming Louisville Attractions

- 2003: The Kentucky Center for African American Heritage, 239 South
  Fifth Street, Louisville 40202; (502) 583–4100

- 2004: The Muhammad Ali Center, honoring the career of one of
  Louisville's most famous residents, 1 Riverfront Plaza, Louisville
  40202; (502) 584–9254; and the Owsley Brown Frazier Historical
  Arms Museum, 4938 Brownsboro Road, Louisville 40208; (502)
  412–2228.

South Louisville

Leave the downtown area via Third Street. You'll pass beautiful Victorian man-
sions in "Old Louisville" and find yourself at the University of Louisville campus, location of two popular family attractions.

THE SPEED ART MUSEUM AND ART SPARKS (all ages)
2035 South Third Street, Louisville 40208; (502) 634–2700, www.speed museum.org. Open Tuesday, Wednesday, and Friday from 10:30 A.M. to 4:00 P.M., Thursday from 10:30 A.M. to 8:00 P.M., Saturday from 10:30 A.M. to 5:00 P.M., Sunday from noon to 5:00 P.M. Closed Mondays. Permanent exhibits **Free**; *Art Sparks Interactive Gallery $.*

When my third-grade class visited the Speed museum, I fell in love with the English Room. This complete room from a Tudor manor has ornately carved wooden panel walls and beautiful tapestries. I felt as if I had been transported back in time. As a parent, it was fun to see my own children discover and enjoy this room. Of course, in the decades (just a few) since I was a child, the Speed has added some things, like Art Sparks Interactive Gallery on the museum's lower level, a terrific place for children to explore their own creativity. Activities range from the extremely high-tech and active Recollections III video and music studio, where children can dance inside a video artwork, to a quiet reading space in a copper teepee. Youngsters can make brass rubbings or create a pop art self-portrait. In Planet PreSchool, especially for ages five and under, there's a puppet theater and a touch-screen computer program called Kiddy Face that helps little ones explore color and shapes. When your children are finished playing at Art Sparks, take one of four gallery packs, including one designed for preschoolers, upstairs to the main galleries for more art discovery. The excellent permanent exhibit includes many works that will interest children, from Greek pottery to contemporary Henry Moore sculptures to the charming Native American cradleboard and amulet. And, of course, the English Room.

GHEENS SCIENCE HALL AND RAUCH PLANETARIUM (all ages)
108 West Brandeis Avenue, Louisville 40208, on the University of Louisville campus; (502) 852–6664, www.louisville.edu/planetarium. Closed Mondays. Afternoon and evening traditional programs Tuesday to Sunday. Several laser shows each Friday night. Hands-on astronomy shows the first Saturday of each month. Adults $$, children $.

Some very cool laser and rock music shows and a lively schedule of traditional and educational programs are offered at this recently updated planetarium. Its Spitz projection system fills the "sky" with more than 4,000 stars, planets, and other celestial objects, while the 15,000-watt sound system fills your ears with music. Saturday morning shows are geared to ages three to eight and use animal characters, puzzles, and games to introduce astronomy. Monthly "Skies over Louisville" shows offer practical guides to local stargazing. "The Tonight Show," the first Saturday of each month, combines a planetarium show with viewing through telescopes (weather permitting). The Friday night laser shows (hourly shows from 8:00 to 11:00 P.M.), for older children and adults, combine star programs with hot music.

A Day Family Adventure

ADay Family Adventure While it's fun to take your children places you went as a child, be prepared to take a little ribbing when you start waxing nostalgic. During one trip to Louisville, I was regaling (or so I thought) my children with memories of the tiny natural history museum that preceded the Science Center, my field trip to the Speed, and so on, when my son piped up from the back seat of the car, "Gee, Mom, we didn't know they had all those things back in the 1800s."

KENTUCKY DERBY MUSEUM/CHURCHILL DOWNS (all ages)
704 Central Avenue, Louisville 40208; (502) 637–1111, www.derbymuseum. org. March 15 to November 30, Monday to Saturday from 7:00 A.M. to 5:00 P.M., Sunday from noon to 5:00 P.M.. Opens at 9:00 A.M. Monday to Saturday December through mid-March. Closed Kentucky Oaks and Derby Day (first Friday and Saturday in May). $$, children 4 and under Free.

Louisville's most famous event is the Kentucky Derby horse race, always run the first Saturday in May and held since 1875. But you can experience the heritage and excitement of the race every day at this museum adjacent to Churchill Downs race track. Youngsters will enjoy climbing aboard a scale model "racehorse" for a jockey's-eye view and meeting the resident thoroughbred and his pony friend out back. Many exhibits are interactive, and the 360-degree video presentation that takes you from foal to finish line is impressive. As for the real race, Derby Day, when some 160,000 throng the historic track, is probably not the best time

Amazing Kentucky Fact Derby Pie, created by the Kerns Family of Louisville, is the world's only copyrighted pie. You can try this delectable concoction of chocolate, sugar and nuts (the actual recipe is secret) at many local restaurants. If the menu doesn't say Derby Pie, but something similar, like Famous Horserace Pie or Winners Circle Pie, they're serving an impostor.

13

to take young children to the races. Many who go this day don't even see a horse; it's all for the party. Choose another day in the spring (May through July) or fall race meets (November) for a more relaxed time with better seating. Ask about the special children's activities and Junior Jockey Club. For more information about the races, call Churchill Downs at (502) 636–4400, or visit www.churchilldowns.com.

KENTUCKY DERBY FESTIVAL (all ages)

Early April through first Saturday in May. Locations around town; (502) 584–6383, www.kdf.org. Many events **Free***.*

The Kentucky Derby isn't just a horse race—it's nearly a month of festivities all over Louisville. There are free concerts, an outdoor "chuck-wagon" for food, contests, big fireworks, a hot air balloon race and several people races, and on and on. For many, the festival is even more enjoyable than the race.

Some of the major events of interest to families are

- Thunder over Louisville, mid-late April at the riverfront. The world's largest fireworks show, this is twenty-eight minutes of intense and incredible pyrotechnics. People watch from Waterfront Park, Bats Stadium, even from boats on the Ohio River.

- Hot Air Balloon Race, late April. Balloons take off from Kentucky Fair and Exposition Center.

- Great Steamboat Race, Wednesday before the race. Boat tickets are available, or join the party on shore at the riverfront.

- Pegasus Parade, Thursday before the race. The parade runs along Broadway in downtown Louisville.

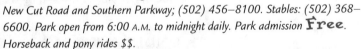

 ### IROQUOIS PARK (all ages)

New Cut Road and Southern Parkway; (502) 456–8100. Stables: (502) 368–6600. Park open from 6:00 A.M. to midnight daily. Park admission **Free***. Horseback and pony rides $$.*

This lushly forested 739-acre park is perhaps best known for Iroquois Hill, traversed by hiking trails that lead to scenic overlooks at the top. This is also one of the few places where you can ride horses in the area: Iroquois Stables offers trail rides (ages eight and up) and pony rides seasonally. The park's outdoor amphitheater is the stage for Music Theatre Louisville productions in the summer months. Call (502) 367–9493 for schedule information. In July folk music fills the amphitheater as musicians from around the world gather for the annual Kentucky

Music Weekend. Call (502) 348–5237 for information about the music festival.

LITTLE LOOM HOUSE (ages 8 and up)

328 Kenwood Hill Road (near Iroquois Park). Open Tuesday and Wednesday from 10:00 A.M. to 3:30 P.M., Thursday by appointment. $

Have your children ever made woven pot holders or interlaced strips of colored paper to make "woven" pictures? If so, they'll enjoy seeing the master weaving on big looms at these three rustic board-and-batten cabins atop a hill in south Louisville. The Little Loomhouse is the legacy of master weaver Lou Tate, who dedicated her life to preserving the traditional craft of hand-weaving. During the tour you'll see hand-spinners and weavers at work, as well as their beautiful finished coverlets and crafts.

LOUISVILLE ZOOLOGICAL GARDENS (all ages)

1100 Trevilian Way, Louisville 40213; (502) 459–2181, www.louisvillezoo.org. Open daily from 10:00 A.M. to 5:00 P.M. April through August, closes at 4:00 P.M. September through March. Adults $$, children under 12 $. Easily accessible from I–264 (Watterson Expressway); take exit 14 and follow the black-and-white signs.

Spacious, attractive, and always adding something new, the zoo has been a perennial favorite of my children since they were preschoolers. Home to more than 1,300 animals, from roaming peacocks to polar bears and penguins, the environments are naturalistic and innovatively designed. For example, the newest exhibit, the four-acre Gorilla Forest, leads you through a dense forested area, then puts you right in the middle of a circular habitat. You're eye to eye with a troop of lowland gorillas, separated only by glass. Younger children especially will enjoy the "African Village" petting zoo. My family has always liked the polar bear exhibit. And the HerpAquarium. And . . . The list goes on and on. A visit involves a lot of walking, so wear comfortable shoes and think strategy: Gauge your group's stamina, and make plans to turn around before everyone is pooped. (Even if you think your toddler has outgrown the stroller, you may want to bring it.) The best times to go are March through June and September through November, when it's not too hot or cold and the animals are most active. The zoo sponsors many enjoyable special events, including the World's Largest Halloween Party, Breakfast with Santa, Summer Camps and Safaris, and Louisville "Roarchestra" concerts.

LOUISVILLE NATURE CENTER/ BEARGRASS CREEK STATE NATURE PRESERVE (all ages)

3745 Illinois Avenue, Louisville 40213 (across from the Louisville Zoo); (502) 458–1328. **Free**.

With over 180 species of trees, shrubs, and flowering plants, 150 species of resident and migratory birds, Beargrass Creek State Nature Preserve calls out to the overwhelmed urban dweller in need of a sanctuary. The Louisville Nature Center serves as a gateway to this secluded getaway and sponsors many classes and camps throughout the year. Kids love the "bird blind," a small building with one-way glass and audio equipment from which visitors can view birds in their natural habitat. When heading for the trails, be sure to grab a map from the Nature Center, or bring a bag of popcorn to mark your trail—one family we know wandered around in circles for an hour.

SIX FLAGS KENTUCKY KINGDOM (all ages)

Watterson Expressway (I–264) adjacent to the fairgrounds and across from Louisville International Airport; (502) 366–2231, www.sixflags.com. Open from 10:00 A.M. to 11:00 P.M. in summer, weekends only in spring and fall. Hurricane Bay Waterpark is open from 11:00 A.M. to 7:00 P.M. seasonally. $$$$, children 48 inches or less $$$, children under 3 **Free**.

If your family thrives on amusement parks, you'll find plenty of stomach-churning action at this medium-sized "kingdom." The roller coaster roster includes T2, a suspended coaster; the twin wood coasters known as Twisted Sisters; and the monstrous 4,155-foot standing coaster Chang. There are other wild rides, too, like the Hellevator, which drops you fifteen stories. Younger, shorter, and less adventurous riders can head to Looney Tunes Movietown for kiddie rides themed after cartoon characters (including a mini-Hellevator). There's also a water park, Hurricane Bay, with a wave pool, water slides, and watersprays. If you plan to visit more than once in a season, check into getting a season pass. It's less expensive than two daily admissions and offers unlimited admission during a season. Other advice: Be sure to pack sunscreen. And be sure to measure your kids before you arrive—you

Amazing Kentucky Fact Louisville's Cherokee, Iroquois, and Shawnee Parks are considered among the finest in the United States and were designed by Frederick Law Olmsted, father of American landscape architecture and designer of New York's Central Park.

don't want to stand in line two hours for a ride, then find out that your child is 47 inches tall, not 48.

CHEROKEE PARK (all ages)

Between Eastern Parkway and Lexington and Cherokee Roads; (502) 456–8100. Park open from 6:00 A.M. to midnight daily. **Free**.

Louisvillians' favorite greenspace, Cherokee Park, with its trails and paths, rock bridges and steps, and towering trees, is a vision of natural beauty—and a place to have a lot of fun. The centerpiece of the park is a 2.4-mile scenic loop in which auto traffic is routed one way and the other half of the road is reserved for pedestrians. On a beautiful day, the loop is a sea of runners, walkers, bike riders, and in-line skaters. At the top of one hill is "Hogan's Fountain," with picnic areas, playgrounds, and a fountain where kids can cool off in summer (bring water shoes or flip-flops). In summer months, many families hold reunions and parties here. The other major hill (Hill Number One to some, Dog Hill to others) has long been a gathering spot for dogs and their people, as well as a favorite kite-flying area. Take a few minutes to drive through Cherokee Park, and you'll see one reason Louisvillians love their city.

Stoneware Stops Louisville has two historic stoneware companies where you can not only shop for delightful hand-painted dishes but take a tour and see how they're made. Children will enjoy these tours because both companies make much more than dishes—everything from mugs to birdhouses. It's also interesting to see how something can come out of playing with dirt. These tours are best for ages six and up.

Hadley Pottery, 1570 Story Avenue, Louisville 40206 (near American Printing House for the Blind); (502) 584–2171, has been making its whimsical hand-painted stoneware since the 1940s. On **Free** tours Monday through Friday at 2:00 P.M. you'll learn about the special single-firing process.

Louisville Stoneware, 731 Brent Street (off East Broadway near Barret), Louisville 40204; (502) 582–1900, is even older—the company started in the 1870s. **Free** tours are offered at 10:30 A.M. and 2:30 P.M. Monday to Saturday, where you'll see the process from raw clay to finish. There's also a paint-your-own pottery area where your children can decorate a piece of pottery for a fee. Be sure your child understands that the piece won't be ready for a few days. (And if you're not going to be in town that long, you'll need to arrange for it to be shipped to you.)

17

FARMINGTON (ages 8 and up)

*3033 Bardstown Road, Louisville 40205; (502) 452–9920, www.historic
farmington.org. (Web site includes "virtual tour").Open Tuesday to Saturday
from 10:00 A.M. to 4:30 P.M., Sunday from 1:30 to 4:30 P.M. $, children under
6* **Free**. *Guided tours on the hour (half hour on Sunday).*

Abraham Lincoln slept here. He really did. In fact, he stayed here for
six weeks, visiting his friend Judge John Speed. The house was based on
plans given to the Speeds by Thomas Jefferson. As you can see, the
Speeds were well connected in antebellum America. And rich, too: This
house was once the center of a 522-acre hemp plantation that was
home to John and Lucy Speed and their eleven children. Modern children will be fascinated by the octagonal rooms and interesting period
treasures, such as the 300-year-old bird cage in the parlor.

THOMAS EDISON HOUSE (ages 5 and up)

*729–31 East Washington Street, Louisville 40202; (502) 585–5247. Open
Tuesday to Saturday from 10:00 A.M. to 2:00 P.M. $, children under 6* **Free**.

Thomas Edison's Louisville story is a good demonstration that success isn't always instant. When Edison lived in Louisville, in 1866 and
1867, he worked as a Western Union telegraph operator and tinkered
with inventions in his spare time. He supposedly got fired when acid
from one of his experiments ate through the floor and dripped onto his
boss's desk on the floor below. A number of Edison's inventions are on
display here, including a Dictaphone, an early movie camera, and a large
collection of lightbulbs. Although Edison lived in the front room of this
house for only
a couple of
years, you can
learn about his
life's work,
from the inven-

Amazing Kentucky Fact Thomas
Edison introduced his incandescent lightbulb at
Louisville's Southern Exposition in 1883.

tions that caught on—like the phonograph and the lightbulb—to those
that didn't, like the "Power Nap" (no kidding).

AMERICAN PRINTING HOUSE FOR THE BLIND
(ages 8 and up)

*1839 Frankfort Avenue, Louisville 40206; (502) 895–2405, www.aph.org.
Factory tours offered Monday to Thursday, except holidays, at 10:00 A.M. and
2:00 P.M. Museum hours are 8:30 A.M. to 4:30 P.M. Monday to Friday.* **Free***;
donations appreciated.*

Did you know that the first braille book was printed in France in 1786? It's one of the items on display in this museum devoted to the history of visual aids. There's also a Bible belonging to Helen Keller, tactile maps and globes, and various other devices that have been used to help vision-impaired people. Your children will enjoy trying to read and write braille, they'll get a sense of some of the challenges of being visually impaired, and they'll learn about the history of one of the oldest and largest braille printing companies. Guided tours of the manufacturing facility show how braille and talking books are made; you're urged to watch your children carefully during the tour, though, since this is a working factory.

 ### LOCUST GROVE HISTORIC SITE (ages 6 and up)
561 Blankenbaker Lane, Louisville 40307; (502) 897–9845, www.locustgrove. org. House tour offered Monday to Saturday from 10:00 A.M. to 4:30 P.M., Sunday from 1:30 to 4:30 P.M.; last tour at 3:30 P.M. $, children 6 to 12 half price. Hands on History Center, open Tuesday to Saturday from 11:00 A.M. to 3:00 P.M. in summer months, $.

Locust Grove was the last home of General George Rogers Clark, the founder of Louisville. An introductory video explains Clark's and the home's historic significance, and guided tours highlight the features of this stately Georgian-style home. Young visitors' favorite part is the Hands on History Center, where they can play with early nineteenth-century-style clothing, log cabin blocks, and the contents of a Revolutionary War soldier's trunk.

A Day Family Adventure

We were driving along River Road east of downtown on our way to visit a friend when we spied something very curious. Set back from the road in a small park was a house—well, the front of a house, anyway—with all kinds of elaborate stone busts and carvings. My children giggled as they scrambled up the steps, through the doorway into . . . open air! We later learned that this fascinating oddity is the facade of the Charles Heigold House. The carved limestone busts and slogans ("All Hail the City of Louisville," "The Union Forever"), added between 1857 and 1866, were his way of expressing faith in democracy at a time when America's unity was threatened and immigrants persecuted. The street where the house was originally located was demolished in the 1950s, but the unusual facade was moved to Thruston Park off River Road, waiting to be rediscovered.

More Historic Houses

- **Brennan House,** 631 South Fifth Street, Louisville 40202; (502) 540–5145. Victorian mansion and doctor's office.

- **Conrad/Caldwell House,** 1402 St. James Court, Louisville 40208; (502) 636–5023. Elegant Romanesque Revival house in Old Louisville.

- **Whitehall,** 3110 Lexington Road, Louisville 40206; (502) 897–2944. Antebellum-style house with formal Florentine garden.

West Louisville

 ### PORTLAND MUSEUM (all ages)

2308 Portland Avenue, Louisville 40212; (502) 776–7678. Open Tuesday to Friday from 10:00 A.M. to 4:30 P.M. $. From downtown, take I–64 west. Exit onto Twenty-second Street, and turn right onto Portland Avenue.

Louisville's west-end Portland neighborhood was once a separate city, settled in 1814 by French immigrants. This interesting little museum delivers Portland history and river history via a sound-and-light show featuring animatronic figures representing such characters as naturalist John James Audubon and Mary Miller, the first woman riverboat pilot. There are also videos of the 1937 flood, the worst in Louisville history, as well as videos made by and featuring children.

Louisville Outskirts

 ### RIVERSIDE, THE FARNSLEY-MOREMEN LANDING (all ages)

7410 Moorman Road, Louisville 40272; (502) 935–6809. Open Tuesday to Saturday from 10:00 A.M. to 4:30 P.M., Sunday from 1:00 to 4:30 P.M. Tours every hour on the half hour beginning at 10:30 A.M.. Last tour 3:30 P.M. $, children 5 and under Free*. To get there, take I–65 south to I–265 west; go 10 miles to flashing yellow light. Make a left on Lower River Road. Turn right at the sign for Riverside.*

Located in far southwestern Jefferson County, this historic house and property offer a view of farm life along the Ohio River during the nineteenth century, when the river was the center of commerce and travel. Besides the spectacularly restored brick house, Riverside includes a nineteenth-century detached kitchen, a kitchen garden where vegetables and herbs of the original era are grown, and an active boat ramp. In late spring or early autumn you may see an ongoing excavation in progress as archaeologists are digging for the remains of former outbuildings. Riverboat cruises on the *Spirit of Jefferson* leave from the landing July through October, but not every day, so call (502) 574–2355 before you promise anyone a boat ride.

HENRY'S ARK (all ages)

7801 Rose Island Road, Louisville 40241; (502) 228–0746. **Free** *(donations appreciated). Off Route 42 near Jefferson–Oldham County line.*

No, your eyes aren't deceiving you; that *is* an emu in the parking lot. Henry's Ark began as a family menagerie, gradually evolved into a refuge for displaced and neglected animals, and along the way became a popular tourist destination. Over 25,000 visitors each year come to see the zebras, bison, camels, elk, Watusi cattle, goats, water buffalo, reindeer, and ostrich in this unusual setting. But Henry's Ark offers more than just a close-up look at exotic animals—its very existence reminds us of what an independent spirit and creative vision can accomplish. Bring carrots and other veggies to feed the animals, but pay attention to all posted notices: Ark staff rely on their visitors to be responsible, and the animals can be very assertive when hungry.

E. P. "TOM" SAWYER STATE PARK (all ages)

3000 Freys Hill Road, Louisville 40241; (502) 426–8950. **Free***. Take the Gene Snyder Freeway (I–265) northeast to the westbound Westport Road exit, and follow the signs.*

Located at the far east end of Louisville, E. P. "Tom" Sawyer State Park may be Kentucky's most urban park. Along with the usual picnic shelters, pool, and playgrounds, this park includes a bicycle motocross track and model airplane field. If you're lucky, members of the Tom Sawyer Model Aircraft Association will be flying their radio-controlled planes during your visit. There are separate trails designated as "fitness" and "nature" trails to keep joggers and amblers apart. In September, the park is the

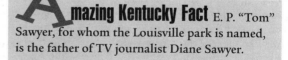

Amazing Kentucky Fact E. P. "Tom" Sawyer, for whom the Louisville park is named, is the father of TV journalist Diane Sawyer.

site of many activities of the Corn Island Storytelling Festival, a major showcase of the art of storytelling.

THE PARK AT MIDDLETOWN (all ages)

201 Park Place Drive, Louisville 40243, off U.S. Route 60 (Shelbyville Road), just inside I–265; (502) 253–9700, www.funatthepark.com. Hours vary widely by season, so check the Web site or call.

You can drop $30 or more fast at this amusement center, but there are times when miniature golf, go-carts, and bumper cars are just what everyone has in mind. The park emphasizes clean fun, so there are no violent video games in the clubhouse, and smoking and alcohol are prohibited. There's a special playground for smaller kids and a picnic area.

Other Things to See and Do

Cave Hill Cemetery, *701 Baxter Avenue, Louisville 40202; (502) 451–5630.* Scenic 300-acre arboretum with lakes, walking paths, and graves of Colonel Harland Sanders and explorer George Rogers Clark. Particularly stunning when dogwoods bloom in the spring.

Filson Club Historical Society Museum, *1310 South Third Street, Louisville 40208; (502) 635–5083.* Includes tree stump carved by Daniel Boone to record the fact that he killed a "bar."

Joseph A. Calloway Archaeological Museum, *Norton Hall, Southern Baptist Theological Seminary, 2825 Lexington Road, Louisville 40202; (502) 897–4039.* Features an Egyptian mummy, rare bibles, a copy of the Rosetta stone, and a room dedicated to Billy Graham.

Louisville Horse Trams Inc., *(502) 581–0100.* Horse-drawn carriage rides through downtown Louisville.

National Society of the Sons of the American Revolution Museum, *1000 South Fourth Street, Louisville 40203; (502) 589–1776.* Historical artifacts, including a replica of George Washington's study and an original thirteen-star flag.

Where to Eat

Baxter Station, *1201 Payne Street, Louisville 40204; (502) 584–1635.* A mixture of international and regional cuisine with a corner bistro feel. Kids will love the model train, which loops the dining room. $$

City Cafe, *505 West Broadway, Louisville 40202; (502) 589–1797.* Very popular downtown lunch place famous for its affordable box lunches. $

Ditto's Grill, *1114 Bardstown Road, Louisville 40204; (502) 581–9129.* Casual restaurant serving burgers, pizzas, and burritos, plus kid-approved side dishes such as cheesy broccoli. Fun atmosphere. $$

El Mundo, *2345 Frankfort Avenue, Louisville 40206; (502) 899–9930.* Mexican with a twist. Outdoor dining and a kid-friendly menu. $$

Kaelin's Kitchen, *1801 Newburg Road, Louisville 40205; (502) 451–1801.* Kaelin's claims to have originated the cheeseburger in 1934, though they are not the only ones to make this claim. Try one anyway and hear their story. Kaelin's used to have a sign out front that read IF YOU CAN'T STOP, JUST WAVE. Now it has a sign that reads YOU'VE WAVED LONG ENOUGH, COME ON IN. $

Kingfish, *3012 River Road, Louisville 40207; (502) 895–0544.* A city favorite since 1948, featuring riverboat decor and all kinds of fried, broiled, and baked seafood. $

Lynn's Paradise Cafe, *984 Barret Avenue, Louisville 40204; (502) 583–LYNN (5966).* A Louisville institution serving three meals a day of creative, "nouvelle comfort food" in a cartoonish atmosphere. The fun starts when you pull into the parking lot and see the oversized animal sculptures and giant perking coffee pot. Lynn's tends to pack up quickly, so plan your arrival accordingly. If you go on New Year's Day for brunch, you may be surprised to see all the patrons in their pajamas. The portions are huge, so plan to share. $$

Nancy's Bagel Grounds, *2101 Frankfort Avenue, 40206; (502) 895–8323.* A variety of delicious homemade bagels, soups, and sandwiches. $

Otto's Cafe, *500 South Fourth Street, Louisville 40202; (502) 585–3200.* Offering casual dining in the elegant Seelbach Hotel, Otto's specializes in themed lunch buffets; also serves breakfast and dinner. $$

Twig and Leaf, *2122 Bardstown Road, Louisville 40205; (502) 451–8944.* Inexpensive neighborhood diner where neither wait staff nor patrons will be perturbed by noise, activity, or even the accidental dropping of food on the floor. $

Where to Stay

Camberley Brown Hotel, *335 West Broadway, Louisville 40202; (502) 583–1234 or (800) 866–ROOM.* Very elegant renovated 1825 hotel, but with larger rooms than many historic hotels. Access to pool and health club, good restaurants. Try a "Hot Brown," a sandwich invented here. Convenient to downtown attractions. Offers family packages. $$$$

Executive West, *830 Phillips Lane, Louisville 40209, next to fairgrounds and Kentucky Kingdom; (800) 626–2708.* Pool, fitness center, restaurants; offers packages. $$–$$$

Fairfield Inn East (Marriott), *9400 Blairwood Road, Louisville 40222; (502) 339–1900.* Off I-64 east of Louisville. Outdoor pool, free continental breakfast. $–$$

Holiday Inn Downtown, *120 West Broadway, Louisville 40202; (502) 582–2241.* Convenient to downtown attractions. Indoor pool, restaurants; pets allowed. $$–$$$

Holiday Inn Hurstbourne, *1325 Hurstbourne Parkway, at I-64, Louisville 40222; (502) 426–2600.* Indoor pool, sauna, sundeck, game room. $$–$$$

Accommodating Thoughts As Kentucky hotel rates go,

Louisville's tend to be pricey. That's not surprising, since it's the biggest city, but it does mean that you'll want to make an effort to look for a way not to pay "rack rate." Think discount! And ask for one: It can make a real difference. For example, for one hotel I checked, the AAA discount knocked $50 off the regular rate. Here are some strategies:

- Ask if there's a better rate, a family rate, or a weekend rate. If you're coming in for a specific reason or event, mention that.

- Visit the Louisville Convention and Visitors bureau Web site (www.gotolouisville.org), or call the bureau at (888) LOUISVILLE to check out special seasonal or tour packages. Hotels in all price ranges and categories offer them. Some packages combine your room with attraction tickets and other freebies.

- Schedule your visit at times other than the busiest—you're not going to find any bargains Kentucky Derby Week.

- Even if you think a hotel or bed-and-breakfast looks too expensive, compare rates. Sometimes you'll be surprised. And remember that closer proximity to where you want to be, better amenities, and more space can make a slightly higher-priced accommodation a better value overall.

Pinecrest Cottage and Gardens B&B, *2806 Newburg Road, Louisville 40205; (502) 454–3800.* An alternative to a hotel, this privately owned lodging offers space and privacy. Guesthouse on six-and-a-half acres with lovely gardens, indoor pool, swings, trampoline, and kids' playhouse. Guesthouse features one bedroom, sleeper sofa, stocked eat-in kitchen, and fireplace. $$$$

For More Information

Greater Louisville Convention and Visitors Bureau, *located in the Kentucky International Convention Center, Third and Market Streets, (888) LOUISVILLE or* *(502) 582–3732; www.gotolouisville.com.* Open Monday to Saturday from 8:30 A.M. to 5:00 P.M., Sunday from 11:00 A.M. to 4:00 P.M.

Annual Events

Edison Birthday Celebration, early February, Thomas Edison House; (502) 585-5247

Kentucky Derby Festival, early April through first weekend in May; (502) 584-6383

Cherokee Triangle Art Fair, late April, Cherokee Park area

Kentucky Shakespeare Festival, outdoor drama, June and July, Central Park, 1114 South Third Street; (502) 583-8738

Waterfront Independence Festival, July 4; (502) 574-3768

Louisville Blues-n-Jazz Festival, mid-July, Water Tower on River Road; (502) 584-6383

National City Kentucky Music Weekend, July, Iroquois Park Amphitheatre; (502) 348-5237

Kentucky State Fair, ten days in mid-August, Kentucky Fair and Exposition Center off I-264; (502) 367-5005 or www.kystatefair.org

Rock the Water Tower, early September, Water Tower on River Road; (502) 584-6383

Farm Fest, mid-September, Farnsley-Moremen Landing; (502) 935-6809

Corn Island Storytelling Festival, late September, E. P. "Tom" Sawyer State Park and Long Run Park; (502) 245-0643

St. James Court Art Show, early October, St. James Court, Old Louisville; Arts, crafts, and food; (502) 635-1842

World's Largest Halloween Party, weekends in October, Louisville Zoo; trick-or-treating and fall activities; (502) 459-2181

Music and Festival of Folkways Weekend, mid-October, Locust Grove; (502) 897-9845

Riverside Heritage Festival, mid-October, Farnsley-Moremen Landing; (502) 935-6809

Dickens on Main Street, late November; (502) 582-3732

North-Central Kentucky

From Louisville, you can drive in any direction and quickly trade the city atmosphere for open countryside. The north-central Kentucky region surrounding Louisville features small towns with museums and quaint shops, major historic attractions such as Abraham Lincoln's birthplace and the famous mansion My Old Kentucky Home, farm tours, and some lovely parks and natural areas. To the west and south, small hills or "knobs" dot the landscape. To the east the terrain begins to take on the graceful rolling silhouette of the Bluegrass. These attractions are easy day trips from Louisville if you want to use the city as a base. But you don't have to: Plenty of comfortable, affordable hotels are available in the smaller cities surrounding Louisville, with special concentration in the Elizabethtown, Bardstown, and Shepherdsville areas. Interstates 65 south and 64 east and western Kentucky parkways—and combinations thereof—will get you into the general area; then take the scenic state and county highways to reach the attractions. Attractions are arranged starting south of Louisville and moving east to position you to continue your travels in northern Kentucky.

Shepherdsville Area

HAWKS VIEW GALLERY (ages 6 and up)

170 Carter Avenue, Brooks 40109; (502) 955–1010. Open Tuesday to Saturday from 10:00 A.M. to 5:00 P.M. Free. *Take I–65, exit 121.*

Blown glass takes on fascinating shapes here. It's fun to watch the artisans create handblown glass fish, candlestick holders that look like flowers, glass "faces," glass boxes, and other items. The tours are self-guided, so keep a close eye on your kids—there's lots of glass everywhere!

NORTH-CENTRAL KENTUCKY

LaGrange

Shelbyville

Taylorsville

Shepherdsville

Clermont

Bardstown

Springfield

Elizabethtown

New Haven

Hodgenville

Leitchfield

N

0   10   20

MILES

Teresa's Top Ten
Picks for North-Central Kentucky

1. Bernheim Arboretum and Research Forest, (502) 955–8512

2. Kentucky Railway Museum and Excursions, (502) 549–5470

3. Fort Duffield, (502) 922–4574

4. Abraham Lincoln National Historic Site, (270) 358–3137

5. My Old Kentucky Home State Park, (502) 348–3502

6. Civil War Museum, (502) 349–0291

7. Gallrein Farms, (502) 633–4849

8. Buffalo Crossing Family Fun Ranch, (502) 647–0377

9. The Schmidt Museum of Coca-Cola Memorabilia, (270) 234–1100

10. Rough River Dam State Resort Park, (270) 257–2311

 KART KOUNTRY (all ages)

At Exit 117 off I–65 south, Shepherdsville 40110; (502) 543–9588. Open daily from 10:00 A.M. to midnight during peak summer months. Hours vary during other seasons, depending on weather; call for hours. Go-cart ride fees are by the lap: $ (but you can drop $$$$ really fast).

For go-cart enthusiasts, it doesn't get much better than this: The track is 1½ miles long. (Kart Kountry is the longest track in the United States.) You pay by the lap, but there are discounted multilap packages that can be divided among drivers. To drive a go-cart, you have to be at least seven years old and 4 feet tall, but younger, shorter children can ride in a double-seater cart with an adult at the wheel. In addition to go-carts, there are batting cages, bumper boats, mini-golf and an indoor arcade. Snack food is available.

 WOODSDALE ONE-ROOM SCHOOLHOUSE (all ages)

Highway 44 East, Shepherdsville 40110; (502) 955–6269. Open from 7:30 A.M. to 5:00 P.M. fall through early summer; Friday in summer from 8:00 A.M. to noon. Free.

To see this restored 1808 schoolhouse, stop in at the Bullitt County Board of Education next door.

SLOWPOKE FARM (all ages)

8910 Cedar Grove Road, Shepherdsville 40110; (502) 921–9632 . No set hours; open when the Bleemels are home, usually daily in summer, though it may be closed around lunchtime. Take exit 116 off I–65, turn left, and go about 9½ miles. Look for the farm sign.

You've got to love a place called Slowpoke Farm. Belonging to the Bleemel family for five generations, Slowpoke Farm is a working cattle, soybean, and tobacco farm that sells seasonal produce and flowers. In recent years the family has started hosting workshops, lunches, and festivals. If your family would like to poke around, call ahead to schedule a lunch or a hayride. Also call to check the schedule of special events, including Mother's Day Brunch on the Farm, Annual Gourd Day on the Farm, and Car Show on the Farm. Or just stop by and see what's in season in the produce shop.

JUNCTION JAMBOREE (all ages)

Highway 434, Lebanon Junction 40150; (502) 833–0800, www.countrycookin band.com. Open Saturday at 7:30 P.M. Adults $$, children $; children under 6 **Free**. *Get off I–65 at exit 105, and go west on Highway 61 to Highway 434.*

If you like country music, you'll enjoy this family-oriented music hall. The house band, Bill Aiken and the Country Cookin' Band, is joined by an array of local, regional, and sometimes nationally known country, gospel, bluegrass, and comedy guest artists. Doors open at 6:00 P.M. Burgers, sandwiches, and snacks are available at the Junction Grill.

Other Things to See and Do

World's Most Awesome Flea Market, *I–65, exit 116, Shepherdsville 40110; (502) 543–8686.* Weekends only.

Shepherdsville Music Show, *Highway 44E, Shepherdsville 40110; (502) 239–8004 or (502) 543–6551.* Friday night bluegrass shows and Saturday night country music shows.

Where to Eat

Country Cupboard Restaurant, *636 Buckman Street, Shepherdsville 40110; (502) 543–2780.* Country cooking with generous portions and a family atmosphere. $

Where to Stay

Best Western Shepherdsville, *211 South Lakeview Drive (I–65, exit 117), Shepherdsville 40110; (502) 543–7097.* Outdoor pool, Denny's '50s-style diner restaurant. $$

Holiday Inn Express, *I–65, exit 121, Brooks 40109; (502) 955–1501.* Outdoor pool, free continental breakfast. $$

KOA Louisville South, *2433 Highway #44E, Shepherdsville 40165; (502) 543–2041.* Primitive and full-hookup camping, pool, game room, mini-golf, playgrounds, nature trail leading to prehistoric Indian rock shelters. $

For More Information

Shepherdsville/Bullitt County Tourism, *395 Paroquet Springs Drive, Shepherdsville 40110; (502) 543–8686,* *(800) 526–2068 or www.travelbullitt.org.* Open Monday to Friday from 8:00 A.M. to 5:00 P.M. Near I-65, exit 117.

Clermont

BERNHEIM ARBORETUM AND RESEARCH FOREST (all ages)
Off KY 245, Clermont 40110; (502) 955–8512, www.bernheim.org. Park open daily from 7:00 A.M. to 5:00 P.M., visitor center open from 9:00 A.M. to 5:00 P.M. Free admission on weekdays; $5.00 per vehicle on weekends and holidays. Take exit 112 off I–65, and follow signs.

Thank you, Isaac W. Bernheim. Back in 1929, this German immigrant, wanting to return something to Kentuckians for the success he enjoyed here as a whiskey distiller, set aside acreage for the Bernheim Research Forest. Generations of Kentuckians have enjoyed his thoughtfulness. A tried-and-true Kentucky getaway spot (I remember coming here on a school field trip), Bernheim Forest just seems to get better as it ages and very much lives up to its slogan "Connecting People to Nature." The 12,000 acres include some 35 miles of hiking trails, several lakes (one for fishing), manicured gardens, playgrounds, tree trails where the species are identified, and picnic areas. Children will enjoy the Nature Center, where they can see birds of prey and visit the deer pen. This is a great place to go for an impromptu picnic or hike (pick up a

Scavenger Hunt list at the Nature Center), but you also may want to call ahead and plan a trip around the many special activities and classes for all ages. Every Saturday at 11:30 A.M., the "Young Explorers" meet by the silo behind the Nature Center. This is an hour-long program for children ages 5 and up that usually focuses on plants or animals. There's usually a hike or animal program for kids on Sunday afternoon.

Elizabethtown Area

THE SCHMIDT MUSEUM OF COCA-COLA MEMORABILIA (all ages)

1030 North Mulberry Street (in the Elizabethtown Tourism and Convention Bureau) Elizabethtown 42701; (270) 234–1100. Open Monday to Friday from 9:00 A.M. to 5:00 P.M., Saturday from 10:00 A.M. to 2:00 P.M. In summer, hours are 9:00 A.M. to 6:00 P.M. $

Looking for the real thing? Here it is. This little museum adjoining the Elizabethtown visitor center is jam-packed with all kinds of things emblazoned with the Coca-Cola logo—toys, trays, radios, signs, clothing, bottle dispensers, you name it—many going back to the very early days of America's classic soft drink. Items on display change from time to time and are from the private collection of the Schmidt family, who used to own Elizabethtown's Coca-Cola bottling plant. Theirs is the world's largest privately owned collection of Coke memorabilia—some 3,000 items in all.

HISTORIC DOWNTOWN WALKING TOUR (all ages)

Leaves from the Hardin County Courthouse, downtown Elizabethtown; (270) 737–8932. Open June through September on Thursdays at 7:00 P.M. Free.

This forty-five-minute tour is part history lesson, part theater. Costumed characters relating to local history, such as Sara Bush Johnston Lincoln (Abe's stepmother), the hatchet-carrying prohibitionist Carry Nation, and even George Armstrong Custer greet you and tell you their stories as you pass twenty-five historic sites and buildings. The costumes, singing, and banjo playing will appeal to children, even if the younger ones don't understand all that's being said.

FREEMAN LAKE PARK (all ages)

North US 31W, Elizabethtown 42701; (270) 769–3916. Park open daily year-round. Historic buildings open Memorial Day to Labor Day, Tuesday to Saturday from 10:00 A.M. to 6:00 P.M., Sunday from 1:00 to 6:00 P.M. **Free**.

In addition to hiking trails, picnic areas, fishing, docks, and rowboat and pedal boat rentals, this park features several historical structures, so you can get a lot of mileage out of a stop here. The One-Room School House, built in Summit, Kentucky, in 1892 and moved to this location in 1978, has original desks and materials, complete with a lesson plan on the chalkboard. Lincoln Heritage House consists of two pioneer cabins built from 1789–1805 with the help of Lincoln's father, Thomas Lincoln, a skilled carpenter. Too tiny to actually enter, The Sara Bush Johnston Lincoln Memorial is a replica of Lincoln's stepmother's Elizabethtown cabin.

SWOPE'S CARS OF YESTERYEARS MUSEUM (all ages)

1100 North Dixie Highway, Elizabethtown 42701; (270) 765–2181. Open Monday to Saturday from 9:00 A.M. to 5:00 P.M. **Free**.

Children must be accompanied by adults at this museum of vintage and rare automobiles. No problem. There are cool cars for all ages here: Children will love the old cars, like the cute 1910 Hupmobile and the 1920 Brush, as well as the more recent, cartoonish '61 Metropolitan, while Dad and Grandpa (and/or Mom and Grandma) can salivate over the '69 Camaro, the pink '55 Dodge Custom Royal Lancer, and the '53 Jaguar XK 120. The collection's twenty cars are in pristine condition.

The Food Run The little town of Glendale, about 8 miles south of Elizabethtown on Highway 22 (from Elizabethtown, take I-65 to exit 86) is chock full of antiques and gift shops. While that may or may not appeal to your family, everyone will enjoy eating at Glendale's two home-cooking restaurants. **The Depot** (270–369–6000) and **The Whistle Stop** (270–369–8586) sit catty-corner to each other near the town's railroad tracks (this was a bustling passenger stop in the early 1800s). Both feature a casual atmosphere and moderate prices. The Depot, as its name suggests, is located in the town's renovated train depot; children will love the bread baked in clay flower pots. The Whistle Stop is decorated with crafts and is known for its homemade pies.

THE GREENBELT (all ages)

Network of trails around Elizabethtown. Pick up a brochure at the Elizabethtown Convention and Visitor Bureau. **Free***.*

This network of trails and parks was created by a private foundation and the city of Elizabethtown. It currently includes more than 13 miles of trails, ranging from short and easy to long and moderately challenging, that go through town and around Freeman Lake, Buffalo Lake, Fisherman's Lake, and other streams in between.

PATTON MUSEUM OF CAVALRY AND ARMOR (all ages)

Keyes Park near the main entrance to Fort Knox Military Reservation; (502) 624–3812. Open daily year-round, except major holidays. Hours are 9:00 A.M. to 4:30 P.M. weekdays, 10:00 A.M. to 4:30 P.M. weekends. Open until 6:00 P.M. in summer. **Free***. To get to Fort Knox from Elizabethtown, take US 31W to Chaffee Avenue.*

From big tanks to toy-sized soldiers (used in dioramas illustrating military strategies), this museum traces the history of armored vehicles from World War I through Desert Storm and Desert Shield. The children will love climbing into a tank; for

Amazing Kentucky Fact The door to the vault in the United States Bullion Depository at Fort Knox weighs more than 20 tons and is made of concrete and steel. No one person has the entire combination to the lock.

adults, there are many informative and interesting items relating to famous World War II general George S. Patton.

FORT DUFFIELD (all ages)

Salt River Drive, off US 31W, West Point 40177; (502) 922–4574. Open daily from 9:00 A.M. to dusk. Take US 31W north from Elizabethtown. **Free***; donations suggested. If coming from Louisville, a quicker way is to take I–265 (Gene Snyder Freeway) to US 31W south; the park is a little over 7 miles from the exit.*

Older children interested in Civil War history will like this preserved Civil War site the most, but all ages can enjoy the open spaces and scenic river views. Fort Duffield was a Union fortification built on orders from General William Tecumseh Sherman to help protect supply routes along the Ohio River. The remote hilltop location (and the fact that for many years this was part of Fort Knox Military Reservation) meant that the earthen-wall fortifications remained little disturbed over the decades. They're reputedly some of the best remaining in the state. In recent years a group of local volunteers has made the fort a labor of love, building Civil War–replica cabins and an amphitheater for living history demonstrations. When you visit, you may see people working on the park dressed in Civil War uniforms. To get to the earthen fort, you have to hike about ¼ mile. On living history weekends (Memorial Day and Labor Day weekends) a shuttle bus is available; small donation suggested. The park also has picnic areas and 10 miles of advanced-level mountain bike paths.

 lso at Fort Knox

- View the **United States Bullion Depository**, where America's gold has been stored since 1969. (Exterior viewing only.) **Free**.

- Make a splash at the **Fort Knox Water Park**, with its slides and outdoor pool. Open to civilians. (502) 624–1253. $

- Just drive around to see the barracks and other buildings; if your children have never been on a military base, they'll find it interesting.

Note: Since fall 2002, security on the base has been tightened. To enter you must present identification, your car registration, and proof of auto insurance.

Other Things to See and Do

Brown-Pusey Community House, *128 North Main Street, Elizabethtown 40271; (270) 765–2515.* Restored Federal-style stagecoach building.

Emma Reno Connor Black History Gallery, *602 Hawkins Drive, Elizabethtown 40271; (270) 769–5204.* Photos and articles on local African-American history. By appointment.

Otter Creek Park, *KY 1638, off US 31W, Brandenburg 40108; (502) 574–4583 or www.ottercreekpark.org.* Hiking trails, nature center, pool overlooking the Ohio River.

Where to Eat

Back Home, *251 West Dixie Highway (U.S. 31W), Elizabethtown 40271; (270) 769–2800.* Home cooking and regional specialties. $

The Depot, *201 East Main Street, Glendale 42740; (270) 369–6000.* Delicious home cooking in a renovated train depot. Children's menu available. Kids love the bread baked in flower pots. $–$$

The Whistle Stop, *216 East Main Street, Glendale 42740; (270) 369–8586.* Home cooking and delicious homemade pies. $$

Where to Stay

Comfort Inn, *1043 Executive Drive, Elizabethtown, 42701; (800) 682–5285, (270) 769–3030.* Indoor pool, restaurant. $$–$$$

Days Inn, *2010 North Mulberry Street, Elizabethtown 42701; (270) 769–5522.* Outdoor pool, laundry, twenty-four-hour restaurant, free continental breakfast. $$

Elizabethtown KOA, *US 62, near I–65, exit 94, Elizabethtown 42701; (270)* 737–7600. Seventy sites, full hookups, playgrounds, miniature golf. $

Hampton Inn, *1035 Executive Drive, Elizabethtown 42701; (I–65, exit 94); (270) 737–7585.* Indoor pool, exercise room, free breakfast. $$–$$$

Otter Creek Park, *KY 1638, off US 31W, Brandenburg 40108; (502) 574–4583.* Two- and four-bedroom cabins overlooking Ohio River; $$–$$$. Camping with hookups, bathhouses also available. $

Outdoor Drama in North-Central Kentucky

If your children are old enough to sit still for a couple of hours, they might enjoy theater "under the stars."

- *Stephen Foster: The Musical.* J. Dan Talbott Amphitheatre, My Old Kentucky Home State Park, Bardstown; (800) 626–1563 or (502) 348–5971. June through late August. Tuesday through Friday at 8:30 P.M., Saturday at 2:00 and 8:30 P.M. Musical (more than fifty songs) about the life of composer Stephen Foster. Adults $$$, children 7 to 12 $$; children 6 and under Free.

- **Pine Knob Theatre,** Pine Knob, 14 miles south of Rough River Dam State Resort Park; (270) 879–8190 or www.pineknob.com. Early June through late September. Saturday at 8:00 P.M. Four shows per season, looking at the past (1800s to 1950s) in song and dance. Old-fashioned store and '50s diner near theater. $$$

For More Information

Elizabethtown Tourism and Convention Bureau, *1030 North Mulberry Street, Elizabethtown 42701 (near I–65, exit 94); (800) 437–0092 or www.toure town.com.* Open Monday to Friday from 8:00 A.M. to 5:00 P.M. Open until 6:00 P.M. weekdays and Saturday from 10:00 A.M. to 2:00 P.M. in summer.

Radcliff/Fort Knox Convention and Tourism Commission, *P.O. Box 845, Radcliff 40159; (800) 334–7540*

West Point Tourism, *City Hall, 509 Elm Street, West Point 40177; (502) 922–4260*

Leitchfield

ROUGH RIVER DAM STATE RESORT PARK (all ages)

KY 79, between Leitchfield and Hardinsburg; (270) 257–2311 or (800) 255–PARK, www.kystateparks.com. Admission and many facilities 𝐅𝐫𝐞𝐞. *From I–65 south at Elizabethtown, get on Western Kentucky Parkway and look for the park exit sign. Lodge rooms $–$$; cabins $$$–$$$$; camping $. Dining room $.*

You're not exactly "roughing it" when you spend a day, weekend, or longer here. This state park, which boasts a 5,000-acre manmade lake, offers fishing and lake sightseeing (boat rentals available), mini-golf, tennis, playgrounds, picnic areas, and a couple of easy nature trails. The lodge features overnight accommodations and a dining room. Cottages and camping are also available. There's a swimming pool for lodge and cabin guests. In July, the park is host to one of Kentucky's premier traditional music events—the **Official Kentucky Championship Oldtime Fiddling Contest.** Fiddle players compete for top bragging rights, as do harmonica, banjo, and mandolin players. Camp and join in the jam sessions and main performances (270–257–2311).

Hodgenville

ABRAHAM LINCOLN NATIONAL HISTORIC SITE (all ages)

US 31E and KY 61, 2995 Lincoln Farm Road, Hodgenville 42748; (270) 358–3137. Opens at 8:00 A.M. daily year-round, closes at 6:45 P.M. Memorial Day through Labor Day; closes at 4:45 P.M. rest of year. Closed Thanksgiving, Christmas, and New Year's Day. 𝐅𝐫𝐞𝐞.

Northeastern Kentucky is the Bluegrass State's "Land of Lincoln," and his birthplace shrine, located on one hundred acres of land that was part of the Lincoln family farm, is a good place to begin your all-Abe adventure. This is one of the most visited shrines in the United States, and it's an imposing sight: The building rises like a granite temple atop fifty-six massive steps (one for each year of Lincoln's life). Make the climb, and inside you'll find a one-room log cabin similar to the one in which Lincoln was born in this area on February 12, 1809. It all symbolizes the humble beginnings that led to great things. Be sure to stop at the visitor center, which includes an audiovisual presentation about Lincoln's childhood and Lincoln family artifacts. My daughter also enjoyed the park's hiking trail and the walk down to Sinking Spring.

A Day Family Adventure The designer of the Abraham Lincoln birthplace shrine must have envisioned coming here as a solemn, thought-provoking experience, and it's true: The amount of time (and effort) it takes to climb those fifty-six huge steps does tend to concentrate your attention. We found it difficult to maintain a serious mood, however, when we overheard a little boy say to his mother, "Gee, the Lincolns sure did have to climb a lot of steps to go to bed at night!"

LINCOLN MUSEUM (ages 4 and up)

66 Lincoln Square, Hodgenville 42748; (270) 358–3163, www.lincolnmuseum ky.org. $

From the Lincoln birthplace, drive into Hodgenville and park near the town square, where there's a bronze statue of Lincoln. This museum is right on the square and features wax figures posed in scenes that re-create sixteen important events in Lincoln's life.

LINCOLN'S BOYHOOD HOME (all ages)

Knob Creek Farm, US 31W, northeast of Hodgenville; (270) 549–3741. Grounds open daily from 8:30 A.M. to 4:30 P.M. Free.

As an adult, Abraham Lincoln said his earliest memories were of the "Knob Creek place," and this is it—the farm where the Lincolns lived from 1811 to 1816, the place where young Abe played, learned to read the Bible, and, by some accounts, nearly drowned in the creek that runs through the farm. LaRue County presented the 228-acre farm to the National Park Service in 2002, and the attraction is in transition. The cabins are closed, at least temporarily, but visitors are welcome to drop by and stroll the grounds.

 LINCOLN JAMBOREE (ages 6 and up)
2579 Lincoln Farm Road, Hodgenville 42748; (270) 358–3545. Open year-round Saturday at 8:00 P.M. $$

I've never heard anything about Lincoln singing, so this family-oriented country music show honors Abe in name only. The folks here do a lot of singing: Local, regional, and some national acts has been giving weekly shows here since 1954. The on-site Joel-Ray's Restaurant serves a cafeteria-style dinner. $

Lincolnmania Does someone in your family look like Abraham Lincoln or Mary Todd Lincoln? If so, head to Hodgenville the second weekend in October, and enter the Lincoln lookalike contests, all part of the fun at the annual **Lincoln Days Celebration** (270–358–3411). There are rail-splitting contests and pioneer games, too.

Where to Eat

Joel Ray's Restaurant, *2579 Lincoln Farm Road, Hodgenville 42748; (270) 358–3545.* Cafeteria-style breakfast, lunch, and dinner. Adjacent to Lincoln Jamboree. $$

Paula's Hot Biscuit, *311 West Water Street, Hodgenville 42748; (270) 358–2237.* Breakfast and lunch. $

Ruthie's Lincoln Freeze, *700 South Lincoln Boulevard, Hodgenville 42748; (270) 358–4987.* Burgers and plate lunches plus ice cream. $

For More Information

LaRue County Chamber of Commerce, *58 Lincoln Square, Hodgenville* *42748; (270) 358–3411 or www.laruecountychamber.org*

Scenic Route From Hodgenville, take US 31E 30 miles to Bardstown, along the Old Kentucky Turnpike Scenic Byway, formerly the main road from Louisville to Nashville.

New Haven

KENTUCKY RAILWAY MUSEUM (all ages)

Exit 10 off Bluegrass Parkway, 15 miles south of Bardstown on US 31E; (502) 549–5470 or (800) 272–0152. Museum open March through December, Monday to Saturday from 10:00 A.M. to 4:00 P.M., Sunday from 1:00 to 4:00 P.M. Train excursion schedule runs year-round but varies by season and day. Museum $; train tickets adults $$$, children $$.

From this restored depot you can take a 22-mile, one-hour scenic excursion on authentic vintage coaches powered either by a diesel locomotive or a restored Louisville and Nashville steam locomotive. In summer there are daily departures from New Haven and weekend departures from both New Haven and the community of Boston to the north. Both are round-trip excursions through scenic Rolling Fork River Valley. Throughout the year there are a variety of special excursions with children in mind, including the Easter Bunny Express, Train Robbery excursions, Haunted Trail and Friendly Ghost excursions in October, and the Santa Express. The depot at New Haven also includes a railroad museum. Your children will probably make a beeline for the model train center, which includes several working trains running through miniature landscapes built with precision and absolute attention to detail. If you have younger children, you might want to bring something for them to stand on or you will be holding them the entire time so they can see.

Bardstown

MY OLD KENTUCKY HOME STATE PARK (all ages)

US 150, Bardstown 40004; (502) 348–3502. Open daily June through August from 8:30 A.M. to 6:30 P.M., September through May from 9:00 A.M. to 4:45 P.M. $

You've already had the 25-cent tour of this lovely Georgian-style house—it's the house featured on the Kentucky state quarter. Pay a little more and you can go inside, visit the gardens, and learn how it supposedly inspired composer Stephen Foster to write the state song. (If you don't know the words to Kentucky's state song, "My Old Kentucky Home," before you visit Bardstown, you will when you leave!) Kentucky's most famous historic house is named Federal Hill, and it dates to 1818. For tours, the Old South atmosphere is re-created complete with tour guides dressed as Southern belles. Children especially enjoy the costumes and hearing about life for the children in the house. The park also includes picnic areas, a playground, and an amphitheater

Amazing Kentucky Fact Stephen Foster, who wrote "My Old Kentucky Home," never had a Kentucky home. He lived in Pittsburgh, Pennsylvania. His distant cousins, the Rowans, owned Federal Hill, and local legend claims that Foster stopped to visit them on his way to New Orleans.

where *Stephen Foster: The Musical* is performed seasonally.

OLD BARDSTOWN VILLAGE, THE CIVIL WAR MUSEUM, AND WOMEN IN THE CIVIL WAR MUSEUM (ages 5 and up)

302 and 310 East Broadway, Bardstown, 40004; (502) 349–0291. Open March through December Monday to Saturday from 10:00 A.M. to 5:00 P.M., Sunday from noon to 5:00 P.M.; open weekends only in January and February. Individual attraction admission $; combo ticket for all three (best deal) $$ adults, $ children.

Three attractions in one complex take you from pioneer times through the Civil War. **Old Bardstown Village** is a collection of replica pioneer cabins, including a forge, as well as Native American items. (*Note:* The village may not be open if it's raining.) The star attraction is the **Civil War Museum,** which several Civil War publications have named as one of the finest in the United States. The museum focuses on the war's western theater, the battles in Kentucky and points west, and includes numerous interesting and rare artifacts, from cannons, uniforms, and flags to hardtack, the food soldiers often lived on. The newest attraction in the complex is the **Women of the Civil War Museum,** housed in a separate 1840 building. You might be surprised to learn that 400 women fought in the Civil War. It was also the first war in which women served as nurses—prior to the Civil War, that was considered men's work. The museum includes costumes, photographs, and other items, and exhibits explain women's roles as wives, soldiers, nurses, and spies.

Bardstown's Boat Man Why is there a monument shaped like a steamboat in Bardstown's town square? Because Bardstown was the last home of inventor John Fitch, who received the first patent for a steamboat in 1791.

Other Things to See and Do

Around-the-Town Carriages, *223 North Third Street, Bardstown, 40004; (502) 348–0331.* Horse-drawn carriage tours of downtown area.

Bardstown Historical Museum, *114 North Fifth Street, Bardstown 40004; (502) 348–2999.* Whiskey museum and local history museum.

Distillery tours. There are several in the "Bourbon Capital of Kentucky." Ask at the visitor center.

St. Joseph Proto Cathedral, *310 West Stephen Foster Avenue, Bardstown, 40004; (502) 348–3126.* First Catholic Church west of the Alleghenies; includes beautiful European paintings.

More Historical Experiences in Bardstown

- Eat lunch or dinner at **Old Talbott Tavern,** 107 West Stephen Foster Avenue, Bardstown, 40004; (502) 348-3494. This was an early stage-coach stop. George Rogers Clark ate here, and Jesse James shot holes in the wall. The regular menu features regional specialties, but children can get chicken tenders, ravioli, a peanut-butter-and-jelly sandwich, and other kid-friendly fare. Lunch $, dinner $$. Open daily.

- Stay overnight at the **Old Stone Jail/Jailer's Inn,** 111 West Stephen Foster Avenue, Bardstown 40004; (800) 948-5551 or (502) 348-5551. Visit this historic jailhouse converted into a bed-and-breakfast. Best for families is the "cell room," decorated in black and white, which features a waterbed and two bunk beds ($$$). Even if you're not an overnight guest, you can take a tour of the adjacent 1819 jail building and the inn. $

Where to Eat

Dagwood's, *204 North Third Street, Bardstown, 40004; (502) 348–4029.* Soup and salad bar, plus burgers and sandwiches, for lunch ($); steak, seafood, and pasta for dinner ($$).

Hurst Discount Drugs Soda Fountain, *Courthouse Square, Bardstown, 40004; (502) 348–9261.* Sandwiches, soups, and ice cream treats at an old-fashioned soda fountain. $

Kurtz Restaurant, *418 East Stephen Foster Avenue, Bardstown, 40004; (502) 348–8964.* Soup/sandwich/pie special for lunch, regional specialties for dinner. Famous for its fried chicken. Lunch $, dinner $$.

Old Talbott Tavern, 107 West Stephen Foster Avenue, Bardstown, 40004; (502) 348-3494. Southern specialties in an inn operating since 1779. Kids menu. Lunch $, dinner $$.

A Day Family Unadventure

Interstate 65, which runs north-south through this region, is such a busy and crowded interstate that it's sometimes nerve-wracking to drive. On the other hand, the east-west parkways through this region, Bluegrass Parkway and Western Kentucky Parkway, can be nerve-wracking for just the opposite reason. Both seem somewhat desolate, and there are few gas stations and restaurants along the exits, except for major city areas like Elizabethtown and Bardstown. Late one Sunday night, I forgot this. The low-gas light had been on for a while, but when we reached Elizabethtown, the traffic was so bad that I didn't want to have to pass the parkway exit, get gas, then turn around and find the parkway entrance. "I'll just wait and get gas on Bluegrass Parkway," I said. Soon everyone in the car realized what a mistake this had been. The first exit had no reentry to the parkway. The next had no gas station in sight. And so on. From the back seat: "Mom, what will we do?" "Are we going to have to spend the night out here?" By the time I saw a sign that read BARDSTOWN 9 MILES, the gas gauge showed "E." We reset the trip odometer and watched the miles tick away, breathing a sigh of relief as each one passed. We did make it to an open station in Bardstown, but I'll never do that (at least on Bluegrass Parkway, late at night) again.

Where to Stay

Days Inn, US 31 and Bluegrass Parkway, Bardstown 40004; (502) 348–9253 or (866) 348–6900. Nine-hole golf, fitness room, game room, outdoor pool. $$

Hampton Inn Bardstown, 985 Chambers Boulevard, off KY 245, Bardstown 40004; (502) 349–0100 or (800) 426–7866. Indoor pool. $$

Jailer's Inn, 111 West Stephen Foster Avenue, Bardstown 40004; (800) 948–5551 or (502) 348–5551; www.jailer sinn.com. Five rooms decorated with antiques; "cell room" features jail motif. $$–$$$

My Old Kentucky Home State Park Campground, US 150, Bardstown 40004; (502) 348–3502. Thirty-nine sites with utility hookups available. On-site grocery, central service building with showers and toilets, laundry, and picnic area. Eighteen-hole golf course and tennis courts. Pets allowed if restrained. Open April through October; no reservations accepted. $

For More Information

Bardstown-Nelson County Tourist and Convention Bureau, 107 East Stephen Foster Avenue, Bardstown 40004; (502) 348–4877 or (800) 638–4877, www.bardstowntourism.com

Springfield

LINCOLN HOMESTEAD STATE PARK (all ages)
5079 Lincoln Park Road, Springfield 40069; (859) 336–7461. Park open year-round; buildings and golf course open May 1 to September 30. Admission to buildings and golf course $; otherwise Free .

While Lincoln's birth is commemorated in Hodgenville, this park pays tribute to the lives of his parents. Two cabins relate to Lincoln history. The Berry House is the original house where Abe's mother, Nancy, lived and, where legend has it, Abe's father, Thomas, proposed to her. It is furnished with period pieces. The other, the Lincoln Cabin, is a reproduction of the home and blacksmith shop where Thomas Lincoln lived and contains furniture he made. There are picnic areas and a playground near the cabins. There's also a small lake for fishing.

BEECH FORK COVERED BRIDGE (all ages)
KY 458 off Highway 55, north of Springfield 40069. Free .

This 211-foot-long span is one of only thirteen covered bridges remaining in Kentucky (there were once several hundred). The bridge is closed to traffic, which means you can leisurely explore the inside and its interesting burr truss construction.

WASHINGTON COUNTY COURTHOUSE (all ages)
Main and Cross Streets, Springfield 40069. Free.

The wedding records of Abe's parents, Thomas and Nancy Lincoln, are among the historic documents on display on the walls of this courthouse. The building itself is historic: The oldest courthouse in continuous use in Kentucky, it dates to 1816.

VALLEY HILL STORE (all ages)
Highway 55, north of Springfield 40069; (859) 336–0255. Open Wednesday to Saturday from 10:00 A.M. to 5:00 P.M., Sunday from 1:00 to 5:00 P.M.

This old post office building turned into a country store features crafts, antiques, foods, and other items, plus friendly service from owner Rosemary Bailey.

Where to Eat

Cecconi's Family Restaurant, *117 West Main Street, Springfield 40069; (859) 336–5136.* Burgers, plate lunches, and homemade pies. $

Linc's Restaurant, *1007 Lincoln Park Road, Springfield 40069; (859) 336–7493.* Country buffet and sandwiches. $, except for Sunday seafood buffet ($$$$).

Where to Stay

Days Inn, *US 150, Springfield 40069; (859) 336–7550 or (800) DAYSINN.* Pool, free continental breakfast. $$

Glenmar Plantation Bed and Breakfast, *2444 Valley Hill Road, Springfield 40069; (800) 828–3330 or (859)*

284–7791. This one-hundred-acre working farm with house (built in 1785) and lovely gardens welcomes children and offers plenty of opportunity for animal lovers to make friends with the resident llamas, horses, dogs, and cats. $$$–$$$$.

For More Information

Springfield/Washington County Chamber of Commerce, *112 Cross Main Street, Springfield 40069; (859) 336–3810.*

Taylorsville

TAYLORSVILLE LAKE STATE PARK (all ages)

1320 Park Road (off KY 248), Taylorsville 40071; (502) 477–8713, campground (502) 477–0086. Open daily year-round. Admission Free*; camping $, boat rental $$–$$$.*

This state park's 3,050-acre lake is the closest major lake to Louisville (about a forty-five-minute drive). With playgrounds and picnic areas, it makes an easy day getaway. Or you can camp and stay longer. There are 16 miles of hiking trails, plus a marina with boat slips and rentals. Horseback riding is allowed on some trails, but you must bring your own horse. The campground includes some horse campsites.

U.S. CORPS OF ENGINEERS TAYLORSVILLE DAM VISITOR CENTER (all ages)

KY 2239, off KY 55; (502) 477–8882. Open daily. **Free**.

Get a good view of the 1,280-foot-long dam over the Salt River that created Taylorsville Lake. Some exhibits about the dam and the area are under development. There's also a hiking trail down to some pioneer cabins.

THE BERRY FARM (all ages)

1168 Wilsonville Road, Taylorsville 40071; (502) 477–2334. Open daily. Gourds available all year; other produce seasonal.

This is a "U-pick-it" place for strawberries in spring; blueberries, blackberries, tomatoes, and grapes in summer; apples, pumpkins, and cushaws (big, green-striped squashes used in pies) in fall; and gourds for drying, painting, and craftmaking year-round.

Other Things to See and Do

JailHouse Arts and Crafts, *Courthouse Alley, Taylorsville; (502) 477–6654.* Homemade local arts and crafts in a former jail building.

Where to Eat

Lynda's Grill, *108 Jefferson Street, Taylorsville 40071; (502) 477–2857.* Plate lunches and sandwiches. $

The Tea Cup, *37 Main Street, Taylorsville 40071; (502) 477–0287.* Hearty breakfast, sandwiches and soups for lunch. $

Shelbyville

GALLREIN FARMS (all ages)

1029 Vigo Road, off Highway 43, Shelbyville 40065; (502) 633–4849. Open daily April through October 31, Monday to Saturday from 9:00 A.M. to 5:00 P.M., Sunday from 1:00 to 5:00 P.M. Admission **Free**; *charges for some seasonal activities.* $

Spring through fall, you'll find something interesting to see and do at this very family-friendly working farm. There's a small petting zoo with donkeys, goats, and rabbits. Children can also feed the ducks and geese at the pond and watch bees making honey in an observation hive. In

Amazing Kentucky Fact Kentucky has about 90,000 farms—more than forty-six other states.

fall, there are hayrides to the pumpkin patch. Produce available varies by season but includes raspberries, blackberries, sweet corn, and pumpkins.

BUFFALO CROSSING RESTAURANT AND FAMILY FUN RANCH
1140 Bagdad Road, Shelbyville 40065; (502) 647–0377 or (877) 700–0047, www.bluegrassbison.com. Open Tuesday to Sunday from 11:00 A.M. to 9:00 P.M. Charges for various activities. $

Imagine—a little bit of the Wild West just a half hour from Louisville. This farm bases its western theme on the fact that Kentucky was America's first western frontier. The centerpiece is a 500-head herd of bison. Start at the visitor center with its exhibits about buffalo and Kentucky history, then take a farm tour to see the herd. You can also rent paddleboats and view a small zoo with exotic animals such as camels and wallabies. As for the buffalo burgers at the on-site restaurant, some children will have to have them, others may be grossed out at the thought. Don't worry: There are other items on the menu ($).

Other Things to See and Do

Science Hill, *525 Washington Street, Shelbyville, 40065.* Shops housed in historic buildings.

Shelby County Flea Market, *off I–64 at exit 28, Shelbyville 40065; (502) 722–8883.* Weekends only.

Standardbred Horse Farms. Arrange tours through tourism office: *(502) 633–6388.*

Where to Eat

Claudia Sanders Dinner House, *3202 Shelbyville Road, Shelbyville 40065; (502) 633–5600.* Open Tuesday to Sunday from 11:00 A.M. to 9:00 P.M. Housed in the former home of Colonel

Sanders of Kentucky Fried Chicken fame and named for his wife, this restaurant serves traditional cooking with family-style service and homemade breads and desserts. $$$

Where to Stay

Best Western Shelbyville Lodge, *I–64, exit 32B, 115 Isaac Shelby Drive, Shelbyville 40065; (502) 633–4400.* Outdoor pool, complimentary breakfast, pets allowed. $$

Holiday Inn Express, *110 Clubhouse Drive, Shelbyville 40065; (502) 677–0109.* Indoor pool, free continental breakfast. $$

For More Information

Shelbyville/Shelby County Tourism Commission, *316 West Main Street,* *Shelbyville 40065; (502) 633–6388 or (800) 680–6388, www.shelbyvilleky.com.*

LaGrange

OLDHAM COUNTY HISTORY CENTER (all ages)

106 North Second Avenue, LaGrange 40031; (502) 222–0826. Open Tuesday to Saturday from noon to 5:00 P.M. $; children under 6 **Free**.

This interpretive history museum traces the history of Oldham County through permanent and changing exhibitions. Of most interest to children is the replica of the railroad that ran through Oldham County on its journey between Louisville and Cincinnati. Be sure to see the outdoor sculpture while enjoying the Heritage Walk.

Downtown LaGrange The Oldham County History Center is at the heart of a very pretty small downtown, so plan a stroll through this historic district before or after your museum tour. The cute shops on Main Street are a popular detour for people traveling between Cincinnati and Louisville. Have Dad take the kids to the region's most beloved toy store, **The Treasured Child** (115 East Main Street, LaGrange 40031; 502-225-9646), or to **Pottery U Paint** (113 East Main Street, LaGrange 40031; 502-225-0006) for some creative expression, while Mom slips into the **1887 Corner Store** for a little gift shopping (101 East Main Street, LaGrange 40031; 502-222-4454) or over to **Christmas in Kentucky** (203 East Washington Street, LaGrange 40031; 502-222-5010) for one-of-a-kind Christmas decorations.

And don't be alarmed when a freight train rumbles through town just feet from where you're standing!

Amazing Kentucky Fact The "Little Colonel" series of children's books by Annie Fellows Johnston were inspired by the community of Peewee Valley near LaGrange. One of the books was made into a film starring Shirley Temple.

Where to Eat

Back-Woods Bar-B-Que, *4205 Highway 146, LaGrange 40031; (502) 222–0300.* Barbecued ribs and chicken with all the fixins. $

Kaelin's Trackside Restaurant, *119 West Main Street, LaGrange 40031; (502) 329–5373.* Chicken, mashed potatoes,

and more at a country-style buffet. $

Red Pepper Deli-Cafe, *103 East Main, LaGrange 40031; (502) 225–0770.* Huge, creative sandwiches served in an artsy cafe atmosphere. $

Where to Stay

Holiday Inn Express, *I–71, exit 22, 1001 Paige Place, LaGrange 40031; (502) 222–5678.* Indoor pool. $$

Super 8 Motel, *I–71, exit 22, 1420 East Crystal Drive, LaGrange 40031; (800) 800–8000.* Continental breakfast, outdoor pool. $

Annual Events

Dulcibrrr Weekend, February, Rough River Dam State Resort Park, Leitchfield; (270) 257–2311

Living History Reenactments, Memorial Day and Labor Day weekends, Fort Duffield, West Point; (502) 922–4574

Native American Heritage Celebration, early June, Bardstown; (502) 348–0425

Pioneer Craft Show, mid-June, Old Bardstown Village; (502) 349–0291

Shelby County Fair and Horse Show, mid-to-late June, Shelbyville; (502) 633–6388

Bardstown Bluegrass Music Festival, late June, Bardstown; (502) 348–9677

Official Kentucky Old-Time Fiddlers Championship, July, Rough River Dam State Resort Park, Leitchfield; (800) 325–1713

Oldham County Fair, late July; (502) 222-5248

LaRue County Fair, late July–early August, Hodgenville; (270) 358-3411

Shelbyville Horse Show Jubilee, late July–Early August, Shelbyville; (502) 633-5029

Living History and Civil War Show, early August, Bardstown; (502) 349-0291

Spirit Fire Native American Music Festival, mid-August, Bardstown; (502) 348-0425

Kentucky Heartland Festival, late August, Elizabethtown; (270) 765-4334

Day of the Wolf PowWow, early October, Bardstown; (800) 638-4877

LaGrange Railroad Days, mid-October, LaGrange; (502) 222-1433

Lincoln Days Celebration, late October, Hodgenville; (270) 358-3411

Glendale Crossing Festival, late October, Glendale; (270) 369-6188

FFA Farm Toy Show, mid-December, Taylorsville; (502) 477-2871

Northern Kentucky

The northern Kentucky region offers both rural and urban entertainment. Northeast of Louisville, small towns hug the Ohio River. Historic sites, state parks, and many interesting community festivals are some of the things to enjoy in this part of the state. Then you reach Boone, Campbell, and Kenton counties (home to the cities of Burlington, Florence, Covington, Newport, Fort Mitchell, Fort Thomas, Highland Heights, Alexandria, and Wilder, among others). In this busy metro area, one of the state's largest, you'll find plenty of hotels, restaurants, and major attractions, such as the Newport Aquarium, Newport on the Levee with its IMAX theater, and the German neighborhood of MainStrasse Village. Cincinnati is just across the Ohio River; in fact, northern Kentucky is a good place to stay if you're visiting downtown Cincinnati attractions such as the Cincinnati Zoo or attending a Reds baseball game. This is big-city driving, so be prepared for heavy traffic and some confusing one-way streets. There are many interesting neighborhoods. Heading east to Maysville, then south into the upper Bluegrass region, your journey becomes rural again, with covered bridges, pioneer cabins, and farm fun.

The major roads in this region are I-71, between Louisville and the Cincinnati area, and I-75, which runs north-south, connecting northern Kentucky and the Lexington/Bluegrass region. I-275 and I-471 are connecting routes that you use to get around the metro area. To see many of the area attractions —or for a more scenic approach wherever you're heading—you can get off the interstates and take the back roads.

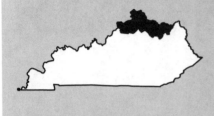

N

0   10   20
MILES

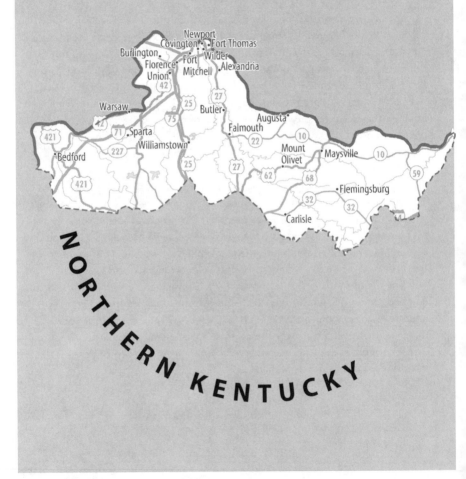

Newport
Covington · Fort Thomas
Burlington · Fort · Wilder
Florence Mitchell · Alexandria
Union
42

Warsaw
25   27
Butler
42   Augusta
71   Sparta   Falmouth
421   Williamstown   22   10
227   Mount   Maysville   10
Bedford   Olivet   59
25   62   68
27   Flemingsburg
32   32

Carlisle

75

NORTHERN KENTUCKY

Teresa's Top Ten
Picks for Northern Kentucky

1. Big Bone Lick State Park, (859) 384–3522

2. Newport Aquarium, (859) 491–FINS

3. Blue Licks Battlefield State Resort Park, (859) 289–5507

4. Dinsmore Homestead, (859) 586–6117

5. Covered Bridges, (606) 845–1223

6. Blue Marble Books, (859) 781–0602

7. MainStrasse Village, (513) 357–MAIN

8. Farm Fun, (Sunrock: 859–781–5502; Farmer Bill's: 859–391–5301; Noah's Ark: 859–635–0803)

9. Sugar Bush Farm, (859) 654–3433

10. Augusta Ferry, (606) 756–3291

Bedford

BRAY ORCHARDS (all ages)

US 42, between Sligo and Bedford; (502) 255–3607. Open daily mid-April through late November, Monday to Saturday from 8:00 A.M. to 7:00 P.M., Sunday from 10:00 A.M. to 7:00 P.M. Admission **Free** *(charge for purchases and some activities).*

The Pyle family's farm market offers all kinds of homegrown seasonal goodies, from strawberries in late May to pumpkins and apples in the fall, with sweet corn, beans, peaches, blueberries, and apples in between, plus jams, jellies, and honey. Always in season, however, is the farm's own rich and delicious homemade ice cream. Many of the fruit flavors are made using the farm's own produce. It's available by the pint and quart as well as by the cone, so bring a cooler. Every weekend in October, there are hayrides out to the pumpkin patch, and youngsters can play in the straw, wander through the corn maze, and enjoy the tricycle race track.

Apple Days The community of Bedford celebrates the apple harvest the second week of September with the **Trimble County Apple Festival.** Events include a children's art workshop along with food, music, crafts, and antiques booths. (502) 255–7196.

Carrollton

GENERAL BUTLER STATE RESORT PARK (all ages)

Highway 227N, off I–71, Carrollton 41008; (502) 732–4384 or (800) 325–0078, www.butlerkentucky.com. Follow the signs from I–71 exit 44. Admission and many activities **Free**.

If you're trying to please a family with varied interests—or want to dabble in a lot of different recreational activities—this state park is a good choice, because there's everything from miniature golf to a historic house tour. Whether you come in just for the day or are staying over in the lodge, cabins, or campground, you can rent pedal boats, canoes, and rowboats at the thirty-acre lake, walk two short (¼- and ½-mile) and easy hiking trails, tour the 1819 Butler-Turpin House, play miniature golf, or take on the nine-hole regulation golf course. There's a swimming pool for overnight guests. There are several

Amazing Kentucky Fact There used to be a downhill ski resort at General Butler State Resort Park. Kentucky winters, however, proved too warm for the resort to make snow.

playgrounds at the park, including a special one for children ages two to six. Picnic facilities are available, and there's a good restaurant in the lodge. The park has one of the best and busiest events schedules of any state park, so call ahead to see if something special is going on. (See sidebar on page 56 for a few of the events.)

THE LITTLE KENTUCKY FLYER RAILROAD (all ages)

Within General Butler State Resort Park; (502) 743–5414. Open Saturday and Sunday afternoons late spring through end of October, weather permitting. $

If you visit General Butler State Resort Park on a weekend in late spring through fall, be sure to take a ride on the Little Kentucky Flyer Railroad. This little train and its ⅓-mile route have been a part of the park for forty-nine years, but it was about out of steam when train enthusiast Chris Pate bought it and restored it in the 1990s. He's the one wearing the engineer's cap.

 OLD STONE JAIL (ages 8 and up)
Courthouse Square, Carrollton 41008; (800) 325–4290. Open Monday to Friday from 9:00 A.M. to 6:00 P.M., Saturday from 10:00 A.M. to 6:00 P.M., and Sunday from 10:00 A.M. to 5:00 P.M. **Free.**

Pick up keys at the tourism and convention bureau (515 Highland Avenue) if you want to see the inside of this jail used from 1880 to 1969. The first floor has been restored to show the old cells.

 MASTERSON HOUSE (ages 5 and up)
304 Ninth Street, Carrollton 41008; (502) 732–5786. Open Sundays in the summer from 2:00 to 4:30 P.M. or by appointment. $

This house overlooking the Ohio River was built in 1790 and is one of the oldest buildings still standing along the river west of the Alleghenies. Your children will notice the basement, which includes the kitchen and servants' quarters, and the family cemetery in front of the house.

Where to Eat

General Butler State Resort Park Lodge, *Highway 227N, off I–71, Carrollton 41008; (502) 732–4384 or (800) 325–0078.* Buffet and regional specialties. Children's menu. $

Ison's Bakery, *1402 Gilloch Avenue, Carrollton 41008; (502) 732–0707.* Famous for its apple dumplings. $

Welch's Riverside Restaurant, *505 Main Street, Carrollton 41008; (502)* 732–9118. Buffet and burgers with a great view of the Ohio. $

*S*cenic Picnic Point Park in Carrollton is a good place for a picnic. The park overlooks the point where the Ohio and Kentucky Rivers meet.

Where to Stay

General Butler State Resort Park, *KY 227, Carrollton 41008; (502) 732–4384 or (800) 325–0078.* Lodge rooms $$, cabins $$$, and campground $.

Days Inn, *I–71 and Highway 227 (exit 44), Carrollton 41008; (502) 732–9301.* Outdoor pool, free continental breakfast, pets allowed. $-$$

Lots of Special Reasons to Visit Carrollton

- **4,000 Easter eggs.** That's how many are hidden during the annual **Easter Celebration**, Easter weekend at General Butler State Resort Park. (800) 325-0078.

- **Shadow dancing.** In late April, Native American dancers and drummers gather at Carroll County Fair Grounds for the **Shadow of the Buffalo** powwow. One day is devoted to special children's activities. (502) 451-0384.

- **Putting with hammers.** That's just an example of the kinds of crazy golf challenges entrants must face in the Wacky Golf Weekend in late June at General Butler Park. Come to enter or just watch. (800) 325-0078.

- **Kilts and bagpipes.** Clans gather at General Butler State Resort Park the second weekend in May for dancing and athletics at **Kentucky Scottish Weekend**. (800) 325-0078 or www.kyscottishweekend.org.

- **Music with a point.** Bring a blanket, or camp over for a weekend of blues at the **Blues to the Point Festival** at Carrollton's riverside Point Park in early September. Children twelve and under admitted free with paying adult. (800) 325-4290.

- **Mud, sweat, and gears.** Several big mountain bike competitions are held annually at General Butler State Resort Park, including MudFest in April and a bike triathlon in August. (502) 732-4384 or www.bike butler.com.

- **Good scares.** The **Family Halloween Weekend** at General Butler State Resort Park the weekend before Halloween features pumpkin-carving contests, ghost stories, hayrides, and "haunted" train rides. (800) 325-0078.

- **Trees, teas, and treats.** December events abound, including a **Festival of Trees, Children's Winter Wonderfest**, and holiday teas at the **Butler-Turpin House** at General Butler State Resort Park. (800) 325-0078.

- **Tiny tracks.** Several toy train shows and swap meets are held throughout the year at General Butler State Resort Park. (800) 325-0078.

For More Information

Carrollton/Carroll County Tourism and Convention Commission, *515 Highland Avenue, Carrollton 41008; (502)* *732–7036 or (800) 325–4290, www. carrollcountyky.com*

Warsaw/Sparta

MARKLAND LOCKS AND DAM (all ages)

Off US 42 on the Ohio River, 3½ miles west of Warsaw; (859) 567–7661. Open daily from 7:00 A.M. to 10:00 P.M. **Free**.

One of twenty lock and dam complexes built on the Ohio River by the U.S. Army Corps of Engineers, Markland offers an excellent view of both the river and the locking process, with displays that explain how it works. The whole point is to maintain a water level suitable for river traffic. Bring a picnic (there are tables, a shelter, and

Amazing Kentucky Fact Over 239 million tons of commodities (everything from coal to grains) are transported by barge along the Ohio River each year. For comparison, about 30 million tons is transported on the Great Lakes system.

rest room facilities), and wait for a barge or boat to come along so you can see the locking process in action.

KENTUCKY SPEEDWAY (ages 8 and up)

Highway 35, Route 1, P.O. Box 15, Sparta 41086; (888) 652–RACE or (859) 567–3400, www.kentuckyspeedway.com. Race and events dates vary. $$$$

Older children might enjoy NASCAR racing at this 66,000-seat 1½-mile track, which opened in summer 2000. There is some free camping, but it's first come, first served and fills up fast. The track includes a restaurant and concessions; many families also come early and tailgate in the parking lot. Keep in mind that races can last up to four hours and that many are held at night and end very late. No children under thirteen are allowed to enter the pit area.

Union

BIG BONE LICK STATE PARK (all ages)

3380 Beaver Road, off KY 338, south of Union; (859) 384–3522. Open daily from dawn to dusk. Museum open daily from 9:00 A.M. to 5:00 P.M. in summer; closed Monday and Tuesday the rest of the year. Admission and many activities

Free. $

Some 12,000 years ago, at the end of the last Ice Age, this was a place where giant bison, sloths, mastodon, and oxen came to lick salt, got stuck in the boggy soil, and died. Today it's a place where the buffalo roam. The combination of old bones and new bison makes for a great family outing. Your children will enjoy the Discovery Trail, an easy 1-mile loop (paved, so you can take a stroller or wheelchair) that meanders through the swampland and past the last remaining salt-sulphur spring. Along the way are diorama displays with models of prehistoric animals. But the best part awaits at the end: the park's bison herd. If you visit in late spring or summer you'll likely see some calves. There's also a seasonal indoor museum with plenty of real bones, including a huge mastodon tooth that you can touch, and changing exhibits about local history. You're not allowed to take any found fossils from the park, but children may have fun looking, anyway, and the museum shop sells some as souvenirs. The park also includes playgrounds, picnic areas, basketball and tennis courts, and a campground with a swimming pool. But don't expect to get a restful night's sleep—those bison can be loud! The **Salt Festival** in mid-October includes demonstrations of pioneer activities and crafts.

Rabbit Hash Take KY 18 and 536 between Big Bone Lick and Burlington for a scenic drive that offers river views and passes right by a shopping spot popular since 1831. Rabbit Hash General Store looks as if it has been around at least that long. Step inside and admire the old wooden display cases, and pick up a soft drink or a bottled version of old-time sarsaparilla. The store carries some crafts, along with snacks and general foodstuffs. (859) 586–7744.

BIG BONE GARDENS (all ages)

Across from Big Bone Lick State Park; (859) 384–1949. Open Saturday and Sunday mid-April through mid-July. Free.

You can look at a variety of demonstration gardens at this privately owned nursery. There are water gardens, herb gardens, and children's favorite, the Gnome Garden, filled with decorative statuary.

Northern Kentucky Metro Area

As you head northeast from Big Bone Lick and Rabbit Hash, you will enter one of Kentucky's largest metropolitan areas, which is also the southernmost part of the Cincinnati, Ohio, metro area. The "Southern Side of Cincinnati," as the area calls itself, is a collection of distinct communities and neighborhoods that make up three large counties, Boone, Kenton, and Campbell. Some parts, like Burlington to the west, seem almost rural (until a big jet from Cincinnati International Airport goes overhead); the riverfront areas of Covington and Newport seem like the neighborhoods in a big city (which they are). I-71/75 is the major north-south artery. I-275 cuts across the metro area from west to east, and I-471 connects certain portions of the northeastern part of the area. We've actually had better luck getting around off the interstates, although it takes longer. The Northern Kentucky Convention and Visitors Bureau dispenses information about all the communities in the metro area and can provide a map. It's a good idea to request one in advance through the Web site at www.staynky.com, or stop at the Florence Welcome Center at exit 177 off I-75. The folks at the main office in Rivercenter are extremely helpful, but getting there can be a hassle with little ones in tow, since you have to park (and pay) in an underground garage complex and find your way to the office inside.

In this section, attractions are listed in the individual communities in which they are located, and communities are listed from west to east. Lodging in any of the areas would be fairly convenient to all the attractions.

Burlington/Florence

DINSMORE HOMESTEAD (all ages)

KY 18 (Burlington Pike), 6½ miles west of Burlington; (859) 586–6117, www.dinsmorefarm.org. Open from April 1 through December 15, Wednesday, Saturday, and Sunday, from 1:00 to 5:00 P.M. Tours on the hour. $

Take a tour of this 1842 house and numerous outbuildings, and you'll learn about family life in Kentucky before and after the Civil War. Five generations of the Dinsmore family lived here, and the house is decorated with a bounty of original possessions, including clothing, furnishings, the elk head bagged by family friend Theodore Roosevelt, and letters. Costumed interpreters add to the illusion with demonstrations of nineteenth-century farm activities and home arts such as cooking and basketmaking. The homestead frequently sponsors wonderful summer educational programs for elementary-school children—everything from archaeology to writing workshops—and there are programs for older children and adults, too. Julia Dinsmore, a daughter of original owners James and Martha Dinsmore, lived here for fifty-four years and wrote many poems and sonnets extensively about her experience; you can buy a book of her poems in the gift shop. The Dinsmore Harvest Festival, on the last weekend of September, features demonstrations of pioneer crafts from cider making to silhouette cutting, plus a petting zoo, children's activities, art display, and live music.

 ## BOONE COUNTY ARBORETUM AT CENTRAL PARK (all ages)

6028 Camp Ernst Road (KY 237), Burlington 41005; (859) 586–6101, www.bcarboretum.com. Open daily year-round from dawn to dusk. **Free**.

Nature meets high tech at this arboretum, the result of a massive county and volunteer planting effort between 1996 and 1999. If you see people walking around this arboretum with handheld computers, here's why: The more than 800 different kinds of trees and 1,500 different kinds of shrubs planted on the 121 acres are not only labeled, they're electronically catalogued using a global positioning system. Using the computers, arboretum staff can easily locate any plant for care and growth tracking. Along the 2 miles of paved paths, you'll pass butterfly gardens, woodland areas, and ornamental plantings. Stop at one of the three information booths for a map, or check the schedule of guided tours. In keeping with the high-tech nature of things, you can check the Web site to find the location of specific plants or to see "what's hot" (blooming).

 ## BOONE COUNTY CLIFFS STATE NATURE PRESERVE (ages 8 and up)

Middle Creek Road off KY 18 west of Burlington; (502) 573–2886, www.ky naturepreserves.org. Open daily from dawn to dusk. No rest room facilities. No picnicking allowed. **Free**.

It's kind of surprising to find so much nature so close to an urban area, but here's another good hiking place. Interesting 20- to 40-foot cliffs, abundant wildflowers (especially in spring), and plenty of birds are what you'll see. (*Note:* Some areas are fairly steep.) Trail maps may not be available on site, so call the state nature preserve commission in advance.

Where to Eat

Karlo's Bistro Italia, *I–75, exit 182, Florence 41042; (859) 282–8282.* Made-to-order pasta and Italian favorites, reasonably priced with generous portions. Lunch $, dinner $$

Little Place Restaurant, *2971 Washington Street (KY 18), Burlington 41005; (859) 586–9421.* Family run for thirty years and a favorite with locals; serves Southern fried chicken and other old-fashioned cooking, chili, Kentucky Silk Pie. $

Matsuya Japanese Restaurant, *7149 Manderlay Drive, Florence 41042; (859) 746–1199.* Extensive menu of authentic Japanese sushi and noodle dishes (the restaurant opened to accommodate Japanese families at Toyota's North American headquarters in nearby Erlanger). $–$$

Ming Garden, *4953 Houston Road, Florence 41042; (859) 268–2688.* Exceptional buffet with Chinese favorites. $

Where to Stay

Courtyard Cincinnati Airport, *3990 Olympic Boulevard, Erlanger 41018; (859) 647–9900.* Indoor pool, restaurant, continental breakfast. $$

Hampton Inn Cincinnati Airport South, *7393 Turfway Road, Florence 41042; (859) 283–1600.* Outdoor pool, free continental breakfast. $$–$$$

Wildwood Inn Tropical Dome and Theme Spas, *7809 US 42, Florence 41042; (800) 758–2335 or www.wildwood-inn.com.* Rooms overlooking pool area with tropical plants, playground equipment, and games. (Unfortunately, the theme spas—including a cave room and African huts—are for two adults only.) $$$–$$$$

For More Information

Florence Welcome Center, *Exit 177 off I–75, Florence; (859) 384–3130. Open daily from 8:00 A.M. to 6:00 P.M.* The easiest and most convenient place to get brochures and maps about the northern Kentucky area. The staff is also very helpful on the phone.

Northern Kentucky Visitors' Center, *50 East River Center Boulevard, Suite 100, Covington 41011; (800) STAY–NKY or (859) 261–4677 (hotel reservations and hotel packages); general info (800) 447–8489 or www.staynky.com.*

Fort Mitchell

VENT HAVEN MUSEUM OF VENTRILOQUISM (ages 6 and up)

33 West Maple Avenue, Fort Mitchell 41011; (859) 341–0461. May 1 to September 31, Monday through Friday, by appointment only. $

So why are there more than 500 "dummies" in Fort Mitchell, Kentucky? This unusual collection is the legacy of a local businessman and amateur ventriloquist, W. S. Berger, who collected ventriloquist "figures" (the term preferred by serious ventriloquists) from the 1930s until his death in 1973. He left a trust fund to maintain and expand the collection. Along with the merely curious, this little museum attracts professional and amateur ventriloquists from around the United States. Along with the figures there are such novelties as a talking cane, a talking painting, and a grandfather clock that turns into a ventriloquist figure. Some children and adults will be fascinated by the rows and rows of staring figures; others might find the experience a bit eerie.

Covington/Kenton County

MAINSTRASSE VILLAGE (all ages)

*Between Fifth and Eighth Streets north and south, Philadelphia and Main Streets west and east, Covington; (859) 491–0458; 24-hour events line (513) 357–MAIN, www.mainstrasse.org. Shop hours vary daily. Public sculpture always on view **Free**. To get there from I–75/71, take Covington Fifth Street exit (exit 192). **Free** parking is available in the Fifth Street lot.*

The historic buildings with their Old World look and the quaint shops and restaurants found along Covington's Main Street and surrounding streets are a reminder of northern Kentucky's nineteenth-century German heritage. Public sculptures have a fairy-tale motif. Read the Grimm Brothers' story of the "Goose Girl" about the princess whose identity is stolen before you come, then see the bronze fountain created by Greek sculptor Elefcherious Karkadoulias. The familiar tale of "The Pied Piper of Hamelin" comes to life on the hour at the **Carroll Chimes Bell Tower** in

Amazing Kentucky Fact Covington, Kentucky, native Haven Gillespie wrote the words to the classic holiday song "Santa Claus Is Coming to Town."

Goebel Park (Fifth and Philadelphia Streets). This Gothic tower includes a forty-three-bell carillon that plays while wooden figures called jacquemarts act out the story of the Pied Piper of Hamelin on the tower's second level. Among the shops in the neighborhood of special interest to children are the **Doll Clinic,** 522 Main Street (859-291-1174); **The Magic Shop,** 526 Philadelphia Street (859-491-1313); **Centerfield,** sports collectibles, 627 Main Street (859-431-7390); and **Mini Splendid Things,** 626 West Main (859-261-5500), with dollhouses and miniatures. Stop by **Strudel Haus,** 520 West Sixth Street (859-491-3663), for ice cream or homemade strudel, or have a complete German dinner at **Wertheim's Gausthaus,** 514 West Sixth Street (859-261-1233).

DEVOU PARK (all ages)

1600 Montague Road, Covington 41011; (859) 491–4003. Open daily. **Free**. *To get to the park from I–75/71, take the Twelfth Street Covington exit.*

Taking the children to the playground here is especially scenic. Devou (pronounced De-VOO) Park offers one of the best overlooks of the river in the area. At nearly 700 acres, this is also Covington's largest park. In addition to playgrounds there are picnic areas, a small lake for fishing, walking trails, and the Behringer-Crawford Museum of Natural History. The park's amphitheater hosts **Free** plays and concerts in the summer.

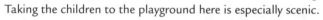
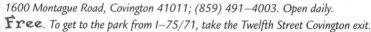

MainStrasse Celebration

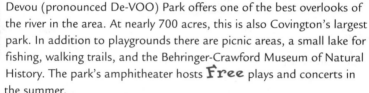

- **Maifest**, the weekend after Mother's Day

- **Christmas in July**, the third weekend in July

- **Oktoberfest**, the weekend after Labor Day

- **Village Harvest Celebration**, in mid-October

- **Santa Claus arrives** in the village in early December—on horseback!—with apples and nuts for the children. The village offers **Lunch with Saint Nick** for children, usually the second and third Sundays in December, with **vintage carousel rides** the second and third weekends in December.

*S*uspense and Suspension At first, you think there's a person sitting on the park bench overlooking the river. Gradually, you realize that it's a statue. The seven bronze statues of local historic figures in the riverfront park along Riverside Drive (between Second and Fourth Streets) in Covington will have you doing double takes, particularly the one of abolitionist James Bradley sitting on a bench. Other things to see from this greenspace are the Cincinnati skyline and the blue Roebling Suspension Bridge. Built in 1868, this was the world's first modern suspension bridge, and it was a prototype for the Brooklyn Bridge in New York. (I hope you'll be better prepared than I was to answer questions about what a suspension bridge is!) One of the statues in the park is of the man who engineered this marvel, John Roebling.

BEHRINGER-CRAWFORD MUSEUM OF NATURAL HISTORY (ages 5 and up)

Devou Park, 1600 Montague Road, P.O. Box 67, Covington 41011; (859) 491–4003. Open Tuesday to Friday from 10:00 A.M. to 5:00 P.M., Saturday and Sunday from 1:00 to 5:00 P.M.; closed Mondays and holidays. $

This museum in Devou Park includes twelve gallery areas showing artifacts and exhibits relating to the local region, from paleontology to fine arts. It's all housed in an 1848 Federal-style farmhouse that belonged to the Devou family (their farm is now the park). The museum takes its name from William Behringer, an amateur archaeologist (he led many of the early excavations at Big Bone Lick), taxidermist, and big game hunter who donated his collections in 1950. The "Crawford" part of the name honors Ellis Crawford, the museum's first curator.

RAILWAY MUSEUM OF GREATER CINCINNATI (ages 4 and up)

315 West Southern Avenue, Covington 41015; (859) 491–RAIL. Open March through October, Wednesday and Saturday from 10:00 A.M. to 4:00 P.M. Guided tours Sunday between 12:30 and 4:30 P.M. $

Train enthusiasts will enjoy strolling through this outdoor museum to see restored cabooses, locomotives, diner cars, and sleepers. You may also see volunteers at work restoring other vintage train cars.

AFRICAN AMERICAN MUSEUM AND CULTURAL CENTER (all ages)

824 Greenup Street, Covington 41011; (859) 431–5700. Open Monday to Friday from 10:00 A.M. to 4:00 P.M. Free.

Housed in a former school, this museum focuses on the lifestyles of African Americans from 1865 to 1965.

Spiritual Experiences

Spiritual Experiences You can't help but notice the many beautiful churches as you drive through northern Kentucky neighborhoods. There are also some out-of-the-ordinary church-related attractions in the area that may interest your family.

- Did you see the animated film *The Hunchback of Notre Dame*? If so, the **Cathedral Basilica of the Assumption** (*Madison Avenue between Eleventh and Twelfth Streets, Covington; 859–431–2060. Open daily from 10:30 A.M. to 4:00 P.M.*) should look familiar; it's modeled after the Paris cathedral. Though smaller in scale, the gargoyles, sculpture, and flying buttresses look so authentic, you expect to see Quasimodo at any minute. Inside are the world's largest handmade stained-glass window and eighty-one others, as well as large-scale oil paintings.

- ·**The Garden of Hope** (699 Edgecliff Drive, Covington 41014; 859–491–1777) is a replica of the tomb of Jesus in Jerusalem, and how it came to be located in Covington is a fascinating story. In 1938, a local minister named Morris Coers visited the Holy Land and was so moved by the experience that he wanted to help others who could not visit there understand what it was like. He spent the next twenty years planning and building this replica tomb, even bringing the caretaker of the Jerusalem garden to Covington to oversee the plans. The garden also includes a chapel patterned after a Spanish mission, a Carpenter Shop, a marble statue of Jesus preaching the Sermon on the Mount, and Holy Land artifacts such as a stone from the Jordan River and ancient tools from Nazareth. The garden is open daily year-round; call to arrange for a tour of the buildings (usually not available on Sunday afternoons).

- Northern Kentucky's **Monte Casino House of Worship** made it into *Ripley's Believe It or Not* as the world's smallest church (just 6 by 9 feet). Only one person at a time can fit inside. It's located across the street from Thomas More College, 2771 Turkeyfoot Road, in Crestview Hills (southwest of Covington and Fort Mitchell). Open from dawn to dusk every day. Take the Turkeyfoot Road exit south off I-275.

MORNING STAR POTTERY PAINTING STUDIO (ages 5 and up)

117 East Fourth Street, Covington 41011; (859) 581–3900. Open Tuesday from 11:00 A.M. to 6:00 P.M., Wednesday to Friday from 11:00 A.M. to 9:00 P.M., Saturday from 10:00 A.M. to 7:00 P.M.

This bright and festive shop welcomes creatively inclined children (and adults) to paint pottery. Staffers will fire your pieces and ship them to your home.

BB RIVERBOATS (ages 4 and up)

Covington Landing, Madison Avenue at the Ohio River, Covington; (859) 261–8500 or (800) 261–8586, www.bbriverboats.com. Cruise year-round; schedule varies. Daily sightseeing and Fun Lunch cruises for children in summer. $$$–$$$$

There are all kinds of excursions offered aboard this cruise company's three sternwheelers, the *Belle of Cincinnati,* the *River Queen,* and the *Mark Twain.* A one-hour narrated general sightseeing cruise is offered daily; the boats are air-conditioned and have snacks available onboard. In summer there are also daily two-hour Fun Lunch cruises with bingo, sing-alongs, and banjo music for ages four and up; the ticket includes a buffet meal. Also ask about combination Newport Aquarium membership/cruises. Cruises are offered year-round, including Santa cruises at holiday time. *Note:* Cruises usually depart from Covington Landing, but in the summer, sightseeing cruises leave from Newport Dock. So make sure you understand which dock you're leaving from, or you'll literally miss the boat.

Where to Eat

Cabin by the Creek, *322 Madison Pike, Covington 41017; (859) 356–7111.* Good seafood featuring crab cakes, frog legs, classic burgers, burgoo, and blackberry cobbler. Ribs on the weekend. $–$$

Mike Fink's, *foot of Greenup on Riverside Drive, Covington 41011; (859) 261–4212.* Northern Kentucky's original floating riverfront restaurant features steaks, seafood, sandwiches, and a popular Sunday brunch. $$

Sports Video Cafe at Jillian's, *1200 Jillian Way, Covington 41011; (859) 491–5388.* Video games and huge TVs, varied menu plus kids' menu; "backyard barbecue picnic" includes ribs, barbecue chicken, corn on the cob, fries, and coleslaw for four plus game tokens for one price. $$

Wertheim's Gasthaus, *514 West Sixth Street, Covington; (859) 261–1233.* Wiener and other schnitzels, plus other hearty German dishes. Toy box for kids, porch and patio dining. $–$$

Where to Stay

Clarion Hotel Riverview, *668 West Fifth Street, I–75, exit 192, Covington; (859) 491–1200.* Indoor pool, revolving restaurant, balconies with great views. $$$

The Drawbridge Inn, *2477 Royal Drive, Fort Mitchell, off I–75's Buttermilk Pike exit 186; (800) 354–9793 or www. drawbridgeinn.com.* This castle-themed hotel (complete with moat) is not the newest in the area, but my children enjoyed staying here. The rooms look like normal hotel rooms. Indoor/outdoor pools and several restaurants. $$$

Hampton Inn Riverfront, *200 Crescent Avenue, Covington, (800) HAMPTON.* Continental breakfast, indoor pool. $$$

For More Information

Florence Welcome Center, *Exit 177 off I–75, Florence; (859) 384–3130. Open daily from 8:00 A.M. to 6:00 P.M.* The easiest and most convenient place to get brochures and maps about the northern Kentucky area.

Northern Kentucky Visitors' Center, *50 East River Center Boulevard, Suite 100, Covington 41011; (800) STAY–NKY or (859) 261–4677 (hotel reservations and hotel packages); general info (800) 447–8489 or www.staynky.com.*

Newport

NEWPORT AQUARIUM (all ages)
One Aquarium Way (in the Newport on the Levee complex), Newport 41071; (859) 491–FINS, www.newportaquarium.com. Open daily from 10:00 A.M. to 7:00 P.M., Memorial Day to Labor Day. Closes at 6:00 P.M. the rest of the year. Adults $$$, children $$. On-site parking $.

"Omigosh, what is that?" "Cool!" "Eeeeyuuuuck!" You'll hear this a lot as you tour the Newport Aquarium—from fellow adults as much as from children. This small but nicely laid out aquarium includes a little bit of everything that swims, floats, and soaks. There are about 11,000 fresh and saltwater animals, from beautiful tropical fish and delicate jellyfish to scary-looking eels, several kinds of sharks, and colorful but deadly dart frogs. You'll see creatures you could hardly

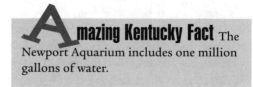

Amazing Kentucky Fact The Newport Aquarium includes one million gallons of water.

imagine, like the stonefish and the flashlight fish, along with familiar creatures such as turtles, alligators, penguins, and an octopus. Seamless acrylic tunnels allow you to view fish swimming above and below you, creating the illusion that you are surrounded by water. All ages seemed to be having a good time both times we've visited. No strollers are allowed; the staff will exchange your stroller for a child pack at the entrance (a good idea, since you may have to lift younger children to see some exhibits, anyway). An on-site restaurant serves sandwiches and snacks, and there's a huge gift store.

A Day Family Adventure Viewing animals is always fun, but often the human animals are every bit as interesting to watch. One time when we visited the Newport Aquarium, we saw a mother and her two daughters closely examining a giant sea turtle. The younger daughter pressed her face right up against the glass, eyeball to eyeball with the creature. "He kind of reminds me of you, Mom," she said in all sincerity. Her older sister glanced mischievously at their mother. "Yeah," she added. "Old and wrinkly."

IMAX THEATRE AT NEWPORT ON THE LEVEE (ages 4 and up)

1 Levee Way (Plaza Level), Newport 41071; (859) 491–IMAX, www.newport levee.com. Open daily; call for show times. $$

Another star attraction at the Newport at the Levee shopping and entertainment complex is the huge 3-D IMAX Theatre, featuring a six-story-tall (and eight-story-wide) screen and an 11,500-watt sound system. A variety of films will be showing at any time, with a varied schedule. Not only can you see movies made for IMAX here, you can also catch larger-than-regular-theater projections of family classics, from Disney films to *Indiana Jones*.

WORLD PEACE BELL (all ages)

403 York Street, Newport 41071; (859) 655–9500. Always on view. **Free**.

While you're in the neighborhood, take a few moments to see this large bronze bell; it's a couple of blocks from the levee. Created to honor the new millennium, this 12-foot-by-12-foot bronze bell was designed by the Verdin Bell Company of Cincinnati, cast in France, shipped to New Orleans, and floated up the Mississippi and Ohio rivers to Newport. The bell was first rung at the moment 1999 became 2000.

Images on the bell include the moon landing; Columbus's ships the *Nina, Pinta*, and *Santa Maria;* and other symbols of human achievement. The bell rings each day at noon, with chimes on the hour.

Amazing Kentucky Fact The World Peace Bell in Newport is the world's largest free-swinging bell. It weighs 66,000 pounds; for comparison, the Liberty Bell in Philadelphia weighs 2,080 pounds.

Other Things to See and Do

Old Courthouse, *Fourth and York Streets, Newport. Open Monday through Friday from 8:30 A.M. to 4:00 P.M..* An 1833 courthouse with skylight depicting the seal of Kentucky.

Stained Glass Theater, *Eighth and York Streets, Newport; (859) 291–7464.* Community theater in a former church building.

More to Do at Newport on the Levee

- Make, name, and dress up a teddy bear at *Adopt-A-Bear* (859–292–0700).

- Play more than 200 video, midway, and virtual reality games—plus eat lunch or dinner—at **GameWorks.** (859–581–PLAY). (Children under eighteen must leave at 10:00 P.M.)

- See a movie at the AMC Newport 20—with twenty screens, there's bound to be something you want to see. (859) 261–8100.

- The complex includes some shops and a variety of eateries, from a pretzel/hot dog stand to full-service seafood, burger, and Italian restaurants.

- Parking is available in an underground garage ($), as well as at nearby pay lots and on the street.

- The complex and surrounding area is the location for concerts and festivals, including the Newport Italian Festival in mid-June and the Newport Arts and Music Festival in late July (859–292–3666).

mazing Kentucky Fact Daniel Carter Beard, born in Covington, was one of the founders of the Boy Scouts of America.

Where to Eat

Dewey's Pizza, *1 Aquarium Way, Newport 41071; (859) 431–9700.* Local favorite; standard toppings plus unusual ones such as goat cheese, capers, and barbecued chicken. Even the crust is good. $

Dixie Chili, *733 Monmouth Avenue, Newport 41071; (859) 291–5337.* Northern Kentucky tradition since 1929; good chili, plus salads and sandwiches; order at counter. Other locations in northern metro area. Open late. $

Green Derby, *846 York Street, Newport 41071; (859) 431–8740.* Family owned since 1947; famous for its fried halibut sandwich, "Derby salad" (hot slaw using lettuce), and potato puffs (breaded, fried, mashed potato balls). Good pork chops and fried chicken; cute hand-painted tabletops. $

Pompilio's, *600 Washington Street, Newport 41071; (859) 581–3065.* Italian favorites. Look for memorabilia from movie *Rain Man.* In summer a bocce ball (lawn croquet) game may be under way out back. $

Sloppy Joe's, *Riverboat Row, Newport 41071; (859) 581–2800.* Seafood is the specialty for adults; good kids' menu and view of river. Kids enjoy the outdoor walkway, where they can feed the ducks. $

Sylvia's Mexican Restaurant, *15 East Seventh Street, Newport 41071; (859) 431–8110.* Show your kids what real gorditas, tamales, sopas, and burritos taste like, or try a roast pork torta (sandwich) or combo platter. $

The Syndicate, *18 East Fifth Street, Newport 41071; (859) 491–8000.* Older children may get a kick out of eating in this "gangster"-themed restaurant, with antique cars out front and inside exhibits relating to local vice history. A few blocks from the Levee complex. Kids' menu. $$$

York St. Cafe, *738 York Street, Newport 41071; (859) 261–9675.* Eclectic menu offered in a converted pharmacy, complete with original floor-to-ceiling wood medicine cases. $$

Where to Stay

Comfort Suites/Riverfront, *420 Riverboat Row, I–471, exit 5, Newport 41071; (859) 291–6700.* $$$

Travelodge, *222 York Street, Newport 41071; (859) 291–4434.* $

For More Information

Florence Welcome Center, *Exit 177 off I–75, Florence; (859) 384–3130. Open daily from 8:00 A.M. to 6:00 P.M.* The easiest and most convenient place to get brochures and maps about the northern Kentucky area.

Northern Kentucky Visitors' Center, *50 East River Center Boulevard, Suite 100, Covington 41011; (800) STAY–NKY or (859) 261–4677 (hotel reservations and hotel packages); general info (800) 447–8489 or www.staynky.com.*

The Sweet Route If you go from Newport to Fort Thomas via Highway 8 (which runs along the river), you'll pass through the community of Bellevue and right by **Schneider's Sweet Shop** (420 Fairfield Avenue [Route 8], Bellevue 41073; 859–431–3545). Instead of getting ice cream at the Levee Complex in Newport, we waited and bought it at this neighborhood confectionery. Schneider's also sells all kinds of homemade candies, Ice Balls (kind of like snow cones), and Ice Balls with ice cream inside, as well as seasonal treats such as candy apples. Open daily from 11:00 A.M. to 8:00 P.M. or so.

Fort Thomas

BLUE MARBLE BOOKS (all ages)

1356 South Fort Thomas Avenue, Fort Thomas 41075; (859) 781–0602. Open Monday to Friday from 10:00 A.M. to 6:00 P.M., Saturday from 10:00 A.M. to 6:00 P.M. Closed Sunday. **Free**.

If your children enjoy (or enjoyed) Margaret Wise Brown's *Goodnight Moon,* stop by this independently owned bookstore to see a veritable shrine to this children's classic. Owner Tina Moore has turned an upstairs room into the replica of "The Great Green Room," down to the "bowlful of mush" (which, thankfully, is synthetic). Older readers will also appreciate the "Secret Garden" behind the store. And all young (and would-be) readers and their parents will appreciate the extensive collection of children's books and knowledgeable recommendations.

TOWER PARK (all ages)

South Fort Thomas Avenue, Fort Thomas. Open daily. **Free**.

This park is named for the Civil War–era tower designed to provide an overlook of the Ohio River. Today, the tower overlooks a playground and sports fields, but the park's trails take you on a tour around some historic buildings that were used as officers' quarters.

Where to Eat

Midway Cafe, *1017 South Fort Thomas Avenue, Fort Thomas 41075, across from Tower Park; (859) 781–7666.* Quesadillas, cheeseburgers, and the house specialty, an Icelandic codfish sandwich, in an 1894 building. $

Wilder

SUNROCK FARM (all ages)

103 Gibson Lane, Wilder 41076; (859) 781–5502, www.sunrockfarm.org. Open Monday to Friday from 2:00 to 3:00 or 4:00 P.M., Saturday from 2:00 to 4:00 P.M. $–$$

This rural oasis, only minutes from urban Newport, is the brainchild of "Farmer Frank" Traina. Its mission is to educate children about the importance of conservation by giving them hands-on experiences. Sign up for a one- or two-hour family tour, and you and your children will have the opportunity to milk a goat, bottle-feed kids, gather eggs, and experience the history and natural beauty of this nineteenth-century farm and farmhouse.

Alexandria

CAMPBELL COUNTY LOG CABIN MUSEUM (ages 4 and up)

234 West Clay Ridge Road, Alexandria 41001; (859) 635–5913. Walking tour daily; guided tours by appointment. Free. To get there, take Highway 27 south, and turn right at Grants Lick Road.

This is definitely a teacher-approved museum—because a teacher built it. Ken Reis, an area middle school art teacher, has reconstructed two pioneer cabins and assembled a variety of interesting things from past times, including turn-of-the-century schoolbooks and antique tractors. You can stop by and walk around, but if you want to go inside the cabins, you'll need to arrange a visit with Mr. Reis. Since he's a teacher, summer is the best time; his availability varies during school months.

Where to Eat

Harry's Hometown Diner, *6875 Alexandria Pike (by Wal-Mart), Alexandria 41001; (859) 635–1943.* Classic '50s diner with metal-and-glass exterior, red vinyl booths, and an oldies jukebox. Great grilled burgers, homemade blue plate specials, and desserts. "Doo Wop Meals" for kids. $

Butler/Falmouth

THAXTON'S CANOE TRIPS (ages 6 and up)

US 27 and Hornbeek Road, Butler 41006; (859) 472–2000. $$$; children under 12 **Free** *with two paid adult fares.*

The Licking River meanders through northern Kentucky from Newport/Covington to Cynthiana. You can follow along it by canoe from this outfitter post south of Alexandria. The guides offer 6- and 12-mile excursions as well as overnight trips and "moonlight floats." Primitive camping and cabins are available for overnight stays.

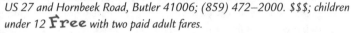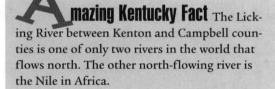

Amazing Kentucky Fact The Licking River between Kenton and Campbell counties is one of only two rivers in the world that flows north. The other north-flowing river is the Nile in Africa.

KINCAID LAKE STATE PARK (all ages)

KY 159 off Highway 27, northeast of Falmouth; (859) 654–3531. Open daily; some activities seasonal. Admission **Free**.

Ever played paddle tennis? (It's kind of a cross between tennis and Ping-Pong.) Give it a try at this recreational park only a half hour south of northern Kentucky's metro area. Equipment is available at the park. You can also rent a boat and go fishing in the 183-acre lake, play miniature golf, walk one of the looped hiking trails, go swimming in the lakeside pool (summer only), enjoy the playgrounds, or have a picnic. There's a nice campground with both tent and RV sites.

SUGAR BUSH FARM (ages 6 and up)

Green Road off Highway 1054, near Falmouth; (859) 654–3433. Hours and activities vary; call first. **Free**.

Now, here's something fun to do in February: See how maple syrup is made. Sugar Bush Farm taps in to some 200 trees using an elaborate system of plastic tubing that runs the sap downhill and into two tanks. In late winter and early spring the sap is boiled down and strained (it takes 40 to 50 gallons of sap to make 1 gallon of syrup). Activities depend on the weather, so call ahead to see if anything is going on. The amount of syrup produced each year varies—a dry summer means less sap. Sugar Bush Farm also makes honey, gathered from thirteen hives. The farm usually has a booth at the annual **Falmouth Wool Festival**, near Kincaid Park, in early October (but there may not be any maple syrup left that late in the year). Activities at the festival include demonstrations of wool spinning and sorghum making, as well as a petting zoo, music, and food.

Williamstown

FARMER BILL'S (all ages)

Windrift Farms, 1790 Baton Rouge Road, Williamstown 41097; (859) 391–5301, www.farmerbill.net. Open June through October; hours vary, so call ahead. **Free**.

Fall and early December are the best times to visit this farm market. In October there are festival activities on weekends, including a pumpkin patch, corn maze, petting zoo, playground, hayrides, and a haunted barn. In December, you can get your tree and wreaths here while enjoying "Country Christmas" activities such as a live nativity scene and carriage rides. Maw-maw's Kitchen at the farm serves country cooking for lunch daily and dinner on Saturday nights.

MULLINS LOG CABIN (all ages)

Scaffold Lick Road, off Highway 36 near Cordova; (859) 824–0565 or (859) 824–3451. No regular hours; call ahead. Take exit 154 off I–75, and follow Highway 35 10 miles to Scafford Lick Road. $; overnight stay for a family of up to six people $$.

Want to really get away from it all? Spend the night in this 1800s log cabin—no electricity, no indoor plumbing, and you have to pump your water. This rustic little cabin was saved from destruction by owner Judy Mullins, who with her husband and son dismantled and moved it to its present location. Special events at the cabin include **Wild Herb Day,** the first Saturday in May, with crafts demonstrations and herb walks, and **Christmas in the Country,** the first weekend in December, with basketweaving and quilting demonstrations.

Other Things to See and Do

Grant County Flea Market, *US 25 between Williamstown and Dry Ridge; (859) 824–3200.* Indoor market Thursday through Sunday, plus outdoor booths on weekends. Mix of old and new, with free entertainment and on-site food vendors.

Where to Eat

The Country Grill, *exit 159 off I–75, Dry Ridge; (859) 824–6000.* Sandwiches, daily specials, and homemade pie. $

Lucas-Moore Drug Store, *112 North Main Street, Williamstown 41097; (859) 824–3349.* Soda fountain serving sandwiches and ice cream. $

Maw-Maw's Restaurant, *1790 Baton Rouge Road, Williamstown 41097; (859) 391–5301 or www.farmerbill.net.* Home cooking for lunch daily, dinner on Friday. $

Where to Stay

Holiday Inn Express, *1050 Fashion Ridge Road, exit 179 off I–75, Dry Ridge; (859) 824–7121.* $$

For More Information

Grant County Tourism and Convention Commission, *1116 Fashion Ridge Road (in the Outlet Center), Dry Ridge* *41035; (859) 824–3451 or (800) 382–7117.*

California

NOAH'S ARK FARM (all ages)

Koehler Road, off Highway 10, California 41007; (859) 635–0803. Open April 1 through November 30, Wednesday to Sunday from 10:00 A.M. to 6:00 P.M. $ ($$ to spend the night).

Bet you didn't even know Kentucky had a California! I didn't either, until I heard about this fun farm located between Alexandria and Augusta. When you take a tour, you'll see all kinds of animals, from regular farm types, like sheep and pigs, to peacocks and emus. You and your kids can bottle-feed lambs and piglets, ask questions of "Dusty the Trick Horse," and watch Max the Macaw put on a show. There are also pony rides and picnic areas. You can even spend the night.

Augusta

AUGUSTA FERRY (all ages)

Ferry Landing, Augusta; (606) 756–3291. Open daily to vehicle or pedestrian traffic (weather permitting) from 8:00 A.M. to 8:00 P.M. $

The quaint river town of Augusta was founded in 1795 because it was a location where you could safely cross the river, and a ferry has been carrying folks across since 1798. Today the Augusta Ferry will take you and your car across. A round trip takes only a few minutes (or you can get off and explore Brown County, Ohio), but my children loved this ride and its simple pleasures—

Amazing Kentucky Fact Scenes from the movies *Centennial* and *Huckleberry Finn* were filmed in Augusta.

seeing the efficient crew at work, peering down into the rushing water, feeling the wind against their faces, and watching the shoreline and its buildings and people recede.

Other Things to See and Do

Augusta Sternwheel Regatta, *on the Ohio River. (606) 756–2183.* Last weekend in June. This is the most exciting time in this quiet river town: There's a steamboat race, arts, crafts, kids' games, food, a petting zoo, and music.

Dover Covered Bridge, *Lee Creek Road off Highway 8 between Augusta and Maysville.* Open to traffic.

Historic Walking Tour. Stroll the historic Row House area near Augusta's Riverside Drive. Many of the buildings date to the 1790s. Most of the shops are galleries and antiques stores.

Pace Yourself From the northern Kentucky metro area, you can get to Augusta and Maysville at a slow and leisurely pace along two-lane Route 8, which follows the river. A faster route is the very modern AA Highway (Route 9), which runs from Alexandria at the southern end of Campbell County all the way to the eastern Kentucky city of Ashland.

Where to Eat

Beehive Tavern, *Main Street, Augusta 41002; (606) 756–2202; reservations recommended.* Traditional Kentucky cuisine along with unusual offerings like Cuban bean soup. With children, lunch is best. $$

McKenzie's, *207 Main Street, Augusta 41002; (606) 756–2014.* A favorite local hangout with homestyle cooking (try the Transparent Pie); go early for breakfast or dinner, because it packs up fast. $

For More Information

Augusta Visitor Center, *116 Main Street, Augusta 41004; (606) 756–2183.*

Maysville Area

 MASON COUNTY MUSEUM (ages 5 and up)
215 Sutton Street, Maysville 41056; (606) 564–5865. Open April through December, Monday to Saturday from 10:00 A.M. through 4:00 P.M. Closed January, Monday and Tuesday in February and March, and all holidays. $

This 1878 building used to be the town's library. And while the Mason County Museum does include a library for genealogists and other researchers, children would rather look at the exhibits on local history. Using dioramas as well as artifacts, the museum tells Maysville's story from settlement, when it was first known as Limestone, to the present day. There are changing exhibits, too, relating to history or visual arts.

NATIONAL UNDERGROUND RAILROAD MUSEUM (ages 5 and up)

115 East Third Street, Maysville 41056; (606) 564–4413. Open Monday to Saturday from 10:00 A.M. to 4:00 P.M. **Free**.

During the Civil War, the Ohio River usually marked the boundary between slavery and freedom, and there was a lot of Underground Railroad activity in this part of the state. This museum, located next to the Maysville visitor center, displays artifacts and photographs relating to slavery and the community's role in helping escaped slaves to freedom in the North. Iron shackles rest in a case next to an original edition of *Uncle Tom's Cabin* by Harriet Beecher Stowe. There's also a rare tobacco press patented by a former slave.

HISTORIC WALKING TOUR

Map of forty-eight sites in Maysville area, available from visitor center. **Free**.

Within walking distance of the Underground Railroad museum is Phillip's Folly (Third and Sutton Streets), thought to have served as both a holding area for slaves brought to Maysville for sale and later a station on the Underground Railroad. Exterior viewing only. The house is one of forty-eight sites on a city walking tour available at the visitor center. Other sites include a Pioneer Cemetery and the girlhood home of singer Rosemary Clooney (tell your children that she was George Clooney's aunt). While walking around, you'll also see the Floodwall Murals portraying Ohio River scenes.

HISTORIC WASHINGTON (ages 6 and up)

Off US 62/68, south of downtown Maysville; (606) 759–7411. Visitor Center on Main Street open Monday to Friday from 11:00 A.M. to 4:30 P.M., Saturday from 10:30 A.M. to 4:30 P.M., and Sunday from 1:00 to 4:30 P.M. Guided tours adults $$, children $.

Although it officially became a part of Maysville in 1990, Historic Washington feels like a separate town. It was, in fact, the first town incorporated west of the Allegheny Mountains (in 1785). Activities are centered on Main Street, where the old buildings house a combination of historic exhibits and modern shops. Start your visit at the **Old Washington Visitors Center** in the 1790 Cane Brake log cabin, where you can watch a video about the town and sign up for one of the guided history tours (the only way to see the inside of some of the buildings). There are one-hour tours focusing on the Underground Railroad, Washington

History, and Log Cabin Learning. If you have the interest and stamina for a longer, more

Amazing Kentucky Fact

Washington, Kentucky, was the first town in America to be named for George Washington. About 500 people lived here in the 1790s; about that same number live here today.

in-depth tour, there's a two-hour **Historic District Walking Tour.** Highlights include the **Simon Kenton Shrine,** a re-creation of a 1790 general store; **the Harriet Beecher Stowe Slavery to Freedom Museum** (while staying here in 1833, the author of *Uncle Tom's Cabin* supposedly witnessed her first slave auction); the **Paxton Inn,** a former stop on the Underground Railroad (look for the hidden stairwell); and **Mefford's Station,** one of the few remaining "flatboat houses" built from the timbers of the flatboats that carried the settlers and their possessions down the river to their new home. While in town you may also want to explore the town's shops, which carry everything from candles to looms, and stop by **The Carriage Museum** on Main Street behind the Carousel Shop. For lunch, there's **Marshall Key Tavern,** *2111 Main Street (606–759–5803; $).* If the kids need to break loose a bit from all this history and shopping, the Maysville Mason County Recreation Park, with an Olympic-size pool, miniature golf course, tennis courts, and twelve-acre fishing lake, is within walking distance.

Festive Washington

The little town of Washington is especially fun during these festivals:

- **Chocolate Festival,** weekend before Easter. Chocolate, chocolate contests, and Easter egg hunt. (606) 759-7423

- **Simon Kenton Frontier Festival,** September. Outdoor drama and pioneer-style activities. (606) 564-3559

- **Civil War Living History Weekend,** second weekend in August. Reenactments and encampment. (606) 759-7411

- **Frontier Christmas,** early December. Caroling and carriage rides. (606) 759-7411

Other Things to See and Do

Cabin Creek Covered Bridge, *off Highway 984, near Tollesboro, east of Maysville. Closed to traffic.*

Paradise Breeze Water Park, *3177 AA Highway, Maysville, 41056; (606) 759–9300. Open daily seasonally. Admission $$; additional charge for some activities. Water slides, go-cart track.*

Where to Eat

Caproni's On the River, *320 Rosemary Clooney Street, Maysville 41056; (606) 564–4321.* Italian and regional food served in a renovated 1930s landmark. $$

Laredo's Restaurant, *545 Tucker Drive, Maysville 41056; (606) 759–8749.* Steaks, burgers, and Southwestern dishes. $$

Magee's Bakery, *212 Market Street, Maysville 41056; (606) 564–5720.* Pastries and sandwiches to go on homemade bread. $

Marshall Key Tavern, *2100 Old Main Street, Washington 41096; (606) 759–5803.* Soups, sandwiches, and daily specials. $

Where to Stay

Best Western Maysville Inn, *US 68 and AA Highway, Maysville 41056; (606) 759–5696.* Free breakfast bar; indoor pool. $$

French Quarter Inn, *25 East McDonald Parkway, Maysville 41056; (606) 564–8000.* Outdoor pool, restaurants; some rooms have river view. $$$

For More Information

Maysville Tourism Commission, *216 Bridge Street, Maysville; (606) 564–9419, www.cityofmaysville.com.* Visitor center is downtown, next to the Simon Kenton Bridge.

Old Washington Visitors Center, *P.O. Box 227, Main Street, Washington 41096; (606) 759–7411.*

Mount Olivet

BLUE LICKS BATTLEFIELD STATE RESORT PARK (all ages)

P.O. Box 66, Highway 68, Mount Olivet 41064; (859) 289–5507; reservations (800) 443–7008. Open year-round; pool and mini-golf seasonal.

This park is kind of a hidden treasure. It has great all-around resort park features—lodge with dining room, cabins, campground, trails, picnic areas, miniature golf, and a pool, plus a Pioneer Museum—but is not nearly as crowded or remote as many other resort parks. Between Maysville and Paris off Highway 68 and an easy drive from either direction, it's an easy day trip. The Pioneer Museum includes artifacts relating to prehistoric animals who came here for the salt licks (the mastodon bones are always a big hit), Native Americans, pioneers, the Revolutionary War battle fought here in 1782, and the springs that made the area a popular nineteenth-century resort area. One of the park's hiking trails takes you past the spot near the Licking River where Daniel Boone was captured by the Shawnee while on a salt-making expedition. In mid-August the park hosts a **Battle of Blue Licks Reenactment,** with pioneer crafts, music, and animal exhibits. In 2003, a buffalo herd exhibit is expected to open.

Carlisle

OLD NICHOLAS COUNTY JAIL AND DUNGEON (all ages)

121 West Main Street, Carlisle 40311; (859) 289–5174. Open by appointment. Free.

The cell area, or "dungeon," of this early 1800s jail and jailer's house complex is what intrigues most visitors of all ages. (At Halloween, it provides the perfect setting for a fun and scary "Haunted House." $. Call for dates: 859-289-5174.) You can also step into the restored caboose outside. While you're in town, stroll by the restored 1912 L&N passenger depot at 101 Market Street.

DANIEL AND REBECCA BOONE HOME (all ages)

Off KY 36 near Carlisle; (859) 289–5174. Open daily; self-guided. Free.

This log cabin was the Boones' last home in Kentucky. If you can find it (in fall and winter you can see it from the road), you're welcome to drive back to it and look around.

Flemingsburg

 COVERED BRIDGES (all ages)
Highway 32 near Goddard; Highway 158 at Rawlings Road in Ringo's Mill; Highway 111 near Hillsboro; (606) 845–1223. **Free**.

Three of Kentucky's thirteen remaining covered bridges are in the Flemingsburg area. The prettiest is Goddard White Covered Bridge, off Highway 32. This 60-foot bridge is still open to traffic, and it's a photographers' favorite because it frames a pretty little country church when you look through it from the west side. Grange City Covered Bridge, off Highway 111 near Hillsboro, is an 86-foot bridge that is closed to traffic. Ringo's Mill Bridge, located on Highway 158 at Rawlings Road, is a 90-foot span not open to traffic. Pick up a bridge brochure from **Fleming County Tourism** (114 West Water Street, Flemingsburg). The drive is pretty, and you'll also pass dairy farms and Amish stores. In late August, there's a Covered Bridge Festival at Goddard White Covered Bridge.

A Day Family Adventure I often take day trips with just one child at a time. These are very special and enjoyable opportunities to spend time together, to talk, and to explore each child's interests or those that we share. One of my most enjoyable trips with my daughter was a day visiting covered bridges in northern Kentucky. We set out early one Saturday and took our time, stopping where we pleased. We started at the three bridges in Fleming County, then drove east of Maysville to Tollesboro. We got lost for a while but finally found the 114-foot Cabin Creek Bridge off KY 984. We stopped in Maysville at the Underground Railroad Museum and visitor center, then drove out to the 63-foot **Dover Covered Bridge,** just south of KY 8 on KY 3113 (Lee Creek Road), between Augusta and Maysville. After a stop in Augusta for a ferry ride (and ice cream), we visited **Walcott Covered Bridge,** southwest of Augusta off KY 1159, near the intersection with the AA Highway. On the way home, we went by Johnson Creek Bridge, off KY 1029 in Robertson County (not far from Blue Licks). Although I was uncertain just how interested a ten-year-old would be, my daughter enjoyed walking through the old bridges and examining the different styles of bracing inside the bridges (and the various states of repair/disrepair and graffiti). I knew the trip had been a success when she asked on the way home, "Can we go back next weekend?"

Amazing Kentucky Fact

Amazing Kentucky Fact Blue Licks Battlefield State Resort Park was the scene of Kentucky's last battle of the Revolutionary War, in 1782. Among the casualties was one of Daniel Boone's sons.

Annual Events

Chocolate Festival, weekend before Easter, Old Washington; (606) 759-7423

Kentucky Scottish Weekend, mid-May, General Butler State Resort Park, Carrollton; (800) 325-4290

Maifest, mid-May, MainStrasse Village, Covington; (859) 491-0458

River Days Festival, early-June, Warsaw; (859) 567-5900

Italian Festival, early June, Newport; (859) 292-3660

Sternwheel Regatta, late June, Augusta; (606) 735-3474

Blackberry Festival, early July, Carlisle; (859) 289-5174

Gallatin County Fair and Horse Show, mid-July, Warsaw; (859) 986-2540

Northern Kentucky Bluegrass Festival, mid-July, Alexandria; (800) STAYNKY

Grant County Fair, late July/early August, Crittenden; (800) 382-7117

Newport Art and Music Fest, late July, Newport; (859) 292-3660

Riverwalk Arts and Crafts Festival, late August, Maysville; (606) 564-9411

Fleming County Covered Bridge Festival, late August, Flemingsburg; (606) 845-1223

Riverfest, early September, Newport; (859) 262-3660

Oktoberfest, early September, MainStrasse Village, Covington; (859) 491-0458

Dinsmore Homestead Harvest Festival, late September, Dinsmore Homestead; (859) 586-6117

Kentucky Wool Festival, early October, Falmouth; (859) 654-3378

Lexington

Kentucky is often called "the Bluegrass State," but to Kentuckians "the Bluegrass" refers to the city of Lexington and the surrounding counties. Both geographically and symbolically, this lovely region of Kentucky is the heart of the state and a place where your family can experience some of Kentucky's most famous traditions firsthand.

Take horses, for example. Although the Kentucky Derby is run in Louisville, it is at the horse farms in Lexington and the surrounding counties that many Kentucky Derby contenders are bred, born, trained, and, after their racing careers have ended, retired. You can visit some of the farms by appointment, and you'll want to be sure to spend a day at the Kentucky Horse Park, a 1,200-acre farm/educational park.

Lexington is also home to an excellent children's museum, children's arts events, and a minor league baseball team, plus a museum celebrating the city's most popular sport—University of Kentucky basketball. Add to this historic and outdoor attractions, and you've got the makings of some great day trips and weekend getaways, almost any time of year.

Lexington is easy to reach: It sits at the crossroads of I–75 north-south and I–64 east-west. Once in town, remember that the city is laid out on a spoke-and-wheel design. Two outer roads—New Circle Road (Highway 4), which encircles the perimeter of the city, and farther out, Man o'War Boulevard—make it almost all the way around. Streets within the city may change names three times as they pass from one end of the city to another. For example, US 27 is Paris Pike north of town, Broadway in town, and Harrodsburg Road south of downtown. Go figure! (Get a map.)

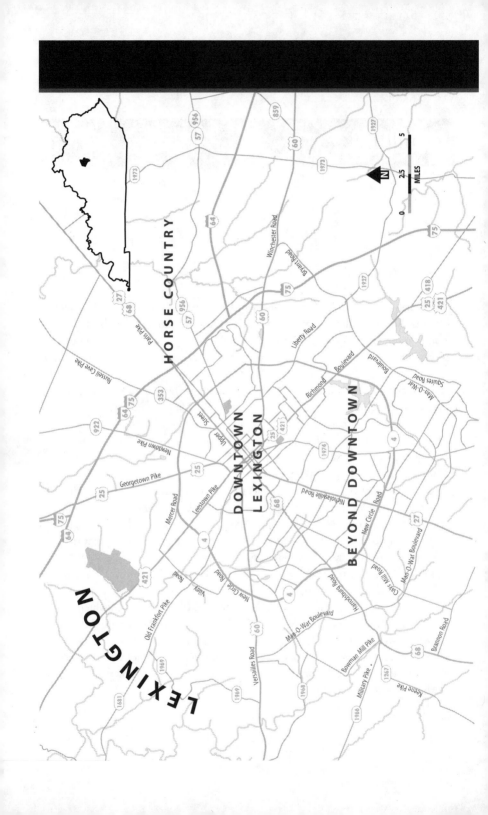

Teresa's Top Ten Picks for Lexington

1. **Kentucky Horse Park,** (800) 678–8813
2. **Lexington Children's Museum,** (859) 258–3256
3. **Lexington Children's Theater,** (800) 928–4545
4. **Lexington Legends,** (859) 252–HITS
5. **Hunt-Morgan House,** (859) 253–0362
6. **Ashland,** (859) 266–8581
7. **Creative Playgrounds,** (859) 288–2900
8. **Raven Run Nature Sanctuary,** (859) 272–6105
9. **Keeneland Race Course,** (800) 456–3412
10. **Hutchinson's Drug Store,** (859) 252–3554

Horse Country

KENTUCKY HORSE PARK (all ages)
4089 Iron Works Parkway, Lexington 40511 (exit 120 off I–75); (859) 233–4303 or (800) 678–8813, www.kyhorsepark.com. Open year-round; some attractions are seasonal. Open daily March 15 to October 31 from 9:00 A.M. to 5:00 P.M., $$$; closed Monday and Tuesday November 1 to March 14, $$. Children ages 6 and under admitted Free *year-round. Additional charge for horseback and pony rides.*

Horses, horses, everywhere—and you can even take a ride at this 1,200-acre kingdom of the horse. Every family with a horse enthusiast will want to spend a day here, exploring the museum and art gallery, watching a farrier at work, taking a trail ride or horsedrawn carriage ride, and coming face to face with dozens of breeds of horses—race horses, working horses, riding horses, and even miniature horses. In addition to the permanent exhibits and activities, there's a packed seasonal schedule of horse shows, riding competitions, dog shows, and other events. You can begin your self-guided tour by visiting the grave and bronze statue of thoroughbred champion Man o' War. Then step into the theater and watch two moving films about horses' roles throughout history. One of our favorite activities is the daily Parade of

Breeds (spring through summer), where you get to see familiar and unusual horse breeds strut their stuff; afterwards you can walk through the Big Barn for a closer look. The daily Mare and Foal Show (late May through July) is a good opportunity for children and baby horses to come eye to eye. The horse park is also a good place for novice riders to take a trail ride; in fact, it's one of the few places in the region where children under twelve are allowed to ride horses as opposed to guided ponies (mid-March through October for ages seven and up). There are pony rides, too, for children ages two to twelve. The park includes a restaurant as well as picnic areas and a campground. Although special events and activities are at their height in spring through fall, the horse park museum can also be a great escape from cabin fever on a winter weekend.

Horse Basics

Has your young horse lover been bugging you for a horse? The summer Youth Riding Program at the Kentucky Horse Park is a chance for youngsters ages ten to eighteen to learn the basics of horse care, handling, and riding. In these weeklong sessions, each participant is assigned a horse (usually one of the park's mustangs) for the week, and it's his or her responsibility to feed, brush, and care for the horse, including cleaning out the stalls and taking care of the tack. Lodging is not included in the fee, but participants have come from across the United States. Your young rider could go to "summer school" at the Horse Park while the rest of the family goes sightseeing in Lexington and the Bluegrass. Call (859) 259–4206 for session dates and more information.

THE AMERICAN SADDLEBRED MUSEUM (ages 4 and up)

Located next to the Kentucky Horse Park; open same hours. Admission included with Kentucky Horse Park.

This museum traces the history and accomplishments of Kentucky's native breed of horse, the American saddlebred. A film presentation fills you in on the history of the breed—it descended from horses shipped to North America from Britain in the 1600s. In other exhibits you'll see saddlebred champions. Then, in an interactive exhibit, you get to see what you'd look like atop the famous champions Imperator, Sky Watch, and Wing Commander.

Horsey Holidays

Horsey Holidays The calendar at the Kentucky Horse Park includes some great events for children:

Young riders from across the state compete at the **Kentucky High School Invitational Rodeo**, late May (859–484–2214). The "minis" parade, prance, and even dance at the **Miniature Horse Association Julep Cup Show**, mid-July (937–787–3248). In late July, collectors of Breyer horse figures gather from around the country for **Breyerfest** (973–633–5090). And in early August, the park sponsor **Kids Weekend**, with many special activities (859–259–4225). The whole family will enjoy **Southern Lights**, a dazzling drive-through-at-your-own-pace holiday lights show at the Kentucky Horse Park, open nightly mid-November through December 31. The animated displays feature horse themes as well as traditional holiday themes (859–255–5727). Also, watch the calendar for dog agility competitions and other activities.

HORSE FARM TOURS (ages 6 and up)

For information about current tours and other farms that are open, contact the Lexington Convention and Visitors Bureau at (859) 233–7299.

Among the farms that are open to visitors is **Calumet Farm,** just minutes from downtown Lexington on Versailles Road. One of the most famous of Bluegrass farms, Calumet has produced a record nine Kentucky Derby winners. The tour is conducted by a longtime employee and includes the farm's horse cemetery, where many of its equine champions are buried. Tours are given Monday, Wednesday, and Friday at 10:00 A.M. Call (859) 231–8272 for reservations. The stallions at **Gainesway Farm,** 3750 Paris Pike, live in an interesting A-frame barn complex. During breeding season (February through July 15), Gainesway allows visitors to watch a breeding session, although this may not be the ideal tour for families. Quiet behavior is essential, and the tour guide will have less time to show you around and answer questions. Call (859) 293–2676 for reservations. See the sections on Versailles and Paris for more horse farm tours.

KEENELAND RACE COURSE (ages 6 and up)

4201 Versailles Road, Lexington 40592; (800) 456–3412 or (859) 254–3412, www.keeneland.com. $ for admission to the races; watching morning workouts or strolling the grounds at other times of the year is **Free***. Take U.S. 60 (Versailles Road) west from downtown Lexington.*

Not far past Calumet Farm on Versailles Road is Keeneland, which is not your typical racetrack. With its tall trees, flowering shrubs, and elegant stone buildings and walls, this place looks more like a park. The races run for several weeks in April and October, and at other times of the year the track is a training center. During race meets the track offers Breakfast With the Works, an early morning backside tour that includes special activities for children. Even if your visit to Lexington doesn't coincide with a race meet, your family might enjoy a visit; go out early (6:00 A.M. to 11:00 A.M. mid-March through mid-November) to watch the horses working out on the track, then have a hearty breakfast at the track kitchen. The Derby Day celebration at Keeneland (always the first Saturday in May) is much more manageable and family-friendly than Churchill Downs in Louisville, with barbecue, music, and special activities for children.

Amazing Kentucky Fact

About 10,000 thoroughbred horses are born each year in Kentucky, generally from February through July. All of the current year's foals officially become one-year-olds (called yearlings) on January 1 of the following year.

Horse Country Dos and Don'ts

There are hundreds of horse farms in and around Lexington, and several allow visitors. All things considered, the Kentucky Horse Park is probably the best place for families to see horses in the Lexington area, especially if your children are younger. If you plan to visit a private farm, just keep these points in mind:

- Do call first. Not all farms welcome visitors, and reservations are always required.

- Do keep a close eye on your children for their own safety. Don't let them wander off into stalls, other barns, or fields. Don't let them get close enough to the horses to be bitten or kicked.

- Do be prepared for your kids to learn about the thoroughbred breeding process. The explanation might be quite detailed.

- Be sure to tip the farm staff member who leads the tour. There's no admission charge for the tours, but a $5.00 to $10.00 tip for the guide is customary.

THE THOROUGHBRED CENTER (ages 5 and up)

3380 Paris Pike, Lexington 40511; (859) 293–1853. Open April through October, tours start at 9:00 and 10:30 A.M. and at 1:00 P.M. Monday to Friday and at 9:00 and 10:30 A.M. Saturday. From November through March, tours start at 10:30 A.M. Monday to Friday only. $$

Like any athletes, racehorses have to train. They work out, eat right, and have a team of advisors. You can find out how a horse is readied for a race at this private training center on Lexington's Paris Pike (nicknamed "Millionaire's Row" because of the many beautiful farms). The guided training center tour begins at the clocking tour, where you'll have a close view of horses working out on the training track. Then you visit one of the barns and meet an owner/trainer. Take an earlier tour to see more horses; by 1:00 P.M. most of the workouts are over for the day. If you visit April through October, it's a good idea to call ahead for reservations.

THE RED MILE HARNESS TRACK (ages 8 and up)

1200 Red Mile Road, Lexington 40504; (859) 255–0752. Racing meets vary. Grounds open year-round from 9:00 A.M. to 3:00 P.M. 𝐅𝐫𝐞𝐞 *to grounds, races $.*

Older children may enjoy seeing harness racing, in which the horses pull riders seated in small carts (the meets run late April through June and a few days in late September). Year-round, you can walk around at this historic track (dates to 1875). Sites to see include the interesting octagonal-shaped Floral Hall building at the entrance, the red soil track from which the name comes, and barn areas. The Red Mile also hosts a variety of other special events, from a chili cook-off on Memorial Day to the Junior League Horse Show, the largest outdoor saddlebred horse show in the nation. Children interested in horses and riding will enjoy seeing the beautiful horses and elegantly dressed riders go through their paces for the judges.

Downtown Lexington

LEXINGTON CHILDREN'S MUSEUM (all ages)

Victorian Square, 440 West Short Street, Lexington 40507; (859) 258–3256, www.lexingtonchildrensmuseum.com. Open Tuesday to Friday from 10:00 A.M. to 6:00 P.M., Saturday from 10:00 A.M. to 5:00 P.M., and Sunday from 1:00 to 5:00 P.M. $

The interactive exhibits at this bright and lively museum give youngsters a hands-on introduction to science, history, geography, and the arts. Even adults in the group will enjoy the well-designed exhibits. There's also a special area for the youngest visitors: In the Wonder Woods, infants and toddlers can slide down a lightning bug, splash in the water, or curl up in a "nest" while Mom and Dad learn how young brains develop. Older children will enjoy such as exhibits as Science Station X (NASA and fighter jet items); Brainzilla, the giant talking brain; and the walk-in anatomy experiences Mighty Mouth and Heartscape. Other favorites include the bubble fun area and the multicultural Home exhibit, which compares houses around the world. Almost every weekend there are special workshops and activities. Some of the special activities require advance registration, so check to see what's going on while you're in town. In late September, the museum sponsors Museum-Go-Round, an arts festival where youngsters can display their art work.

UNIVERSITY OF KENTUCKY BASKETBALL MUSEUM (ages 5 and up)

Second floor of the Civic Center, Lexington Center, 410 West Vine Street, Lexington 40507; (800) 269–1953. Open Monday to Saturday from 10:00 A.M. to 5:00 P.M., Sunday from noon to 5:00 P.M. $

If you're into college basketball, you've heard of the UK Wildcats. The Cats have long been a national powerhouse and have captured five NCAA championships. Just a covered pedway walk away from Victorian Square across Main Street, in the Civic Center complex, is an engaging collection of memorabilia relating to the team's history and accomplishments. The hands-on activities are the most fun: You can play trivia at a computer monitor, take your turn at the microphone to call the action of a videotaped play (then listen to yourself), and even shoot some hoops on a small court that includes part of the real floor from the Meadowlands, where UK won one of its championships. Don't miss the Virtual Court, where video cameras and computer technology enable you to go one-on-one against some of Kentucky's top players from the past. For a small additional fee, you can take a guided tour of nearby Rupp Arena, the Wildcats' home court. At the entrance to the museum is a display of some of the art Wildcats created for a citywide exhibit.

LEXINGTON LIVERY COMPANY (all ages)

Make reservations by calling (859) 259–0000, or catch a coach in front of the Radisson Plaza Hotel, Vine Street and Broadway. April through January 1 (weather permitting), 7:30 A.M. to 11:00 P.M. Sunday through Thursday, 7:30

P.M. *to midnight Friday and Saturday. Cost: $25 for half-hour tour; up to four passengers. www.lexingtonlivery.com.*

This horse-drawn carriage tour winds through Lexington's downtown and historic Gratz Park neighborhood, but what youngsters will love most are the giant Percheron draft horses (sweet and pettable) and the thrill of clippity-clopping through the city.

FOUCAULT PENDULUM AND HORSE CLOCK (all ages)

Lexington Public Library, 140 East Main Street, Lexington 40507; (859) 231–5500. Library hours are Monday to Thursday from 9:00 A.M. to 9:00 P.M., Friday and Saturday from 9:00 A.M. to 5:00 P.M., and Sunday from 1:00 to 5:00 P.M. The Book Cellar is open Monday to Thursday from 11:00 A.M. to 6:00 P.M., Saturday from 11:00 A.M. to 3:00 P.M., and Sunday from 1:00 to 5:00 P.M. **Free**.

The atrium of the main branch of Lexington's public library includes a Foucault pendulum suspended 70 feet from the top of the atrium. Also of interest is the handless clock: sixty horses around the perimeter of the clock face light in sequence to look like a horse racing around the edge. The library also includes a small art gallery off the lobby and a used bookstore, the **Book Cellar,** on the lower level. The library adjoins Phoenix Park, a good place to rest or have an outdoor lunch in warm weather.

LEXINGTON CHILDREN'S THEATER (ages 5 and up)

418 West Short Street, Lexington 40507; (859) 254–4546 or (800) 928–4545, www.lctonstage.org. $

In a typical season, LCT will bring folk tales, historical characters, and great children's stories to life onstage. Founded in 1938, it's one of the longest operating professional children's theater companies in the United States. The company performs in its own theater just down the street from the Lexington Children's Museum. The performance season runs from October through May. In summer, there are day camps and workshops in which youngsters rehearse and perform plays; if you're planning to be in town for a week or so, this might be a special experience your child would enjoy.

MARY TODD LINCOLN HOUSE (ages 6 and up)

578 West Main Street, Lexington 40507; (859) 233–9999, www.mtlhouse.org. Open March 15 through November 30, Monday to Saturday from 10:00 A.M. to 4:00 P.M. $$; children under 6 **Free**.

At this fourteen-room Georgian-style brick house, you'll learn about the childhood of Mary Todd, who later became First Lady as the wife of Abraham Lincoln. Mary's family lived here, and she and Abe visited after they married. The house features authentic memorabilia of the Todd family, and the tour focuses on Mary's cultured upbringing as a member of a prominent early Lexington family. The house is within easy walking distance of the Lexington Children's Museum and the UK Basketball Museum.

More Arts for the Kids Other Lexington arts attractions geared to families include:

- **Thoroughbred Center Theatre.** Variety of Saturday children's productions throughout the year. (859) 293–1853.

- **Lexington Philharmonic.** Three fun one-hour family concerts each season: Halloween, Candy Cane Holiday concert, and spring concert. Performances at Singletary Center, with preconcert Instrument Petting Zoo and games. (859) 233–4226.

- **Lexington Ballet** (859–233–3925) and **Ballet Theatre of Lexington** (859–252–5245). The city often has two versions of the popular holiday ballet *The Nutcracker*, as well as other kid-friendly ballet performances.

- **Art a la Carte ArtsPlace**, 161 North Mill Street. **Free** lunchtime concerts one day a week; in summer, the concerts are specifically geared toward children. (859) 233–1469.

- **UK Art Museum and Singletary Center for the Arts**, University of Kentucky campus. Variety of works in permanent exhibit; small, easily maneuvered space. Children may also enjoy the contemporary outdoor sculptures on the center grounds. There are many free concerts and recitals at Singletary, as well as paid events by top artists. (859) 257–4929.

- **Central Kentucky Youth Orchestras.** Fall, December, and spring concerts by outstanding young middle school and high school musicians. (859) 254–0796.

A Fountain of Fun Before or after a visit to the Lexington Children's Museum, UK Basketball Museum, or a Lexington Children's Theater performance, enjoy a soda, malt, milkshake, or sundae at **Hutchinson's Drug Store** (859-252-3554), on the first floor of Victorian Square. This authentic old-time soda fountain is a real treat for modern youngsters. Open Monday to Friday from 9:30 A.M. to 7:00 P.M., Saturday from 10:00 A.M. to 5:00 P.M.

LEXINGTON CEMETERY (all ages)

833 West Main Street, Lexington 40508; (859) 255–5522. Cemetery open daily from 8:00 A.M. to 5:00 P.M. Office open Monday to Saturday from 8:00 A.M. to 4:00 P.M. **Free**.

With hundreds of varieties of trees and plants, lovely lakes and gardens, and an abundance of birds, this nationally acclaimed arboretum makes an excellent nature walk. There are also many interesting monuments. Stop at the office and pick up the Children's Tour, an oversized map with interesting information and a list of things for children to look for as they walk through the arboretum. History and tree guides and a bird list also are available.

HUNT-MORGAN HOUSE (ages 8 and up)

201 North Mill Street, Lexington 40508; (859) 253–0362. Open March 1 through December 22, Tuesday to Saturday from 10:00 A.M. to 4:00 P.M., Sunday from 2:00 to 5:00 P.M. $

This elegant Federal-style house just a few blocks north of Main Street has a lot of great history attached to it. It was built by John Wesley Hunt, reputedly Kentucky's first millionaire. Hunt's grandson, who also lived in the house, was a flamboyant figure of the Civil War. Confederate General John Hunt Morgan and his "Raiders" caused trouble all over Kentucky, and his escapades give the house tour guides some great material. Ask about the time Morgan rode his horse into the house—and the ghost with red shoes. A small Civil War museum on the second floor includes uniforms and other

An Amazing Kentucky Fact West to Lexington? Kentucky was the first American frontier, and as its first big city, Lexington was called the "Athens of the West" in the early 1800s.

artifacts relating to Morgan and his "Raiders." The surrounding Gratz Park neighborhood was Lexington's poshest suburb in the early 1800s. The small park with its bronze statues and fountain is a pleasant place to rest or romp after a tour.

Lexington's "Transylvania"

If your family is up for a little more walking, stroll from Gratz Park across Third Street to the campus of Transylvania University, the oldest university west of the Alleghenies. Sites to see include a 1783 log cabin and the massive Greek Revival–style administration building, Old Morrison. Despite the name, there are no vampires here, although there is a tomb. Constantine Rafinesque, an eccentric nineteenth-century professor, is buried underneath Old Morrison. Every Halloween students are selected to spend the night in "Rafinesque's tomb."

LEXINGTON LEGENDS (all ages)

Applebee's Park, 1200–1295 North Broadway, Lexington 40505 (next to Northland Shopping Center); (859) 252–HITS. Ticket prices from $ to $$$, depending on seat location.

A devoted group of baseball fans worked for years to bring a minor league team to town. The Lexington Legends arrived in 2001 and won the South Atlantic League championship their very first year. Any Legends home game (about seventy per season, April through October) is a winning experience for baseball-loving families. The stadium design puts you very close to the action and includes many family-friendly features, such as picnic areas, family rest rooms, and a kids' play area complete with merry-go-round. If you live in the region, you may want to sign your child up for the Kids Club; for $10, each member gets special

Haunted Hotel?

Some people have had an absolutely ghostly time at the **Gratz Park Inn**, 120 West Second Street, in downtown Lexington. The ghost of a little girl has been seen playing in the hall. Guests have complained about noise from the rooms on the floor above, only to discover that they are staying on the top floor. And hotel workers have spotted specters in the basement. (Maybe it's not too surprising when you learn that this historic building once housed the city morgue!)

perks, including a T-shirt, newsletter, and opportunities to "run the bases" at some games.

THOROUGHBRED PARK (all ages)

Main and Midland Streets, Lexington. Open daily year-round, 24 hours. ℱᵣₑₑ.

It just isn't a visit to Lexington without snapping a few photos of the family with the life-sized, realistic-looking bronze horses that "race" and "graze" in this two-and-a-half-acre park at the east end of downtown.

More Sports Fun in Lexington

- **University of Kentucky Wildcat football.** Commonwealth Stadium. Tickets: (859) 257–4929.

- **University of Kentucky Wildcat basketball.** Rupp Arena. (Tickets can be hard to get.) (859) 257–4929.

- **Lexington Men O'War minor-league hockey.** Rupp Arena. (859) 233–3656.

- **Kentucky Boys "Sweet Sixteen" State Basketball Tournament.** Mid-March at Rupp Arena. (859) 299–5472.

THE LIVING ARTS AND SCIENCE CENTER (all ages)

362 North Martin Luther King Boulevard, Lexington 40508; (859) 252–5222, www.livingartsandscience.org. Open Monday through Friday from 9:00 A.M. to 4:00 P.M.; Saturday from 10:00 A.M. to 2:00 P.M.; closed Saturdays June through August. ℱᵣₑₑ.

Although this center is best known for its workshops and classes, even if you're in town just for a day you may want to stop by to see the changing science and visual arts exhibits.

Beyond Downtown

ASHLAND, THE HENRY CLAY ESTATE (ages 8 and up)

120 Sycamore Drive, Lexington 40502; (859) 266–8581, www.henryclay.org. Tours start on the hour from 10:00 A.M. to 4:00 P.M. Monday through Saturday, 1:00 to 4:00 P.M. Sunday. Closed in January and on Monday from November to March. Admission for house tour: adults $$, children ages 6 to 18 $; children 5 and under ℱᵣₑₑ. *Admission to grounds and garden* ℱᵣₑₑ.

Henry Clay was one of early Kentucky's most prominent citizens, a U.S. senator, secretary of state, and three-time losing presidential candidate.

("I'd rather be right than President," he reportedly said.) Away from Washington, at his 672-acre estate in Lexington, Clay was a gentleman farmer who bred prize livestock and entertained notables such as the Marquis de Lafayette and James Monroe. Twenty acres of Clay's Lexington estate are preserved as a historic site, including an elegant Italianate house built by his son James. The house includes many family artifacts. Young visitors will especially enjoy the parklike setting. The formal garden is a fun place to take a walk. Check the events calendar during your visit; special children's events range from an Easter Egg Hunt to Victorian teas. Spring through fall you can have lunch (sandwiches and wonderful desserts) on the grounds at the Gingko Tree cafe.

A Day Family Adventure

Because I love old houses so much, I've dragged my children through many of them over the years. Even when they were little, I would often give it a try, with varying degrees of success. Here are some "survival" tips for old house–loving parents:

- Go through when the house is not crowded (the first or last tour of the day often fits this bill). This gives you and the tour guide more flexibility to shorten the narrative or focus it to children's interests. (A smart tour guide at the Hunt-Morgan House fascinated my children by telling them about the horse hair chair in the parlor.)

- If the tour is self-guided, be prepared to take it all in quickly. Your children won't want to linger, but even a whirlwind walk-through can still be enjoyable.

- Many homes have materials such as scavenger hunts used with school tour groups. Ask for a copy.

- If your child is tired or cranky, come back another time.

- Don't try to cram too many historic houses or passive activities into one day. Balance the historic house tour or educational activity you want your children to see with an activity or attraction they choose. My children quickly discovered that touring an old house made Mom a much more enthusiastic miniature golfer!

Play Time Bring your skateboard when you visit Lexington: The **Skatepark in Woodland Park** (East High Street at Kentucky Avenue; 859–288-2900) offers 12,000 square feet of pipes, platforms, and ramps. **Free**.

Other good spots when it's just time to play include three elaborate wooden **Creative Playgrounds** for climbing, swinging, sliding, and imagining (Jacobson Park, off Richmond Road; Shillito Park, off Reynolds Road; and behind Picadome Elementary School, 1642 Harrodsburg Road.) **Free**; (859) 288-2900. If it's raining, take younger kids to **Kids-Place** at the Lexington Athletic Center (3992 West Tiverton Court, 859–272-5433), a two-story indoor playground. Older youngsters will enjoy the laser gun game at **Laser Quest** (224 Bolivar Street; 859–225-1742, $$).

Kids got you climbing the walls? Get them climbing the 35-foot-high climbing walls at **Lexington Rocks** (near Laser Quest at 200 Bolivar Street; 859–381-9000, $) or the 25-foot walls at **Climb Time** (2416 Over Drive; 859–253-3673, $$).

LEXINGTON ARBORETUM (all ages)

Alumni Drive, between Nicholasville and Tates Creek Roads, Lexington; (859) 257–9339 or www.uky.edu/Arboretum. Open dawn to dusk daily year-round. **Free**; *$ for the Shakespeare Festival performances.*

Paved pathways and a variety of plant displays make this one-hundred-acre greenspace (Kentucky's Official State Botanical Garden) an enjoyable place for a city hike. The "Walk Across Kentucky" is a 2-mile path encircling the arboretum, with a variety of plants designed to show the geophysical regions of the state. If that's too far for your group, it's just a short stroll from the parking lot to the vegetable, herb, flower, and water-plant display gardens. Stop by the visitor center for maps and information. The arboretum is the site of the annual Shakespeare Festival in July, which includes three different productions (usually two Shakespearean and one non-Shakespearean play) over three weekends. Come early with a picnic to claim your blanket or lawn-chair spot. The atmosphere is very casual, and there are oodles of children—parents of little ones can go to the theater after all!

RAVEN RUN NATURE SANCTUARY (all ages)

5886 Jacks Creek Road, Lexington 40515 (from Lexington, take Tates Creek Road to Spears Road to Jacks Creek Pike); (859) 272–6105. Open daily, October through March, from 9:00 A.M. to 5:00 P.M. April through September from 9:00 A.M. to 7:00 P.M. Admission **Free**; *some programs $.*

This 470-acre acre park includes 8 miles of hiking trails through beautiful meadows and woodlands. Although some of the trails are too rugged for young children, there are some easy options, including a ½-mile Freedom Trail accessible to strollers and wheelchairs. Spring through fall, Raven Run offers terrific evening and weekend programs in which families can explore nature together, including stargazing, "bug walks," nocturnal walks with owl calling and storytelling, and learn-to-camp nights. There are special programs for children under five. The schedule varies and reservations are recommended, so call ahead.

A Day Family Adventure One spring break, appointments and budget prevented us from taking a trip, so for a few days we checked into a local hotel that had a big swimming pool and game room. We went to free places in the area that we had never visited before and enjoyed the feeling of a getaway without major expense or the long drive.

WAVELAND HISTORIC HOME (ages 8 and up)

225 Waveland Museum Road, Lexington; 6 miles south of Main Street off Nicholasville Road (US 27 south); (859) 272–3611 or (800) 255–PARK. Open March 1 through mid-December, Monday to Saturday from 10:00 A.M. to 5:00 P.M., Sunday from 1:00 to 5:00 P.M. Adults $$, students $.

Waveland, built by the Bryans, distant relatives of Daniel Boone, offers a glimpse of life on an antebellum Kentucky plantation, from the mansion to the slave quarters. The tour guides tell young visitors about popular children's games of the time, as well as household items that today's children might not be familiar with, such as feather beds. Pack a picnic lunch and let your children play on the playground, or take a family walk on the easy hiking trails near the house. *Note:* No wheelchair-accessible rest rooms.

MCCONNELL SPRINGS (all ages)

McConnell Springs Road (take Old Frankfort Pike out of downtown, and turn left across from the fire training tower); (859) 225–4073. Open year-round, daily. Hours are 9:00 A.M. to 5:00 P.M. January through April and October through December, 9:00 A.M. to 6:00 P.M. May and September; and 9:00 A.M. to 7:00 P.M. June through August. Free.

This twenty-six-acre nature sanctuary includes the campsite where early settlers heard the big news about the Revolutionary War Battle of Lexington—and decided to name their settlement in its honor. You'll see a variety of plants and wildlife along its 2 miles of hiking trails. The ½-mile paved section accommodates strollers and wheelchairs. The Education Center includes displays and rest rooms.

HEADLEY-WHITNEY MUSEUM (ages 8 and up)
4435 Old Frankfort Pike, Lexington 40510; 6½ miles from downtown Lexington; (800) 310–5085 or (859) 255–6653, www.headley-whitney.org; $; Free *for children under 5.*

Have you ever seen a room in which the walls and doors are covered with thousands of seashells? You'll find one at this eclectic museum, along with a Jewel Room showcasing tiny bibelots encrusted with gems and precious metals. A third building houses a variety of permanent and changing decorative arts exhibits from around the world, from textiles to porcelain. Although there is definitely a "fragile" nature to this museum, older children in particular will enjoy the interesting and odd items on display.

Kids Shopping in Lexington

- **Joseph-Beth Booksellers,** *Lexington Green, Nicholasville Road, Lexington 40503; (859) 273–2911.* Award-winning independent bookstore with large children's department and Free activities for children six and under each Wednesday and Friday.

- **Mad Potter,** *3385 Tates Creek Road, Lexington 40502; (859) 269–4591.* Paint your own pottery.

- **Zany Brainy,** *Crossroads Plaza, Nicholasville Road, Lexington 40503; (859) 245–8697.* Creative and educational toys and games.

AVIATION MUSEUM OF KENTUCKY (all ages)
Bluegrass Airport, P.O. Box 4118, 4316 Hangar Drive, Lexington 40544; (859) 231–1219, www.aviationky.org. Open Tuesday, Thursday, Friday, and Saturday from 10:00 A.M. to 5:00 P.M., Sunday from 1:00 to 5:00 P.M. $; children under 6 Free.

Airplanes big and small are on display in this hangar museum located next to Lexington's Bluegrass Airport (just across Versailles Road from

Keeneland). Youngsters can learn about some Kentucky aviation pioneers, view an

Amazing Kentucky Fact Famous Lexingtonians include Backstreet Boys Brian Littrell and Kevin Richardson.

F-4 Phantom jet and other antique and modern airplanes, and try their own hands at flying in a kid-sized flight simulator.

Other Things to See and Do

Kentucky Living History Farm,
(859) 293–9367

Lexington Farmers Market, mid-April through early December; Saturdays on Vine Street, Tuesdays and Thursdays at Broadway and Maxwell.

Lexington Walk and Bluegrass Country Driving Tour, Pick up at Lexington Convention and Visitors Bureau.

William S. Webb Museum of Anthropology, UK. *(859) 257–8208*

Where to Eat

deSha's, *101 North Broadway in Victorian Square, Lexington 40507; (859) 259–3771.* Varied menu; specialties include meatloaf and honey cornbread. $$–$$$

Gattitown, *2524 Nicholasville Road, Lexington 40503; (859) 277–2323.* Pizza buffet plus bumper cars, cartoons, and video games.

Jalapeno's, *295 New Circle Road NW, Lexington 40505; (859) 299–8299; and 1030 South Broadway, Lexington 40504; (859) 281–5171.* Mexican classics in a colorful setting. $$

Joe Bologna's, *120 West Maxwell, Lexington 40508,* near the University of Kentucky campus; (859) 252–4933. Enjoy pizza, huge garlic breadsticks, and other Italian favorites in a former synagogue building. $

Magee's Bakery, *726 East Main, Lexington 40502; (859) 255–9481.* Yummy doughnuts, muffins (the pumpkin ones are our favorites), scones, and ham biscuits for breakfast; sandwiches or quiche and cookies for lunch. "Pablo," a painted, almost life-sized horse, is on display just inside the front door. This was one of dozens of art horses featured in a citywide exhibit in 2000. $

Parkette Drive-in, *1216 New Circle Road NE, Lexington 40505; (859) 254–8723.* A real '50s drive-in, where carhops serve burgers, fries, shakes, and chicken right to your car. $ (No credit cards accepted.)

Ramsey's Diner, *496 East High Street, Lexington 40507; (859) 259–2708.* Comfort food like meatloaf, chicken and dumplings, and locally grown veggies. You can even get a peanut butter sandwich. $$

Where to Stay

Holiday Inn North, *1950 Newtown Pike (exit 11, I–75).* Restaurant, indoor pool, huge activity center with video games and Ping-Pong, tennis courts. $$$

Holiday Inn South, *5532 Athens-Boonesboro Road (exit 104, I–75, Lexington 40509); (859) 263–5241 or (800) HOLI-DAY.* Indoor and outdoor pools, restaurant, laundry, exercise room, and recreation room. $$$

Kentucky Horse Park Camp-ground, *4089 Iron Works Parkway,*

Lexington 40511; (859) 233–4303 or (800) 678–8813, www.kyhorsepark.com. Offers 260 paved campsites with water and electric hookups. Primitive sites also available. Swimming pool, tennis courts, horseshoes, activities pavilion, bathhouse/laundry. $

Marriott's Griffin Gate Resort, *1800 Newtown Pike, Lexington 40511; (859) 231–5100 or (800) 228–9290.* Indoor and outdoor pools, tennis courts, recreation room, restaurant, laundry. $$$$

For More Information

Lexington Convention and Visitors Bureau, *301 East Vine Street, Lexington* *40507; (800) 845–3959 or (859) 233–7299, www.visitlex.com*

Annual Events

Rolex Three-Day Event, late April, Kentucky Horse Park; (859) 254-8123

Kentucky Derby Day at Keeneland, first Saturday in May, Keeneland Race Course; (800) 456-3412

Kentucky High School Invitational Rodeo, May, Kentucky Horse Park; (859) 484-2214

Memorial Day Summer Fest, Memorial Day, Red Mile Harness Track; (859) 255-0752

Annual Egyptian Event, early June, Kentucky Horse Park; (859) 255-0752

Festival of the Bluegrass, early June, Kentucky Horse Park; (859) 846-4995 or www.kyfestival.com

Junior League Horse Show, early July, Red Mile Harness Track; (859) 252-1893

Lexington Lions Club Bluegrass Fair, July, Masterson Station Park; (859) 233-1465

Woodland Jubilee, July, Woodland Park; (859) 288-2925

Shakespeare Festival, July, UK Arboretum; (859) 257-4929

Breyerfest, late July, Kentucky Horse Park; (973) 633-5090

Roots and Heritage Festival, early September, downtown; (859) 533-7668

Museum-Go-Round, late September, Woodland Park; (859) 258-3256

Sheiks and Shrieks Fun Show, last Saturday in October, Kentucky Horse Park (The horse park's Parade of Breeds takes on a Halloween theme, with both horses and riders in costumes.)

Southern Lights, mid-November through December 31, Kentucky Horse Park; (859) 255-5727

Bluegrass Region

The Bluegrass region is rich in history. You can tour replicas of pioneer forts in Harrodsburg and near Richmond, the nation's largest restored Shaker community at Shaker Village of Pleasant Hill, and the site of Kentucky's most important Civil War battle at Perryville. You can visit a contemporary landmark—Toyota's state-of-the-art automaking plant in Georgetown—and explore museums featuring everything from a "talking crow" to an undertaker's table. This region includes the state capital, Frankfort, with its many museums and public buildings, including the Kentucky History Center, the state's largest and most comprehensive history museum. Take a riverboat ride, see how dulcimers and quilts are made, watch a pro football team train, and enjoy drama under the stars—so much awaits families in this beautiful and tradition-laden part of the state.

The Bluegrass is a compact region, too. All of the cities mentioned here are an easy day trip from Lexington, northern Kentucky, Louisville, most of north-central and south-central Kentucky, and much of eastern Kentucky. I-75 and I-64 can get you to some of the cities, but you're probably going to have to get off the interstates and take the old US highways, like 68, 62, 27, 127, and 460. In general, these are pretty good roads, though two-lane for the most part. Get a good map, take your time, and enjoy the beautiful view.

Attractions are arranged in a loop around Lexington, starting at the northeast and moving counterclockwise around Lexington. You'll end up poised to explore eastern Kentucky.

BLUEGRASS REGION

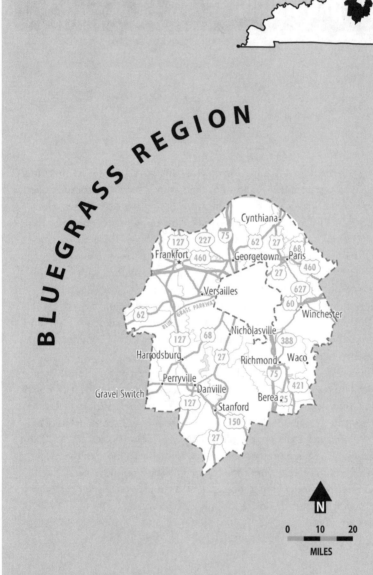

Cynthiana

127 227 75 62 27 68
Frankfort 460 Georgetown Paris
460
Versailles 27
627
62 60 Winchester
BLUE GRASS PARKWAY
Nicholasville
127 68 388
Harrodsburg 27 Richmond Waco
Perryville Danville 75 421
Gravel Switch Berea 25
127 Stanford
150
27

N

0   10   20
MILES

Teresa's Top Ten
Picks for the Bluegrass Region

1. Salato Wildlife Education Center and Game Farm, (800) 858–1549
2. Buckley Wildlife Sanctuary, (859) 873–5711
3. Kentucky History Center, (502) 564–1792
4. Farm Fun in Scott County, (502) 863–2547
5. *Dixie Belle* at Shaker Village, (800) 734–5611
6. Hummel Planetarium and Space Theater, (859) 622–1547
7. Old Fort Harrod State Park, (859) 734–3314
8. Fort Boonesborough State Park, (859) 527–3131
9. Toyota Motor Manufacturing Kentucky, Inc., (800) TMM–4485
10. Bluegrass Scenic Railroad and Museum, (800) 755–2476

Paris

CLAIBORNE FARM (ages 8 and up)
Highway 627, southeast of Paris; (859) 233–4252. Tours by appointment only. **Free** *(tip for guide is customary).*

The Claiborne family has been raising thoroughbred racehorses for several generations. When you tour this beautiful farm, you'll see the barn areas as well as the grave of great Triple Crown champion Secretariat. A $5.00 to $10.00 tip for the guide is customary.

HOPEWELL MUSEUM (ages 5 and up)
800 Pleasant Street, Paris 40361; (859) 987–7274. Open Wednesday to Saturday from noon to 5:00 P.M., Sunday from 2:00 to 4:00 P.M. **Free**.

In pioneer times, travelers going from Maysville to Lexington or vice versa hoped they'd make it to this town north of Lexington before dark. But in 1790, the community of Hopewell was renamed Paris to honor America's Revolutionary War allies. In 2000, residents revived the old name for this community museum. Here you can learn about famous Bourbon Countians such as Garrett Morgan, the inventor of the stoplight and the gas mask, and see photographs of local history as well as changing fine arts exhibits. The building itself is a work of art, built in 1909 as the community post office.

CANE RIDGE MEETING HOUSE AND SHRINE (ages 5 and up)

KY 537, off US 460, northeast of Paris; P.O. Box 26, Paris 40362; (859) 987–5350. Open April 1 through October 31, Monday to Friday from 9:00 A.M. to 5:00 P.M., Sunday 1:00 to 5:00 P.M. Free*; donations requested.*

If your family is a member of the Christian Church (Disciples of Christ) or Church of Christ denominations, you'll particularly enjoy visiting this shrine and museum. Encased in a golden limestone building is a large log meeting house. Cane Ridge was the site of some of the huge religious revivals of the early 1800s (they attracted 20,000 to 30,000 people), and in 1804 the Reverend Barton Warren Stone and other Presbyterian ministers signed a document here that led to the creation of the new Christian denominations. The museum includes early church documents, Stone family items, and a collection of nineteenth-century farm and home artifacts. You can picnic on the grounds.

NANNINE CLAY WALLIS ARBORETUM (all ages)

616 Pleasant Street, Paris 40362; (859) 987–6158. Hours vary; call first. Free*.*

The four-acre backyard of the headquarters of the Garden Club of Kentucky is both scenic and educational. The arboretum features six theme areas: a Walk Garden, Rose Garden, Perennial Garden, Wildflower Garden, Bird Border, and Shade Garden. The trees are marked, and you can borrow a study guide to use as you explore. The fish pond is always a big hit with young visitors. The arboretum is especially pretty in spring, when the dogwoods are in bloom. In early December, there's an open house, with greenery and other natural decorations for sale.

For More Information

Paris/Bourbon County Tourist Commission, *525 High Street, Paris 40361; (859) 987–3205.*

Cynthiana

CYNTHIANA/HARRISON COUNTY MUSEUM (ages 5 and up)

112 South Walnut Street, Cynthiana 41031; (859) 234–7179. Open Friday and Saturday from 10:00 A.M. to 5:00 P.M. Free*.*

All kinds of things have been donated by local residents to help this museum tell Cynthiana's story. You'll see old photos, Civil War uniforms, vintage wedding dresses, a model of a long-gone covered bridge, and many other items as you learn about the founding of the town in 1793, Cynthiana's two Civil War battles, and other events large and small in the history of the town.

QUIET TRAILS NATURE PRESERVE (all ages)

Pugh's Ferry Road, off Highway 1284 near Sunrise; (502) 573-2886 or www. kynaturepreserves.org. Open daily year-round. No rest room facilities. **Free**.

This lovely preserve offers several easy hiking trails and relatively unspoiled views of the Licking River Valley. There's a box on site that usually contains trail maps. Pets are not allowed.

Where to Eat

Biancke's Restaurant, *3 Main Street, Cynthiana 41031; (859) 234-3443. A local favorite since 1894. Specialties* include the Big Joe Burger, fried green tomatoes, and homemade cream pies. $

Georgetown

TOYOTA MOTOR MANUFACTURING KENTUCKY, INC.
(tour ages 6 and up; visitor center all ages)

2002 Cherry Blossom Way, Georgetown 40324 (from I-75, exit 126, head east 2½ miles on Cherry Blossom Way); (800) TMM-4485 or (502) 868-3027, www.toyotageorgetown.com. Visitor center open Monday through Friday from 9:00 A.M. to 4:00 P.M. Tours at 10:00 A.M., noon, and 2:00 P.M. daily, with an additional 6:00 P.M tour on Thursday. **Free**.

Learn about the Toyota Production System, *kaizen* (a philosophy of continuous improvement), and Kentucky teamwork at this modern, bright, and noisy automaking facility. About half a million vehicles (Camry and Avalon sedans and Sienna minivans) and nearly as many engines are made at the Georgetown plant every year. The tour is by tram, and you'll wear headphones to hear the guide over the sound of the factory. The tram visits several areas of the plant: Stamping, where giant presses turn steel into car body parts; Body Weld, where robotic and human welders put the body together; and Assembly, where the engine and other interior components are installed. To go on the plant tours, children must be at least in the first grade and be accompanied by an adult. Reservations are strongly recommended for the tour. No cameras are allowed on the tour, nor are shorts (for safety reasons). All ages can explore the visitor center, which includes interactive exhibits, a video, and the first Camry made at the plant in 1986. Because of tightened security since 2001, no purses or bags are allowed inside, and you'll need to show a photo ID.

CINCINNATI BENGALS SUMMER TRAINING CAMP (ages 5 and up)

Georgetown College Athletic Complex, Lemons Mill Road, Georgetown 40324; (502) 863–8009. Open mid-July through mid-August; days and times vary. **Free** *most days; scrimmage game $.*

Is there a little (or big) football fan in the house? If so, you may want to brave the sweltering heat to watch Cincinnati Bengals players go through their paces to get ready for the fall season. The daily schedule varies, but the camp includes practice sessions, a scrimmage, and workouts, with some opportunities for autographs and pictures. Warning: It gets very hot sitting in those open-air bleachers—you really gotta love football (or the Bengals).

ROYAL SPRING PARK (all ages)

South Water and West Main Streets, Georgetown 40324; (502) 863–2547. Log cabin open mid-May through mid-October, Tuesday to Sunday from 10:00 A.M. to 4:00 P.M. View the spring and see the chainsaw sculpture daily year-round. Note: Cabin not wheelchair-accessible. **Free**.

You may see local youngsters fishing near the old stone bridge when you visit this historic site—just as children of Georgetown have done for over 200 years. Royal Spring or Big Spring was discovered by surveyors in 1774, and the town grew up around this amazing water source (which produces some 25 million gallons of water a day). The small park next to the spring includes a viewing area, a Revolutionary War monument (on the bluff above the spring), and two small cabins that were built at other locations. One of the cabins is a museum of pioneer life, with tours and occasional workshops. The sculpture at the park's entrance is of Elijah Craig, a Georgetown founder. Believe it or not, this Baptist minister of the late 1700s is reputed to have made the first batch of bourbon whiskey near the spring. Believe it or not again, the statue was created by local craftsman Sandy Schu using a *chainsaw*.

Farm-Fresh Fun

Farm-Fresh Fun Fall is an especially fun—and delicious—time to spend a day or weekend in Scott County because the county's numerous farm markets are in full swing. These are great places to pick your Halloween pumpkin, buy farm-grown mums, and take some wonderful fall photos of your children.

- **Double Stink Hog Farm** (502-868-9703), 6 miles east of Georgetown on Highway 460, features crafts displays, wagon and camel rides, pony rides, pig races, and all kinds of delicious food during **Pumpkinfest**, weekends late September through October.

- Not to be outdone, **Bi-Water Farm and Greenhouse** (north of Georgetown on US 25; 502-863-3676) holds **Autumnfest**, which features a five-acre corn maze, a Spooky Farmhouse, a petting zoo and the Autumnfest Express Train.

- **Evans Farm Orchard and Cider Mill**, 180 Stone Road (502-863-4550), not far from Double Stink, is the place to get fresh apples, fresh-pressed apple cider, and homemade apple slushies, then take on the challenge of the Corn Maze and Straw Mountain. Call for date of Kids Day, when children get free access to the mazes, free cider slushies, and other special treats.

- In the midst of all the farm fun comes **Festival of the Horse** (a weekend in late September), with all-horse-drawn parades (including a Children's Parade on Friday evening), music, and children's activities. Call (502) 863-2547 for more information.

 GEORGETOWN/SCOTT COUNTY MUSEUM (ages 5 and up)
229 East Main Street, Georgetown 40324; (502) 863-6201. Open Monday to Friday from 9:00 A.M. to 4:00 P.M. **Free**.

You can learn all about Georgetown history at this interesting museum housed in the town's elegant 1900s post office building. Items on display include paper made by city founder Elijah Craig at his early paper mill, photographs by noted Georgetown landscape and portrait photographer Eugene Bradley, arrowheads, World War II items, pens made in Georgetown, and a changing exhibit about the history of Georgetown College. Some of the exhibits have signage and information in Japanese as well as English, resulting from an exhibit that was on display in Georgetown's sister city of Tahara-cho, Japan. Railroad enthusiasts will want to see the $40,000 model train replica of the 1931 DeWitt

Clinton. And be sure to see the animated talking replica of Pete the Crow and get the story on Georgetown's most famous animal resident of the early 1800s.

CARDOME CENTRE/YUKO-EN ON THE ELKHORN (all ages)

800 Cincinnati Pike (US 25) north of downtown Georgetown; (502) 863-1575. Open daily. **Free**.

Children will love the giant wooden buffalo—more chainsaw art—that "stand watch" in front of this former monastery, just a short drive from Royal Spring Park. Next to Cardome is **Yuko-en on the Elkhorn,** a five-acre Japanese-style garden and the official "Japanese–Kentucky Friendship Garden." The garden opened in 2002, so exhibits are still growing (literally!), but there are the beginnings of several garden areas, a Zen garden, wooden bridges, statuary, a tiny lake, and very huge, interesting wooden doors leading onto it all. It's an easy, paved pathway. In late April, Cardome is the site of Georgetown's **International Kite Festival** (502-863-1575, ext. 44), which features Japanese kite makers and kite flying from Georgetown's sister city, Tahara-cho, Japan—plus hot air balloon rides and a variety of international foods. In early June, Civil War enthusiasts come to Cardome for the reenactment of **Morgan's Raid on Georgetown** (502-868-0975), with skirmishes, Civil War–era music, costumed historic figures of the time, and "sutlers" (vendors) tents.

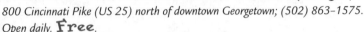

Up a Creek The Elkhorn Creek is a lovely and historic waterway that flows through six Bluegrass counties. A canoe excursion is a fun way to see the creek and the countryside. You can rent one from **Canoe Kentucky** *(7323 Peaks Mill Road, 8 miles north of Frankfort; (502) 227-4492 or (800) K-CANOE; www.canoeky.com. $$$$).* Although it's based north of Frankfort, you can make a reservation by phone and meet the guide at a creek entry point. Tell them the ages of the children in your family, your canoeing experience level, and what you're interested in seeing and doing (fishing, history, picnicking, rapids, etc.), and they'll suggest a route. Guided excursions are also available. There are several good entry points to the Elkhorn in and near Georgetown: **Cardome Park** (US 25N) in Georgetown, **Great Crossings Park** (US 227, off US 460 west of Georgetown), and underneath Switzer Bridge (KY 1689 off US 460 between Georgetown and Frankfort). At Great Crossings Park, there's a nature trail along the creek, including a short paved section. The trail leads to an elementary school with a playground.

KENTUCKY JAMBOREE (all ages)
*Georgetown Convention Center, 292 Connector Road, Georgetown 40324
(I-75, exit 125 or 126); (502) 867-7424 or (888) 806-7424, www.kentucky
jamboree.com. Every Saturday at 8:00 P.M. $$*

If your family enjoys country and gospel music, plan to spend a Saturday evening at this friendly and wholesome musical gathering. Entertainer Kenny Whalen started the jamboree to give young performers a smoke-free, alcohol-free place to get a start. Talented youngsters, along with guest gospel and country groups, join Whalen and his band, The Travelers, each week.

Other Things to See and Do

Country World Flea Market, *3036 Paris Pike, Georgetown 40324; (502) 867–0831.* Huge outdoor/indoor weekend flea market with food and live music.

Where to Eat

Bella Vella, *751 Slone Drive (Indian Acres Shopping Center), Georgetown 40324; (502) 863–1877.* Italian favorites and good pizza. $

Fava's Restaurant, *159 East Main Street, Georgetown 40324; (502) 863–4383.* Fava's has been a Georgetown institution since 1910. Join the regular "courthouse crowd" for home cooking, grilled cheese sandwiches and burgers, and homemade pies. There's an all-you-can-eat catfish special on weekends. $

Jessie Pearl's Kitchen, *124 Opera Alley (behind Georgetown Antique Mall), Georgetown 40324; (502) 570–8700.* Jessie Bledsoe and her family will serve you beans and cornbread, catfish, burgers, and homemade bread pudding. $

Sam's Truckstop, *US 25S, Georgetown; (502) 863–5872.* Before the interstates, US 25 was the main route in and out of Georgetown. These days you'll find more local families than truckers dining at this restaurant south of town. The menu includes everything from steaks to Samburgers. $

Where to Stay

Best Western, *132 Darby Drive, Georgetown 40324; (502) 868–0055 or (877) 868–6555.* Breakfast buffet, indoor pool, refrigerators in rooms. $

Country Inn Suites, *131 Darby Drive, Georgetown 40324; (502) 868–6868 or* *(800) 456–4000.* Complimentary breakfast, indoor pool, laundry. $

Hampton Inn, *128 Darby Drive, Georgetown 40324; (502) 867–4888 or (800) HAMPTON.* Indoor pool, some rooms with kitchenettes. $

For More Information

Georgetown/Scott County Tourism, *40324; (502) 863–2547 or (888) 863–*
339 Outlet Center Drive, Georgetown *8600, www.georgetownky.com.*

Frankfort

KENTUCKY HISTORY CENTER (all ages)
100 West Broadway, Frankfort 40601; (502) 564-1792, www.kyhistory.org.
Open Tuesday, Wednesday, Friday, and Saturday from 10:00 A.M. to 5:00 P.M.,
Thursday from 10:00 A.M. to 8:00 P.M., and Sunday from 1:00 to 5:00 P.M.
Free.

This beautiful, relatively new facility shows off Kentucky artifacts that
the Kentucky Historical Society has been collecting for decades. The central exhibit is the "Kentucky Journey," a chronological look at the state
from presettlement to the present day, with numerous interactive and
animated displays. You go through at your own pace, and the open
design is well suited to active children. The history center conducts many
special programs for children, including hands-on "Super Saturday"
workshops and dramatic presentations, so check into the schedule.

STATE CAPITOL (ages 5 and up)
Capital Avenue, Frankfort; (502) 564-3449. Guided tours offered Monday to
Friday, except holidays, from 8:30 A.M. to 4:30 P.M. Although all ages can visit,
the tour is for ages 5 and up. **Free**.

Kentucky's Capitol Building, with its impressive rotunda, was modeled after the federal Capitol in Washington, D.C. Features include
murals of Kentucky history, a collection of dolls dressed like Kentucky's
First Ladies in their inaugural gowns, and the legislative chambers. Statues of both Abraham Lincoln and Jefferson Davis commemorate the fact
that both Union and Confederate presidents during the Civil War were
Kentuckians. Behind the Capitol is the Floral Clock—a 34-foot-diameter
clock made of plants and flowers.

KENTUCKY GOVERNOR'S MANSION (ages 5 and up)
Adjacent to the Capitol Building, Frankfort; (502) 564-8004. Open Tuesday to
Thursday from 9:00 A.M. to 11:00 A.M. **Free**.

Home to Kentucky's chief executive since 1914, the house was patterned after Marie Antoinette's summer villa, the Petite Trianon. The tour
includes the elegant ballroom, state dining room, and reception room.

OLD STATE CAPITOL (ages 5 and up)

Broadway and Lewis Streets, Frankfort; (502) 564-3016. Open Tuesday to Saturday from 10:00 A.M. to 5:00 P.M., Sunday from noon to 5:00 P.M. **Free**.

The Kentucky legislature met in this building from 1830 to 1910; it's interesting to compare the scale and size of the legislative chambers to the present Capitol. Many early portraits and artifacts are on display, but one of the most interesting features is the unusual self-supporting winding staircase.

REBECCA-RUTH CANDY (ages 4 and up)

112 East Second Street, Frankfort; (502) 223-7475 or (800) 444-3766, www. rebeccaruth.com. Tours offered January through October, Monday to Saturday from 9:30 A.M. to 4:30 P.M. Store hours are Monday to Saturday from 8:30 A.M. to 5:30 P.M., Sunday from noon to 5:00 P.M. **Free**.

Chocoholics the world over know about Frankfort because of Rebecca-Ruth Candy. Take a candy factory tour and find out about the hundreds of confections made here (most famous are its Kentucky Bourbon candies) and about Ruth Hanly and Rebecca Gooch, former schoolteachers who started this candy company in 1919. Best part of the tour: free samples.

 ### LIBERTY HALL AND ORLANDO BROWN HOUSE (ages 6 and up)

Liberty Hall: 218 Wilkinson Street, Frankfort 40601; (502) 227-2560 or www. libertyhall.org; Orlando Brown House, 202 Wilkinson Street, Frankfort 40601; (502) 875-4952.Open March through December. Tours at 10:30 A.M., noon, and 1:30 and 3:00 P.M. Tuesday to Saturday; 1:30 and 3:00 P.M. Sunday. **Free**.

John Brown, one of Kentucky's first two U.S. senators, built Liberty Hall for his wife, Margaretta, and their family in 1796. The Orlando Brown House next door was built for his son, and lovely lawns and gardens connect the two. The houses remained in the Brown family until they became museums in the 1950s, and so many lovely furnishings and family portraits remain. Ghost enthusiasts, take note: Liberty Hall is home to one of Kentucky's most famous ghosts, the "Grey Lady," frequently sighted and thought to be the spirit of an aunt who died while visiting the Browns to help console them over the death of their daughter.

 ### GRAVE OF DANIEL AND REBECCA BOONE (all ages)

Frankfort Cemetery, 215 East Main Street, Frankfort 40601; (502) 227-2403. Open daily from 8:00 A.M. to 5:30 P.M. in winter, 8:00 A.M. to 8:30 P.M. in summer. **Free**.

Kentucky's most famous pioneer couple are buried at a lovely site high on a hill overlooking the Kentucky River. This is a large cemetery, with monuments dating to the Revolutionary War period, and some children may like to walk around and look at the interesting Victorian monuments or read the often poetic inscriptions.

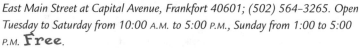

Amazing Kentucky Fact U.S. Senator George Graham Vest, who coined the famous saying "Dog is man's best friend," grew up in Frankfort. You can tour the house he lived in, the Vest-Lindsey House, at 401 Wapping Street. (502) 564-6980.

KENTUCKY MILITARY HISTORY MUSEUM (ages 7 and up)
East Main Street at Capital Avenue, Frankfort 40601; (502) 564-3265. Open Tuesday to Saturday from 10:00 A.M. to 5:00 P.M., Sunday from 1:00 to 5:00 P.M. Free.

My son's interest in Civil War uniforms led to our first visit here, and sometimes when we're in Frankfort we just stop by. He sees something he never noticed before each time. It doesn't take a long time to tour the collection of uniforms, guns, flags, cannons, swords, and other battle memorabilia. The museum covers a time span from before the Revolutionary War to the present day. The building itself is a military artifact: A former Union arsenal building, it looks appropriately fortress-like and sits atop a hill overlooking downtown Frankfort.

KENTUCKY VIETNAM VETERANS' MEMORIAL (all ages)
Coffee Tree Road, Frankfort. Open daily. Free.

Before visiting, you might explain how a sundial works, so your children can appreciate the unusual design of this monument. The names of Kentuckians who died in the Vietnam War are etched in granite beneath a giant sundial; the gnomon's shadow falls on the veteran's name on the anniversary of his death.

SALATO WILDLIFE EDUCATION CENTER AND GAME FARM (all ages)

#1 Game Farm Road, Frankfort 40601; US 60, west of Frankfort (take exit 53 B off I-64 to US 127 north; travel 1½ miles and turn left on US 60); (800) 858-1549 or (502) 564-7863. Open year-round. November through April hours: 10:00 A.M. to 4:30 P.M. Tuesday to Friday, 10:00 A.M. to 5:00 P.M. Saturday,

and 1:00 to 5:00 P.M. Sunday. May through October hours: 9:00 A.M. to 5:00 P.M. Monday to Friday, 9:00 A.M. to 6:00 P.M. Saturday, 1:00 to 6:00 P.M. Sunday. $ admission to education center, rest of the complex is **Free**.

Bald eagles, deer, bison, elk, fish, venomous snakes, and wild turkeys live at this state-operated nature complex. There are also two fishing lakes, a songbird area, and picnic grounds. The staff does an excellent job of educating young visitors in an engaging way. One of the three fishing lakes is for children ages twelve and under only (and is abundantly stocked to increase the odds of a successful catch). Forgot your pole? No problem—they have some you can use. (*Note:* Those over sixteen must have a state fishing license; also available at the game farm.)

SWITZER BRIDGE (all ages)

Take US 460 east from Frankfort, turn left at KY 1689.

If you take US 460 from Frankfort to Georgetown, make a side trip to Switzer Bridge. This 120-foot span across Elkhorn Creek was originally built in 1855, when Kentucky had hundreds of "kissing bridges." Today there are only thirteen left—but there would be only twelve if not for a bit of luck and a lot of hard work. In 1997, intense spring floods swept the Switzer Bridge off its foundation; luckily, a nearby concrete bridge prevented it from being washed down the creek. An amazing federal/state rebuilding partnership made it nearly good as new. The bridge is closed to traffic, so youngsters can explore it without worry of cars. The small surrounding park is a good place for a summer picnic, splashing in the water, and fishing. It's also a convenient entry point for a Kentucky canoe excursion.

Where to Eat

Gibby's Deli, *212 West Broadway, Frankfort 40601; (502) 223–4429. Pasta, salads, and sandwiches.* $

Jim's Seafood, *950 Wilkinson Boulevard, Frankfort 40601; (502) 223–7448.* Fried seafood with kids' menu and scenic view of the Kentucky River. $$

Melanie's on Main, *238 West Main Street, Frankfort 40601; (502) 226–3322.* Good lunch place with kids' menu. $

Where to Stay

Bluegrass Inn, *635 Versailles Road, US 60, Frankfort 40601; (502) 695–1800 or* *(800) 322–1802.* Outdoor pool, pets accepted. $

Elkhorn Campground, *165 Scruggs Lane, off US 460, Frankfort 40601; (502) 695–9154.* Tent and full hookup sites, pool, showers, playground, laundry. $

Hampton Inn, *1310 US 127S, Frankfort 40601; (502) 223–7600.* Outdoor swimming pool, free breakfast buffet. $$–$$$

Holiday Inn Capitol Plaza, *405 Wilkinson Boulevard, Frankfort 40601; (502) 227–5100 or (800) HOLIDAY.* Indoor pool, restaurant, exercise room, continental breakfast. $$$

For More Information

Frankfort Visitor Center, *100 Capitol Avenue, Frankfort 40601; (800) 960–* *7200 or (502) 875–8687, www.visitfrankfort.com.*

Versailles

THREE CHIMNEYS FARM (ages 8 and up)

Old Frankfort Pike, Versailles; (859) 873-7053. Tours except December and January. **Free.**

A classic horse farm with a well-organized tour program, Three Chimneys—home to racing champion Silver Charm and other top stallions—offers tours of the stallion barn, breeding shed, and mare receiving barn.

THE CASTLE (all ages)

US 60, west of Bluegrass Airport. Exterior viewing only.

Youthful imaginations are sure to be stirred by the site of this authentic-looking castle. What's the story? In 1969, a businessman began building a castle, turrets and all, with the intent of living in it. He never finished it, but he inadvertently created the Bluegrass region's most unexpected roadside attraction. Alas, no tours, but you can pull off the road out front or at Old Pisgah Pike, just west of the castle, to snap exterior photos.

NOSTALGIA STATION TOY AND TRAIN MUSEUM (ages 3 and up)

279 Depot Street, Versailles 40383; (859) 873-2497. Open Wednesday to Saturday from 10:00 A.M. to 5:00 P.M., Sunday from 1:00 to 5:00 P.M. $

You'll enjoy talking with Wanda and Winfrey Adkins and seeing their collection of model trains and other antique toys. This must-see attraction for railroad buffs is housed in a restored passenger depot.

BLUEGRASS SCENIC RAILROAD AND MUSEUM (all ages)

Woodford County Park (US 62 at Beasley Road), about 1½ miles west of Versailles, P.O. Box 27, Versailles 40383; (859) 873-2476 or (800) 755-2476. Three excursions on Saturday and two on Sunday, early May through late October. $$

Before or after you see the model trains at Nostalgia Station, take a ride on the real thing. The ninety-minute excursion crosses through scenic farmland and stops before returning to allow passengers to walk up to Young's High Bridge, a nineteenth-century railroad trestle over the Kentucky River. In addition to the regular sightseeing excursions, there are numerous themed runs great for families, including special Mother's Day and Father's Day excursions, Clown Daze in early October, a Wild West Train Robbery in late June, a Civil War Train Robbery in early September,

Amazing Kentucky Fact Both Versailles, Kentucky, and its French namesake are spelled the same, but they're pronounced differently. In Kentucky, it's not "Ver-SIGH," it's "Ver-SALES."

and Halloween and Santa Claus runs. It's a good idea to get your tickets in advance for these special excursions, since they often sell out. Conclude your day in the museum looking at the 1960s caboose, a restored engine, and other classic rail cars.

JACK JOUETT HOUSE (ages 5 and up)

Craig's Creek Pike, off McCowan's Ferry Road, Versailles 40383; (859) 873-7902. Open April through October, Wednesday from 11:00 A.M. to 1:00 P.M., Saturday and Sunday from noon to 5:00 P.M. **Free.**

Your children may have heard of Paul Revere, but how about Jack Jouett? He has been called the "Paul Revere of the South" for galloping through Virginia countryside to warn of the coming British invasion. His Kentucky house, built around 1797, has just five rooms, a good size for young historians with short attention spans.

BUCKLEY WILDLIFE SANCTUARY (all ages)

1035 Germany Road, between Frankfort and Versailles; (859) 873-5711. Open Wednesday to Friday from 9:00 A.M. to 5:00 P.M., Saturday and Sunday from 9:00 A.M. to 6:00 P.M. From Versailles, take US 60 west, turn left onto Highway 1681. Take 1681 to Millville, and turn left onto Highway 1659. Go just under 2 miles, and turn right onto Highway 1964. Go 1 mile and turn right onto Germany Road, then keep going straight—do not go left when the road forks—for a little over a mile. $

Though it can be a little tricky to find, this pretty 364-acre sanctuary is worth the effort. There are a variety of hiking trails, educational exhibits, bird-blinds, and picnic areas, and you're likely to see all kinds of wildlife from deer to butterflies. Spring through fall, there are many weekend events geared to children. One of the most popular is "Fantasy Forest" in October, which features hayrides, storytelling, music and a forest walk in which children encounter animals along the way (costumed volunteers) who tell them about forest life. There's also a Family Fun Day in early August, with animal exhibits and entertainment.

Where to Eat

Kessler's 1891 Eatery, *197 South Main Street, Versailles 40383; (859) 879–3344.* Great barbecue, plus steaks, pork chops, and country ham croquettes. $

Uptown Chatter, *160 South Main Street, Versailles 40383; (859) 873–1102.* Sandwiches, soups, and daily specials in a casual downtown cafe. $

Where to Stay

Western Fields, *Fords Mill Road (Highway 1965), near Nonesuch; (859) 879–0066.* If you'd like to stay in a private house as opposed to a hotel, this is a good one that welcomes families. An artistically decorated three-bedroom guest house on an eighty-acre farm with llamas, hiking trails, gardens, and even a pottery studio. $$$$

Nicholasville

CAMP NELSON HERITAGE PARK (ages 6 and up)
Along US 27, about 20 miles south of Lexington and 6 miles south of Nicholasville; (859) 881–9126 or www.campnelson.org. White House tours Wednesday to Saturday from 10:00 A.M. to 4:00 P.M. Interpretive trail and restored buggy shed offering site overview open daily dawn to dusk. **Free.**

After your visit, you can go home and tell your friends you have toured the White House. This White House, however, was the officers' headquarters of a sprawling 4,000-acre Union Army supply depot and enlistment site. After Abraham Lincoln made the Emancipation Proclamation, more than 10,000 African Americans came to Camp Nelson to receive their freedom. Many also came to enlist, followed by their families, who set up camp nearby. The heritage park includes 400 of the original 4,000 acres. In addition to the headquarters' tour, there's an interpretive trail and a restored buggy shed with site overview.

HARRY C. MILLER LOCK COLLECTION (ages 6 and up)

Lockmasters Education Center, 1014 Main Street, Nicholasville 40356; (859) 887-9633. Usually open Monday to Friday from 9:00 A.M. to 4:00 P.M., but hours may vary, depending on what else is going on. 𝔽ree.

This is a private company that trains locksmiths, but visitors are welcome to stop by and look at the amazing collection of vintage locks, some dating to the 1300s. The collection was assembled by lock industry legend Harry C. Miller, an inventor of more than forty locks as well as a renowned safecracker. In the 1940s he worked with the federal government to develop locks to protect national security, and later was president of the Sargent & Greenleaf lock company. His descendants own Lockmasters.

For More Information

Jessamine County Chamber of Commerce and Tourism Center, 611 *North Main Street, Nicholasville 40356; (859) 887-4351.*

Harrodsburg

SHAKER VILLAGE OF PLEASANT HILL (all ages)

3501 Lexington Road (off US 68), Harrodsburg 40330; (800) 734-5611 or (859) 734-5411, www.shakervillageky.org. Open daily except December 24 and 25, April through October from 9:30 A.M. to 5:30 P.M. Admission: adults $$$, children $$; under 6 𝔽ree. *November through March, some buildings are closed, and hours and admission are reduced.*

Children may not want to tour all the buildings that are open, but they'll be interested in the main building, with its kitchen and large cellar, double staircases, and rooms with chairs hung on wooden pegs (an efficient way to keep things neat and clean). They'll also enjoy the animals (the village has an old-breeds preservation program and includes many interesting varieties of farm animals) and wide open spaces at the nation's largest restored Shaker community. My children were also intrigued by the Shaker premise of separating the men and women, and they enjoyed the singing and dancing presentations. The Shakers lived here from 1805 until 1910. At its height, the

> # Amazing Kentucky Fact Kentucky
> has its own Brooklyn Bridge, crossing the Kentucky River in the scenic Palisades area. It's on the way from Lexington to Shaker Village/Harrodsburg via US 68.

community owned 4,000 acres of land and had 500 residents, and was a major producer of tools, animals, and seeds. There are many special events throughout the year celebrating Shaker customs and activities as well as the village's role in local history. There are also trails for hiking and, if you bring your own horse, riding. You can walk through the village at your own pace and let the kids run and play for a while if they get restless.

DIXIE BELLE (all ages)

Departs several times daily from Shaker Landing May through October; (800) 734–5611. $$. If you're going to both tour the village and take the boat ride, save money by getting a combo ticket. Boat ride tickets only $$. Buy tickets and get directions to landing from Shaker Village.

Though their interest in Shaker Village varies from visit to visit, my children always enjoy a boat ride on the *Dixie Belle,* a little sternwheeler that departs from Shaker Landing near the village spring through fall. You may spot people canoeing and turtles sunning themselves on the water, and you're sure to enjoy the beautiful scenery of the Palisades area. This is always a good way to end a day at Shaker Village.

OLD FORT HARROD STATE PARK (all ages)

US 127 and US 68, Harrodsburg 40330; (859) 734–3314. Open daily 9:00 A.M. to 5:00 P.M. mid-March through October 31, 8:00 A.M. to 4:30 P.M. November through mid-March. Closed Thanksgiving, Christmas week through New Year's Day, and Mondays in January. Extended fort hours the evenings of outdoor drama performances. $

Harrodsburg lays claim to being the first permanent English settlement west of the Allegheny Mountains; it's where James Harrod founded a fort in 1774. The fort here is a full-scale replica of that original fort. The cabins and blockhouses are filled with pioneer artifacts. April through October, costumed craftspeople demonstrate pioneer crafts. We especially enjoyed seeing the blacksmith at work and visiting the schoolhouse. The park's Mansion Museum (open in summer only) includes Native American artifacts, Lincolniana, antique musical instruments, documents relating to George Rogers Clark and Daniel Boone, and many other items relating to Kentucky history. The park also includes the Lincoln Marriage Temple, which houses the cabin where Abraham Lincoln's parents were married (it was moved here from Springfield, Kentucky), and a Pioneer Cemetery.

A Day Family Adventure I turned my back for just a second when we were visiting Old Fort Harrod State Park, and when I looked around not a child was in sight. I soon heard a giggle from above. There they were, all three perched on the branches of the giant osage orange tree near the fort's entrance. This immense tree—with some of its huge branches almost parallel to the ground for easy maneuvering—is always a favorite part of our visit to Fort Harrod.

THE LEGEND OF DANIEL BOONE (ages 4 and up)
James Harrod Amphitheatre, Old Fort Harrod State Park, Harrodsburg 40330; (800) 852–6663 or www.boonedrama.com. Performances 8:30 P.M. Tuesday to Saturday, 7:00 P.M. Sunday, mid-June through late August. Adults $$$, children $$.

This outdoor theater production weaves documented history with romantic legend to pay tribute to Kentucky's most famous pioneer. Be warned: There's a lot of rough-and-tumble action (including a "scalping").

OLDE TOWN PARK (all ages)
Main Street between Poplar and Office Streets, Harrodsburg 40330; call tourism office at (859) 734–2364 for information. Open daily, 24 hours. **Free**.

If you decide to walk around Harrodsburg and look at the many old buildings (walking tour guide available from the visitor center), stop and rest at this little park on Main Street. The centerpiece of the park is an interesting cascading fountain by Harrodsburg artist Zoe Strecker. The fountain was inspired by the rock and cliff formations in the nearby Palisades area of the Kentucky River.

HARRODSBURG POTTERY (ages 5 and up)
US 68, 1026 Lexington Road, Harrodsburg 40330; (859) 734–9991. Open Monday to Saturday from 10:00 A.M. to 5:30 P.M. Closed in January and February.

The hand-dipped candles at this shop attracted my children. The shop also carries handmade stoneware and has some interesting herb gardens and small fountains made of pottery shards.

Herrington Lake

A 3,600-acre manmade lake, Herrington Lake is accessible from Highway 33 or Highway 152. The lake is pretty but gets very crowded, especially on weekends. You can rent a fishing boat or pontoon at

- Cane Run Fishing Marina, 360 Cane Run Camp Road; (859) 748–5487

- Chimney Rock Marina, 250 Chimney Rock Road; (859) 748–9065

- Pandora Marina, #1 Pandora Cove; (859) 748–9121

- Royalty's Fishing Camp, 940 Norman's Camp Road; (859) 748–5459

- Cummins Falls Marina, 2558 Cummins Ferry Road (Highway 1988); (859) 865–2003; also rents canoes and paddleboats

Where to Eat

Beaumont Inn, *US 127 South, 638 Beaumont Inn Drive, Harrodsburg 40330; (859) 734-3381 or (800) 352-3992.* Open Wednesday to Sunday, mid-March through mid-December. Homey atmosphere and Kentucky specialties, plus an excellent Sunday brunch. $$-$$$

Old Happy Days Diner, *112 East Lexington Street, Harrodsburg 40330; (859) 734-4607. Closed Sunday.* Known for its barbecue and homemade pies. $

Shaker Village of Pleasant Hill, *3501 Lexington Road, off US 68, Harrodsburg 40330; (800) 734-5611.* The village dining room serves three family-style meals a day. The menu features traditional Southern cooking, but for the health conscious, there is always a vegetarian option, and fresh vegetables are plentiful. The food is kid-friendly, and the desserts are homemade. No tipping allowed, but reservations are a good idea. $-$$. On weekends in summer, you can get soup, sandwiches, and desserts at the Summer Kitchen; no reservations necessary. $

Where to Stay

Beaumont Inn, *US 127 South, 638 Beaumont Inn Drive, Harrodsburg 40330; (859) 734–3381 or (800) 352–3992, www.beaumontinn.com.* Open mid-March through mid-December. Though historic (a former girls' school), this hotel is very family friendly. Rooms are housed in several buildings in the neighborhood and decorated with period antiques. Outdoor pool. $$$–$$$$

Best Western Harrodsburg, *1680 Danville Road, Harrodsburg 40330; (859) 734–9431.* Continental breakfast, outdoor pool; pets accepted. $$

Chimney Rock Campground, *160 Chimney Rock Road, Harrodsburg 40330; (859) 748–5252.* Open April through November. Tent camping and hookups, laundry, showers, and pool. $

Shaker Village of Pleasant Hill, *3501 Lexington Road, off US 68, Harrodsburg 40330; (800) 734–5611.* Stay in one of the restored buildings. Rooms are furnished with Shaker pieces but include modern amenities such as TV and phones. $$–$$$

For More Information

Harrodsburg/Mercer County Tourism Commission, *103 South Main Street, P.O. Box 283, DEPT KTG01,* *Harrodsburg 40330; (859) 734–2364 or (800) 355–9192, www.harrodsburgky.com.*

Danville

CONSTITUTION SQUARE STATE HISTORIC SITE (all ages)
134 South Second Street, Danville 40422; (859) 239–7089. Open daily year-round. **Free.**

Younger children won't necessarily take in all the history, but they'll enjoy exploring the mix of original and replica pioneer buildings in this small park in Danville. The collection commemorates Danville's role as the center for political activity that led to Kentucky statehood in 1792. The self-guided tour includes a replica of the courthouse where early political leaders held ten constitutional conventions to prepare for statehood, a replica of an early jail made of 9-inch-thick logs, an original pre-1792 post office, and a replica of an early meetinghouse. At the center of the park is a bronze statue of Kentucky's state seal surrounded by plaques denoting Kentucky governors. The old brick buildings adjacent to the park date to the early 1800s and house art galleries and a local museum operated by the Danville/Boyle County Historical Society. There's a small charge to tour the museum, which includes an eclectic collection of items relating to Danville history.

Lunch on the Square Get a sandwich from Burke's Bakery, 121 West Main Street, across the street from Constitution Square, and have lunch at the picnic tables in the park.

MCDOWELL HOUSE, APOTHECARY, AND GARDENS (ages 6 and up)

125 South Second Street, Danville 40422; (859) 236-2804, www.mcdowell house.com. Open Monday to Saturday, 10:00 A.M. to noon and 1:00 to 4:00 P.M., Sunday 2:00 to 4:00 P.M. Closed Monday November through February. $

On Christmas Day 1809, in a back bedroom of this house, Dr. McDowell removed a 20-pound ovarian tumor from Jane Todd Crawford without benefit of anesthesia. (Mrs. Crawford, who rode more than 60 miles on horseback to get to Danville, recited psalms during the operation.) Five days after surgery, she was making her own bed, and twenty-five days later, she returned home. The operation became a milestone in modern medicine. Adults, more than children, are fascinated by this harrowing tale of America's first abdominal surgery, but all ages will enjoy touring the house and attached apothecary shop to see interesting items such as a comb-back rocker and early dental tools.

PIONEER PLAYHOUSE OF DANVILLE (ages 6 and up)

840 Stanford Road, Danville 40422; (859) 236-2747, www.pioneerplayhouse. com. Performance Tuesday to Saturday. Tickets can be purchased for dinner and the play ($$) or just the play ($$$). Children under 6 $.

Not all the plays at the open-air Pioneer Playhouse will be of interest to young children, but there are usually at least a couple of shows each season that are appropriate. Come

Amazing Kentucky Fact John Travolta is among the famous actors who have performed at Pioneer Playhouse.

just for the show, or come early to look at the pioneer-style shops and to have dinner in the on-site restaurant.

OLD CROW INN AND ELEMENTS POTTERY (ages 5 and up)

471 Stanford Road, Danville 40422; (859) 236–1808.

There's all kinds of interesting stuff going on here—a pottery studio and shop, hiking trails, the beginnings of a winery. There's also overnight lodging.

KENTUCKY SCHOOL FOR THE DEAF (ages 6 and up)

South Second Street, Danville 40422; (859) 236-5132. Open Monday to Friday from 8:30 A.M. to noon and 1:00 to 4:00 P.M. **Free**.

This school, founded in 1829, was the first state-supported institution created to educate deaf children. The small museum located in Jacobs Hall includes a recreation of an 1850s classroom and student dorm. There are also a video and exhibits of photographs, letters, historical records, and auditory aid equipment.

DANVILLE MODEL RAILROAD MUSEUM (all ages)

314 West Main Street, Danville 40422; (859) 236-8090. Open Sunday from 2:00 to 5:00 P.M., Monday evenings at 7:00 P.M. and by appointment. **Free**.

Train enthusiasts will want to see the operating model trains at this small museum.

Top Brass Danville has one of the best musical events in the state—the annual Great American Brass Band Festival in mid-June. Dozens of bands and some 40,000 people from around the world converge on Danville for a weekend of Dixieland, march tunes, even Civil War music using authentic period instruments. Concerts are free and held at various locations on the Centre College campus and around town. Other events include a hot air balloon race.

Where to Eat

Dunn's Restaurant, *215 Stanford Road, Danville 40422; (606) 238–2207.* Home-style cooking and barbecue. $

Freddie's, *126 South Fourth Street, Danville 40422; (859) 236–9884.* Terrific Italian favorites plus daily specials. $

Where to Stay

Comfort Suites, *864 Ben Ali Drive, Danville 40422; (859) 936–9300.* Continental breakfast, indoor pool. $$

Country Hearth Inn, *US 150 Bypass, Danville 40422; (800) 325–2525.* Outdoor pool, restaurant; pets accepted. $$

Gwinn Island Camping, *off Highway 33 North, Danville 40422; (859) 236–*

4286. Campsites and rustic cabins on Lake Herrington. Marina, boat rental, swimming pool. $

Holiday Inn Express, *US 150 Bypass, Danville 40422; (859) 236–8600.* Pool, continental breakfast. $$

Pioneer Campground, *Pioneer Playhouse, Danville 40422; (859) 236–2747.* Hookups and tent sites; showers. $

For More Information

Danville/Boyle County Convention and Visitors Bureau, *304 South Fourth*

Street, Danville 40422; (800) 755–0076 or (859) 236–7794, www.danville-ky.com.

Perryville

PERRYVILLE BATTLEFIELD STATE HISTORIC SITE (all ages)
1825 Battlefield Road, on KY 1920, just north of the junction of US 68 and US 150, Perryville 40422; (859) 332–8631 or (800) 755–0076. Open daily April through October from 9:00 A.M. to 5:00 P.M. Admission to museum $; admission to grounds Free.

On October 8, 1862, Kentucky's deadliest and most important Civil War battle was fought here. More than 6,000 soldiers were casualties in this last serious effort of the Confederacy to claim Kentucky. Today, the battle is commemorated with monuments to the soldiers of both sides and a museum detailing the history of the battle. There are also trails that allow families to take a self-guided walking tour over these historic grounds. The gift shop has a large selection of books about the Civil War. The first weekend in October, reenactors and spectators gather for a battle reenactment. Very crowded!

Gravel Switch

PENN'S STORE (all ages)

257 Rollings Road, off Highway 243; (859) 332-7715. Open May through October, Monday to Saturday from 10:00 A.M. to 6:00 P.M., Sunday from 2:00 to 5:00 P.M.; November through April, closes at 5:00 P.M. and closed most Sundays.

This is a real old-timey country store, right down to the cigar-box cash register. In fact, it's the oldest continuously operating family store in the United States, in business since 1850. Your children will enjoy the old-fashioned candies, homemade dolls, potbellied stove, and general tumbledown appearance.

Stanford

WILLIAM WHITLEY HOUSE STATE HISTORIC SITE (ages 4 and up)

625 William Whitley Road, off US 150, east of Stanford; (606) 355-2881. Tours offered March 15 through December 31, Tuesday to Sunday from 9:00 A.M. to 5:00 P.M. Also open Monday in summer. $

This beautiful estate, built in 1788, was one of the first brick houses in Kentucky. It was the home of William Whitley, a Revolutionary War veteran and Indian fighter. One of its most fascinating features for children is the hidden staircase, so the family could hide in case of Indian attacks, a real possibility in pioneer Kentucky. Whitley's long rifle and engraved powderhorn hang over one of the fireplaces. The lovely grounds make a nice place for a picnic (tables available), and there's playground equipment for the children.

HISTORIC STANFORD DEPOT (all ages)

1866 North Depot Street, Stanford 40484; (606) 365-4518. **Free.**

You're welcome to stop by the restored 1860s depot and see such items as a velocipede (a machine used to do small errands on the railroad tracks) and large brass bell. A restored caboose is set up to show a cabooseman's home away from home.

HARVEY HELM MUSEUM (ages 6 and up)

Lincoln County Library, 315 West Main Street, Stanford 40484; (606) 365–7513. Open Wednesday from 1:30 to 3:30 P.M., Saturday from 1:00 to 4:00 P.M. **Free**.

You'll find a little bit of everything in this local history museum, but what usually gets youngsters' attention are the Victorian wicker "body basket" and antique undertaker's table.

Where to Eat

Cree-Mee Drive-in, *816 East Main Street, Stanford 40484; (606) 365–9100.* Burgers in a '50s atmosphere.

Kentucky Depot Restaurant, *119 Metker Trace, Stanford 40484; (606) 365–8040.* Home cooking and daily specials. $

Berea

BEREA COLLEGE TOURS (ages 6 and up)

Register for tours at Boone Tavern Hotel, College Square, Berea 40404; (859) 985–3000 or www.berea.edu. Historical tours offered Monday, Wednesday, and Friday at 9:00 A.M., 1:00 and 3:00 P.M., Tuesday at 9:00 and 10:00 A.M., 1:00 and 3:00 P.M., and Saturday at 9:00 A.M. and 2:00 P.M. College Craft tours Monday to Friday from 10:00 A.M. and 2:00 P.M. **Free**.

Berea College's past and present are equally interesting. The school was founded in 1859 with the goal of dividing its student population evenly between blacks and whites—an interracial college in the South, and this was before the Civil War. Today Berea is known for its student industries, which enable low-income students from Kentucky's mountains to obtain a quality college education. All students must work, but they pay no tuition. The historical tour focuses on the college's story and historical buildings. Most children will find the crafts tour, with its demonstrations of blacksmithing, weaving, and woodworking, more enjoyable.

BEREA ARTISAN SHOPS (ages 6 and up)

Shops are concentrated in the College Square area and Old Town (North Broadway area, near visitor center). Hours vary.

Berea is internationally renowned for its craftspeople and artisans who work and display here, making everything from pottery to jewelry in both traditional and contemporary styles. Some shops are working studios; others are display galleries. If your children enjoy shopping and/or crafts, they might like to explore some of the stores; mine have become impatient here after a few stops. Here are a couple of noteworthy stops:

- **Churchill Weavers,** *100 Churchill Drive off Lorraine Court; (606) 986–3127.* Visitors are welcome to walk through the production area (no strollers allowed) where weavers work at huge wooden looms to create the company's hallmark blankets, shawls, and scarves.

- **Warren A. May Woodworker,** *110 Center Street, Berea 40403; (606) 986–9293.* Young musicians in particular will enjoy seeing Mr. May's beautiful handmade mountain dulcimers. There's usually a work in progress as well.

- **Log House Craft Gallery,** *College Square; (800) 347–3892.* This shop showcases student-made crafts; upstairs is a museum of early American Wallace Nutting furniture.

- A Berea Artisan Center showcasing traditional mountain crafts is scheduled to open in 2003. The center will be located right off I–75.

 KENTUCKY GUILD OF ARTISTS AND CRAFTSMEN SPRING AND FALL FAIRS/BEREA CRAFT FESTIVAL (all ages)
Indian Fort Theater, Highway 21E, 3 miles east of Berea; (800) 598–5263. Guild fairs weekends in mid-May and mid-October; craft festival in mid-July. $

Berea's open-air fairs are an enjoyable way for families to see a wide variety of crafts and craft demonstrations. You'll see everything from garden art and painted gourds to textiles and fine jewelry. There's also entertainment, as well as traditional foods. Artisans must have their work juried to join the guild, and only members display at these two fairs. The Berea Craft Festival brings in top-quality craftspeople from across the United States.

Where to Eat

Boone Tavern Hotel, *100 Main Street, Berea 40403; (859) 986–9358.* Excellently prepared Kentucky cooking; try the spoonbread and Chicken Flakes in the Bird's Nest. Staffed by Berea College students. Reservations recommended; no shorts or athletic clothes. $$

Hometown Cafeteria, *at I–75, exit 76, Berea 40403; (606) 986–7086.* Home cooking served cafeteria-style. $

Sweet Betty's, *at I–75, exit 76, Berea 40403; (606) 986–3824.* Home cooking, buffet, and homemade pies. $

Where to Stay

Boone Tavern Hotel, *100 Main Street, Berea 40403; (859) 986–9358 or (800) 366–9358.* Historic hotel decorated with handmade crafts and staffed by Berea College students. $$$

Holiday Inn Express, at I-75, exit 77, Berea 40403; (800) HOLIDAY. Continental breakfast, indoor pool. $$

For More Information

Berea Welcome Center, *201 North Broadway (in restored L&N Railroad Depot), Berea 40403; (606) 986–2540 or (800) 598–5263, www.berea.com.*

Valley View Ferry If you're heading to Richmond or Berea from Lexington, make a Free ride on the Valley View Ferry a part of your route. This ferry has been in operation since 1785, making daily crossings over the Kentucky River between Jessamine and Madison counties. Many people who work in the Lexington/Bluegrass area use it to help them get to work and back each day. To get to the ferry from Lexington, take Tates Creek Road (Highway 169) all the way south to the Kentucky River. Once you get across you can take Highway 169 into Richmond, and from there get on I-75 or US 25 if you're continuing to Berea. The ferry runs year-round, river conditions permitting, Monday to Friday from 6:00 A.M. to 8:00 P.M., Saturday from 8:00 A.M. to 6:00 P.M., and Sunday from 9:00 A.M. to 6:00 P.M. Call (859) 885–4500 or (859) 258–3611 for more information.

Waco

BYBEE POTTERY (ages 6 and up)

610 Waco Loop (Highway 52), 9 miles east of Richmond, Waco 40385; (859) 369–5350. Self-guided tours Monday to Friday from 8:00 A.M. to noon and 12:30 to 3:30 P.M. Free.

The log Bybee Pottery building looks ancient—this family-owned company has been making pottery here since 1845, maybe since 1809, if local legend is correct. The simple-lined, solid-colored and speckled pieces are made from local clay that is ground and stored in a vault before it is hand-thrown, glazed, and fired. Visitors are welcome to walk through the production area and see the process firsthand. Bybee makes some cute piggy banks and other items children will like, but if the shelves in the attached sales room seem bare, it's because dealers and collectors line up at daybreak to get first crack at the stock on kiln-emptying days, Monday, Wednesday, and Friday at 8:00 A.M. These become grab fests once the doors are opened; people take everything they can reach, then trade with other shoppers for the pieces they really want.

Richmond

HUMMEL PLANETARIUM AND SPACE THEATER (all ages)

Kit Carson Drive, Eastern Kentucky University campus, Richmond 40475; (859) 622-1547, www.planetarium.eku.edu. Children's shows at 6:00 P.M. Thursday and Friday and 2:00 and 6:00 P.M. Saturday; main features at 7:30 P.M. Thursday and Friday and 3:30 and 7:30 P.M. Saturday. $

"Explore" Mars, get an astronomical glimpse of the future or distant past, see how the sky would look from the space shuttle—visions like these are available on earth through the sophisticated equipment of the Hummel Planetarium. With a starball capable of projecting up to 10,164 stars, a multimedia system capable of creating sophisticated special effects, and Dolby sound, this is one of the largest and most sophisticated planetariums in the world. Programs for younger children incorporate characters, stories, and games. Both the children's and the main program topics change several times a year. Each program includes a "Star Talk" about that night's sky.

 ## IRVINTON HOUSE MUSEUM (all ages)

345 Lancaster Avenue, Richmond 40475; (859) 626-1422. Open Monday to Friday from 9:00 A.M. to 5:00 P.M. **Free**.

This beautiful early 1800s house is located in Irvine McDowell Park, and the Richmond Visitor Center is at the back of the house. So touring is very convenient; when you stop to pick up a map or brochures, see if the curator is around to take you through. (And if you have restless little ones, let them play in the park before or after.) The tour is highly personalized and friendly, and the elegant house includes an eclectic collection of items relating to local history. The vintage clothes are great, and children will enjoy seeing the Revolutionary War uniform and artifacts from Boonesborough.

LAKE REBA RECREATIONAL COMPLEX (all ages)

876 Eastern Bypass, Richmond 40475; (859) 623-9408. Open daily. **Free**.

This 450-acre park features a variety of recreational facilities, including nature and walking trails, picnic areas, and volleyball courts. The seventy-five-acre fishing lake is stocked with largemouth bass, bluegill, and catfish.

A Boone for You? According to local tradition, it's good luck to rub the foot of the Daniel Boone statue on Eastern Kentucky University's campus. The Daniel Boone Monument is located on University Drive. (859) 628-8474.

WHITE HALL STATE HISTORIC HOUSE (ages 6 and up)

500 White Hall Shrine Road, Richmond 40475; follow the signs from the I-75 Winchester–Boonesboro exit; (859) 623-9178. Open daily April 1 through October 31 from 9:00 A.M. to 5:30 P.M.; closed Mondays and Tuesdays after Labor Day. $

Cassius Clay, this house's most famous resident, was quite a character. At various points in his life he was an emancipationist, newspaper publisher, flamboyant U.S. ambassador to Russia under Abraham Lincoln, and local eccentric (there's a hole in one of the walls where he shot at an unwanted visitor). The house itself is a bit eccentric. It's actually a house within a house, an older Federal-style building over which an elegant Italianate structure was built. A costumed guide fills you in on the details as you tour the house; the forty-four rooms include many family items and interesting early bathroom facilities. Picnic facilities are available on the grounds.

DEER RUN STABLES (all ages)

2001 River Circle Drive, off Highway 627 between White Hall and Fort Boonesborough, Richmond 40475; (859) 527-6339. Open year-round Tuesday to Friday from 9:00 A.M. to 7:00 P.M., Saturday from 11:00 A.M. to 7:00 P.M., Sunday from noon to 7:00 P.M. Closed Monday unless it's a holiday. Trail rides $$$– $$$$; pony rides $$.

Deer Run offers forty-five-minute and one-hour trail rides for ages seven and up. The guided ride at a walk pace takes you up and down hills, along a creek, and past an old cabin or cemetery. Pony rides are available for younger children. Only groups of ten or more need reservations. If you're driving along Highway 627 heading from Fort Boonesborough to White Hall, look for the sign.

FORT BOONESBOROUGH STATE PARK (all ages)

4375 Boonesboro Road, Richmond 40388 (between Richmond and Winchester); follow the signs from I-75, exit 99; (859) 527-3131. There are separate entrances for the park and for the fort. Fort admission: $.

Start your visit to this pioneer fort, a re-creation of the settlement founded in this area by Daniel Boone in the 1770s, with a short video presentation. Then walk around the village to see how pioneers in the eighteenth century lived and watch artisans demonstrate weaving, rifle making, baking, pottery, soap making, and wool carding. There's also a small general store with maple candy and other treats and souvenirs. In the center of the fort is a blacksmith shop with a giant bellows that

Amazing Kentucky Fact The famous scout and pioneer "Kit" Carson was born on Christmas Eve 1809, in a log cabin near Richmond, Kentucky.

is certain to fascinate young ones. Once you have finished touring the old fort, you can enjoy more modern fun in this state park, including a junior Olympic-size pool with a waterslide, fountain, special children's area, and a rain tree. There are also picnic shelters, a fishing area, and nature trails. From the park, you can see the locks on the Kentucky River, where you can watch the interesting process of boats "locking through."

Other Things to See and Do

Camp Catalpa Bird Sanctuary, US 25E off Eastern Bypass, Richmond 40475; (859) 623–8753. One-mile scenic walking trail through shaded forest. Shelters, playgrounds, and picnic tables.

Driving Tour of Battle of Richmond, guide to 1862 Civil War battle sites; available at visitor center; (859) 626–8474.

Krazy Karts Family Fun Park, 1958 Berea Road, Richmond 40475; (859) 623–7240. Go-carts, bumper cars, miniature golf, a special track for younger children, and concession stands.

Where to Eat

Bellagio's, *1103 Kim Kent Drive, Richmond 40475; (859) 626–3800.* Good pasta, calzones, pizza, and subs. $

Burns Family Restaurant, *107 Big Hill Avenue, Richmond 40475; (859) 623–8265.* Home cooking, varied menu. $

Casa Cafe, *709 Big Hill Avenue, Richmond 40475; (859) 623–8582.* Traditional Mexican food made from scratch each day. $

Woody's Restaurant and Bar, *246 West Main Street, Richmond 40475; (859) 623–5130.* Eclectic menu with interesting lunch and dinner specials. $$

Where to Stay

Fort Boonesborough State Park Campground, *4375 Boonesboro Road, Richmond 40475; (859) 527–3131.* Primitive and full hookup camping. Showers, laundry, access to park pool, grocery. $

Days Inn, *I–75, exit 90, Richmond 40475; (800) 325–2525.* Continental breakfast, outdoor pool, pets accepted. $

Econolodge, *I–75, exit 87, Richmond 40475; (800) 424–4777.* Continental breakfast, outdoor pool; pets accepted. $

For More Information

Richmond Visitor Center, *345 Lancaster Avenue, Richmond 40475; (800)* *866–3705 or (859) 626–8474, www.richmond-ky.com.*

Winchester

DOWNTOWN AREA (all ages)

Main Street and surrounding streets; (859) 744-0556. **Free**.

   Winchester has a cute, old-fashioned downtown area, and you can pick up a guide for a short walking tour at the Tourist Information Center, 2 South Maple Street. Sites include the county courthouse, where a portrait of Daniel Boone hangs; the "American Doughboy" statue by E. M. Visquesney on the courthouse lawn; and the restored Leeds Theatre, a performing arts center that features some drama and music performances appropriate for children.

ALE-8-ONE "COMPANY STORE"
25 Carol Road, Winchester 40391; (859) 744-3484, www.ale-8-one.com. Open Monday to Friday from 8:30 A.M. to 4:30 P.M. **Free**.

Ale-8-One is a sweet, gingery soft drink made only in Winchester, with many devoted fans in the region. If you've never heard of it, be sure to try one while you're in the area. (It's sold in vending machines as well as at some restaurants in Lexington and the Bluegrass region.) Ale-8-One has been made since the 1920s using a secret formula developed by a Winchester entrepreneur named G. L. Wainscott. He held a contest to name his new soft drink, and since other soft drinks were already on the market, a little girl suggested "A Late One." Wainscott changed her suggestion a little to become Ale-8-One, or so the story goes. The Company Store carries clothing and souvenirs with the Ale-8-One logo, as well as memorabilia and, of course, Ale-8-One. Tours of the bottling operation are not offered.

Coming Attractions in Winchester

- Bluegrass Heritage Museum, scheduled to open 2004 in Victorian house downtown.

- Civil War encampment site, restoration in the works near Fort Boonesborough.

Where to Eat

Hall's on the River, *1225 Athens-Boonesboro Road, near Boonesborough, between Winchester and Richmond; (859) 255–8105.* Popular family restaurant overlooking the Kentucky River. Famous for its fish, fried battered banana peppers, and beer cheese. Children's menu available. $$

Jazzman Cafe, *1100 Interstate Drive (exit 96 off I–64), Winchester 40391; (859) 744–6425.* Regional dishes including ribs, barbecue sandwiches, and fried fish. Live music on weekends. $-$$

Where to Stay

Days Inn, *I–64, exit 96, Winchester 40391; (859) 744–9111.* Outdoor pool, free continental breakfast. $$

Holiday Inn Express, *5250 Revilo Road (I–64, exit 94), Winchester 40391; (859) 745–3009.* Indoor pool, free continental breakfast. $$

Annual Events

International Kite Festival, late April, Georgetown; (502) 863-1575, ext. 44

Kentucky Guild of Artists and Craftsmen Spring Fair, late May, Berea; (800) 598-5263

Horsey Hundred Bicycling Weekend, Memorial Day weekend, based in Georgetown; (859) 266-6419

Old Fort Harrod Heritage Festival, early June, Old Fort Harrod State Park, Harrodsburg; (859) 734-3314

Pioneer Kids Day, mid-June, Versailles; (859) 873-7902

Great American Brass Band Festival, mid-June, Danville; (859) 236-7794

Woodford County Fair and Rodeo, mid-late June, Versailles; (859) 879-0670

Scott County Fair, mid-late June, Georgetown; (502) 863-2547

Morgan's Raid on Georgetown Civil War Reenactment, mid-late June, Georgetown; (502) 863-1575

Berea Crafts Festival, mid-July, Berea; (800) 598-5263,

Kentucky Shaker Music Weekend, late July, Shaker Village of Pleasant Hill; (800) 734-5611

Kentucky River Fest, late July, Frankfort; (502) 223-8261

Annual Pleasant Hill Craft Fair, early August, Shaker Village of Pleasant Hill; (800) 734-5611

Family Fun Day, early August, Buckley Wildlife Sanctuary, Versailles; (859) 873-5711

Daniel Boone Pioneer Festival, Labor Day weekend, Winchester; (800) 298-9105

Kentucky Folklife Festival, September, downtown Frankfort; (502) 564-1792

Battle of Cynthiana Reenactment, late September, Cynthiana; (859) 234-5236.

Constitution Square Festival, late September, Danville; (859) 236-7794

Autumn Fest at Bi-Water Farm, weekends late September-late October, Georgetown; (502) 863-3676

Pumpkinfest at Double Stink Hog Farm, weekends late September–late October, Georgetown; (502) 863-9703

Festival of the Horse, late September, Georgetown; (502) 863-2547

Perryville Battle Reenactment, early October, Perryville; (859) 332-8631

Bluegrass Festival and Burgoo Festival, early October, Winchester; (800) 298-9105

Kentucky Guild of Artists and Craftsmen Fall Fair, mid-October, Berea; (800) 986-2540

Storytelling at the River, late October, Shaker Village of Pleasant Hill; (800) 734-5611

Shaker Order of Christmas, early December, Shaker Village of Pleasant Hill; (800) 734-5611

Frontier Christmas at the Jack Jouett House, early December, Versailles; (859) 873-7902

Eastern Kentucky

Eastern Kentucky is a region of incredible natural beauty, abundant recreational opportunities (especially if you like to hike, camp, or fish), and constant surprises. You never know what you might find around the next bend—a classy performing arts center, a coal-mining museum (or a coal mine), a craft shop, or a snake venom research collection center. Rolling in the north, mountainous in the south, this area contains some of Kentucky's most rugged and interesting geography. There are lush forests, massive stone arches, and rushing waterfalls. State parks are the prime ways to take advantage of the outdoor opportunities.

I-64 runs through the northern part of eastern Kentucky to the largest city in this region, Ashland, and Mountain Parkway and Daniel Boone Parkway (the latter one of the state's few remaining toll roads) are four lanes for at least part of the way. But in many places you will be on winding two-lane highways. As a result, travel time is longer, so bring along plenty of books, CDs, tapes, and games for your passengers. Some areas have little development, so don't defer necessity stops assuming there will be another place just up the road.

Attractions are listed in a circuitous route that begins east of Winchester, heads northeast to Ashland, then south along Kentucky's eastern border and west to the Cumberland Gap area. This will position you to explore south-central Kentucky.

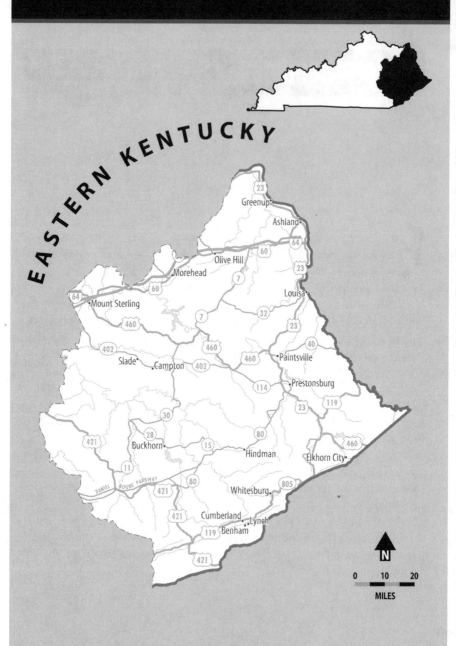

EASTERN KENTUCKY

Teresa's Top Ten
Picks for Eastern Kentucky

1. Natural Bridge State Resort Park, (606) 663–2214
2. Kentucky Reptile Zoo, (606) 663–9160
3. Kentucky Folk Art Center, (606) 783–2204
4. Carter Caves State Resort Park, (606) 286–4411
5. Kentucky Opry/Mountain Arts Center, (888) 622–2787
6. Appalshop, (606) 633–0108
7. Hindman Settlement School, (606) 785–5475
8. Kentucky Coal Mining Museum, (606) 848–1530
9. Kingdom Come State Park, (606) 589–2479
10. Lilly Cornett Woods, (606) 633–5828

Slade

NATURAL BRIDGE STATE RESORT PARK (all ages)

2135 Natural Bridge Road (off KY 11), Slade 40376; (606) 663–2214; reservations: (800) 325–1710. Admission and many activities **Free**. *Sky lift ride $.*

Because it's so close to Lexington (just about an hour and a half via I-64 and Mountain Parkway), this getaway spot is very popular and often crowded. Nonetheless, we've always had a good time. The park takes its name from its huge natural stone arch, one of many in the area. The main trail up to the arch is scenic and fairly easy (I've done it with a four-year-old walking and an infant in a front pack). The worst part is seeing your little one go scampering across the top of the arch: There are no side rails. (The arch is fairly wide, but for your own peace of mind, be ready to hold a younger child's hand.) You can also take a sky lift to a level walking trail at the top (April through October). Other features include pedal boat rental, a small nature center, miniature golf, picnic areas, playgrounds, and weekly square dances and music on Hoedown Island. Some activities are seasonal. There are nine hiking trails, ranging from ½ mile to 8½ miles in length, with interesting views year-round (in winter you can see the rock formations more clearly, since there's less vegetation).

Red River Gorge

Red River Gorge Natural Bridge State Resort Park is a good place to begin exploring the Red River Gorge Geological Area. This federally designated 26,000-acre geological area is located within Daniel Boone National Forest and is the state's most visited hiking area. The more than eighty natural stone arches add a special beauty to the landscape, and the area is abundant in wildflowers and wildlife. Red River Gorge is popular with rock climbers as well as hikers, and there are so many trails that entire books have been written about this area alone.

Take the 30-mile driving loop, beginning at Highway 15, west of the Slade exit off Mountain Parkway. Along the way are scenic overlooks and other points of interest:

- Nada Tunnel, on Highway 77, is an 800-foot-long tunnel cut in the early 1900s to give trains access to timber in the area.

- Gladie Creek Cabin, a restored 1884 cabin, also has a blacksmith shop, a buffalo herd, and logging exhibits.

- At the Gladie Creek Forest Service station, you can pick up maps and information, essential for safe hiking. It's open daily in summer; hours vary other times of the year. (606) 663–2852.

The gorge is beautiful, but it's a place where you should know what you're getting into if you plan to hike or camp (backcountry camping allowed with permit and small fee). The steepness and the remoteness of the area make many trails inappropriate for novice hikers and younger children, and every year even experienced backpackers are injured here. Keep in mind that the area is also open to hunting.

Another way to see the gorge is a canoe excursion on the Red River. Canoe Kentucky offers both guided and unguided trips (800–522–6631).

 KENTUCKY REPTILE ZOO (ages 4 and up)
1275 Natural Bridge Road, Slade 40376; (606) 663-9160. Open daily Memorial Day through Labor Day from 11:00 A.M. to 6:00 P.M., weekends only at other times of the year. $

The big painting in front of this place of a man riding an alligator should get your children's attention. Don't worry: This isn't a tacky tourist trap but an educational center run with a good sense of humor. Reptile and amphibian fans in the family will want to see the turtles, alligators, lizards, and hundreds of varieties of snakes from around the world and learn how poisonous snakes are "milked" to obtain venom used for medical research.

A Day Family Adventure With it beautiful scenery, eastern Kentucky is a great place for photography. On one of our day trips to Natural Bridge we took along several cameras, so everyone would be able to take photos of the rock formations, trees, wildlife, and, of course, each other. We had a great time sharing and comparing each others' shots and perspectives.

Where to Eat

Miguel's Pizza, *1890 Natural Bridge Road, Slade 40376; (606) 663–1975.* Open March through Thanksgiving. A favorite hangout for serious rock climbers in the area, this small spot serves delicious pizza made with home-grown veggies. $

Natural Bridge State Resort Park, *2135 Natural Bridge Road (off KY 11), Slade 40376; (606) 663–2214.* Regional specialties and daily buffet. Children's menu. $

Rose's Restaurant, *1289 Natural Bridge Road, Slade 40376; (606) 663–0588.* Beans and cornbread, sandwiches, and daily specials. $

Where to Stay

Natural Bridge State Resort Park, *2135 Natural Bridge Road (off KY 11), Slade 40376; (606) 663–2214; reservations: (800) 325–1710.* Lodge rooms ($-$$), cabins ($$-$$$$), and camping ($). Campground closed in winter.

Shadow Mountain Mist Bed and Breakfast, *30 Lee Lane, Slade 40376; (606) 663–8018 or (888) 663–2600.*

Themed rooms, including a Wild West room, and country cabin. $$$

Tecumseh Resort and Cabin Country Rentals, *3435 Natural Bridge Road, Slade 40376; (888) 663–0283.* Wide variety of lodgings, from two-bed treehouses to A-frames and chalets. Kids' cabin includes an indoor basketball court. $$$$

For More Information

Gladie Creek Information Center, *Stanton Ranger District, 705 West College Avenue, Stanton KY 40308; (606) 663–2852.*

Natural Bridge/Powell County Chamber of Commerce, *Caboose Visitor Center, 30 L&E Railroad Place, Slade 40376; (606) 663–9229 or www.powellcountytourism.com.*

Campton

TORRENT FALLS FAMILY CLIMBING ADVENTURES
(ages 10 and up)

1435 Highway 11, Campton 41301; (606) 668–6441. Open daily in summer from 9:00 A.M. to about 8:30 P.M.; last climbers admitted around 6:30 P.M. Over 17 $$$, children 10–17 $$. From exit 33 off Mountain Parkway, go right.

If you and your older children enjoy those rock-climbing walls, here's a chance to go big time. This is an outdoor activity based on a European sport called *via ferrata*. The idea is to climb and maneuver around a vertical hiking/climbing path. You use a harness and steel cables to climb up and around iron rungs that have been drilled into the rock around a U-shaped canyon. (This isn't for those with a fear of heights—it goes about 100 feet up!) Admission is for an all-day pass, so you climb at your own pace and where you want to. The course includes a suspension bridge and ledges to rest along the way. You'll get a short training session; also, guides are available for an additional hourly fee and are required for minors not climbing with a parent. Sturdy shoes are a must, and gloves are also a good idea since your hands will get sore. Climbers must be at least ten years old, and you're required to sign a liability waiver. Food is available on site.

Forest Info Daniel Boone National Forest covers 672,000 acres in eastern and south-central Kentucky, offering all kinds of spectacular sites and recreational opportunities, from camping and picnicking to whitewater rafting and rock climbing. The Sheltowee Trace National Recreation Trail runs 257 miles from one end to the other (now, there's an ambitious family project!). There are six ranger stations throughout the forest, which are great sources of information and maps. The stations in eastern Kentucky are

- **Morehead** (Cave Run Lake) (606) 784–6428

- **Stanton** (Red River Gorge) (606) 663–2852

- **Redbird** (Redbird Crest Trail) (606) 698–2192

Or visit www.fs.fed.us/recreation/recgov/visit_danielboone.shtml.

Where to Stay

Torrent Falls Bed and Breakfast and Cabins, *1435 North Highway 11, Slade 41301; (606) 668–6441.* Homey rooms with quilts or cabins on forty-two acres. Full breakfast and nightly bonfire. Adjoins Torrent Falls Family Climbing Adventures. $$–$$$$

Mount Sterling

COURT DAYS (all ages)
The weekend before and the third Monday in October, downtown Mount Sterling; (859) 498-8732. **Free.**

The main event in the pretty little town of Mount Sterling is this wild swapfest. "Court Days" has been going on here for some 200 years: Back in the early 1800s, each county court met once a month, and the days became occasions for celebration and trading. This event gets incredibly crowded; some 100,000 people converge upon this town of 5,400 over the three days (go on Monday if you can, when it's less crowded). But it's fun, even for youngsters. Just make sure you bring a stroller or pack carrier for little ones. Vendors offer just about everything—old stuff, new stuff, strange stuff—plus barbecue, funnel cakes, and other delicious festival fare.

RUTH HUNT CANDIES (all ages)
550 North Maysville Street, Mount Sterling 40353; (859) 498-0676. Open Monday to Saturday from 9:00 A.M. to 5:30 P.M., Sunday from 1:00 to 5:30 P.M.

Ever hear of a Blue Monday? It's a dark chocolate candy bar with pulled cream in the center, the creation of Ruth Tharpe Hunt, who started this candy business in 1921. Other homemade goodies include caramel, sweet chocolate balls, and hot cinnamon suckers. Take a peek in the kitchen, where they make the candy in huge copper kettles.

GALLERY FOR THE ARTS (ages 6 and up)
44 East Main Street, Mount Sterling 40353; (859) 498-6264. Open Tuesday to Saturday from 11:30 A.M. to 4:30 P.M.

Youngsters will love the gourd-geous and very detailed painted gourd characters at this shop. In April, there's an exhibit of local student work.

Good Old Days Have a chili hot dog and shake for dinner at Berryman's Tasty Treat, 639 East Main Street in Mount Sterling (859–498–6830), then catch the show at the Judy Drive-in, 4078 Maysville Road, Mount Sterling; (859) 498–1960. (Both are closed in winter.)

For More Information

Mount Sterling/Montgomery County Tourism Commission, 51 *North Maysville Street, Mount Sterling* 40353; (859) 498–8732 or *www.mountsterling-ky.com.*

Morehead

KENTUCKY FOLK ART CENTER (ages 5 and up)
102 West First Street, Morehead 40351; (606) 783–2204, www.kyfolkart.org. Open Monday to Saturday from 9:00 A.M. to 5:00 P.M., Sunday from 1:00 to 5:00 P.M. $

This museum features fascinating walking sticks, carved animals and figures, paintings, assemblages, painted furniture, and other folk art created by Kentuckians. You may see anything from carved walking sticks and animals to figures of Elvis and Abe Lincoln to clothing woven from strips of plastic bags. Like Minnie Adkins, who makes the wonderful carved foxes and chickens, some of the artists live nearby in eastern Kentucky, but urban Kentuckians create folk art, too. Your family will get a broadened perspective of what art is, and you're bound to see something that will make you smile.

CAVE RUN LAKE (all ages)
Off KY 801 (take I–64, exit 133). Forest Service visitor center on KY 801: (606) 784–5624. Open year-round. Day use fees in recreational areas for noncampers. $

On a summer weekend at this lovely 8,270-acre lake at the northern end of Daniel Boone National Forest, you'll see fishing boats and maybe even a sailing regatta. It's a big muskie fishing area. Both the U.S. Army Corps of Engineers, who built the dam, and the U.S. Forest Service manage recreational areas here for camping and day use. Two major areas are Zilpo, a 355-acre wooded peninsula (877–444–6777), and Twin Knobs (606–784–8498). Both have campgrounds, picnic areas, hiking, and boat ramps. Stop at the Cave Run Ranger Lake Morehead Ranger Station on KY 801, 2 miles off US 60 for lake information and to see exhibits about the area.

For a scenic overview, drive the Zilpo National Scenic Byway, an 11-mile route from US 60 in Salt Lick to Highway 211 south to Forest Service Road 129; you'll end at Tater Knob Fire Tower, where there's an interpretive trail.

 MINOR CLARK STATE FISH HATCHERY (all ages)
120 Fish Hatchery Road (KY 801; take I-64, exit 133), Morehead 40351; (606) 784-6872. Open Monday to Friday from 7:00 A.M. to 3:00 P.M. **Free.**
Where do fish come from? The fish in Cave Run and many other Kentucky lakes come from this 300-acre hatchery, one of the largest warm-water hatcheries in the nation. You can view breeding ponds of muskie and bass and learn about the hatching process.

Where to Eat

Dixie Grill, *172 East Main Street, Morehead 40351; (606) 784–9051.* Beans and cornbread, daily specials, and homemade pies. $

Where to Stay

Ramada Inn, *KY 32 near I-64, exit 137, Morehead 40351; (606) 784-7591.* Restaurant, outdoor pool, free continental breakfast. $–$$

Twin Knobs Recreation Area, *KY 801, 7 miles from I-64, exit 133; (606) 784-6872.* U.S. Forest Service campsites on Cave Run Lake. $

For More Information

Morehead Tourism Commission, *150 East First Street, Morehead 40351;* *(606) 784–6221 or www.moreheadchamber.com.*

Olive Hill

GRAYSON LAKE STATE PARK (all ages)

314 Grayson Lake Park Road (KY 7, south of Grayson), Olive Hill 41164; (606) 474-9727. Open daily year-round. Admission and many activities **Free***; outdoor drama $$.*

The main attractions here are the fishing in the 1,500-acre lake and the serene atmosphere. Mid-June through mid-July a historical drama about the Civil War, *Someday,* is performed in the outdoor amphitheater Friday and Saturday nights. (606) 286-4522.

CARTER CAVES STATE RESORT PARK (all ages)

344 Caveland Drive (KY 182 off US 60 and I-64), Olive Hill 41164; (606) 286-4411 information; (800) 325-0059. Open year-round. Last cave tour leaves between 4:00 and 6:00 P.M., depending upon cave. Admission and many activities **Free***; cave tours $ each cave.*

Three of the twenty caves located in this scenic state resort park are open for guided tours. These are good cave tours for children: The tours are generally easy walking, and they don't last too long (a half hour to ninety minutes). Families with older children may be able to tour all three in a day. The biggest and prettiest tour is of Cascade Cave, which includes a small waterfall. The Saltpetre Cave tour is more historically oriented, and there are fewer formations in the cave, but you'll learn how saltpeter was mined to make gunpowder. X Cave has the coolest name and the shortest tour (about a half hour); it's just two tunnels that make an X. If you're really into spelunking, plan to come for the park's Crawlathon Weekend in late January. There are also Ghosts in the Cave tours at Halloween. Aboveground activities abound as well: You can canoe, swim, play miniature golf, picnic, or take a hike. The park offers a lodge with restaurant, cottages, and a campground.

NORTHEASTERN KENTUCKY HISTORY MUSEUM (all ages)

1385 Carter Caves Road, Olive Hill 41153; (606) 286-4411. Open daily April through October from 9:00 A.M. to 5:00 P.M. **Free***.*

Learn a little bit about area history and view Native American artifacts, fossils, and pioneer items as well as exhibits about World War II and the present day.

Where to Eat

Carter Caves State Resort Park, 344 Caveland Drive (KY 182 off US 60 and I–64), Olive Hill 41164; (800) 325– 0059. Kentucky regional foods and buffet, plus a children's menu. $

Where to Stay

Carter Caves State Resort Park, 344 Caveland Drive (KY 182 off US 60 and I–64), Olive Hill 41164; (800) 325– 0059. Lodge rooms ($-$$), cottages ($$$$), and year-round campground with seasonal pool, tent and full hookups, showers, laundry, and grocery.

Grayson Lake State Park Campground, 314 Grayson Lake Park Road (KY 7, south of Grayson), Olive Hill 41164; (606) 474-9727. Open year-round. $

Greenup

GREENBO LAKE STATE RESORT PARK (all ages)
KY 1, 18 miles from I-64, Grayson exit, Greenup 41114; information: (606) 473-7324, reservations: (800) 325-0083. Admission and some activities Free.

Not all of eastern Kentucky is mountainous, as a visit to this 3,008-acre park demonstrates. There are easy hiking trails along even to gently sloping terrain. Good as a day destination as well as for longer stays, Greenbo has a public swimming pool with wading pools and waterslide, a lake for fishing and pontoon sightseeing (boat rentals available), miniature golf, bicycle rentals, and tennis courts. The lodge is named for Jesse Stuart, the famous Kentucky author and poet who lived not far from here, and in the reading room at the lodge you can sample his works and learn about his life.

Covered Bridges Two of Kentucky's thirteen remaining covered bridges are located near Greenbo Lake State Resort Park. On your way to or from the park, stop to see 192-foot-long **Oldtown Bridge**, off KY 1, 9 miles south of Greenbo Lake State Resort Park. This bridge is closed to traffic. You can drive through the 155-foot-long **Bennett's Mill Bridge**, north of the park, on KY 3112, off KY 7.

Where to Eat

Greenbo Lake State Resort Park,
KY 1, 18 miles from I-64, Grayson exit,
Greenup 41114; (606) 473-7324. The
lodge restaurant serves Kentucky
regional foods and a buffet. Children's
menu available. $

Where to Stay

Greenbo Lake State Resort Park,
KY 1, 18 miles from I-64, Grayson exit,
Greenup 41114; information: (606) 473-
7324, reservations: (800) 325-0083.
Lodge rooms $. Campground (open
April through October) with laundry,
showers, grocery $.

Ashland

HIGHLANDS MUSEUM AND DISCOVERY CENTER (all ages)
1620 Winchester Avenue, Ashland 41101; (606) 329-8888, www.highlands museum.com. Open Tuesday to Saturday from 10:00 A.M. to 4:00 P.M. $

Located in a 1917 mansion, this museum includes exhibits on everything from early Native American cultures to the country music stars The Judds, who are from the Ashland area. Of special interest to children are the nineteenth-century one-room schoolhouse exhibit and the Discovery area with hands-on activities.

Jesse's Stories Jesse Stuart (1906–1984) wrote short stories, novels, and beautiful poems about his native eastern Kentucky. His books for elementary-school-age children include *The Beatinest Boy, A Penny's Worth of Character,* and *Andy Finds a Way.* You'll find them at Greenbo Lake State Resort Park and other resort park gift shops, as well as at the Jesse Stuart Foundation, 1645 Winchester Avenue, Ashland 41101; (606) 326-1667 or www.jsfbooks.com.

PARAMOUNT ARTS CENTER (ages 6 and up)
1300 Winchester Avenue, Ashland 41101; (606) 324-3175, www.paramount artscenter.com.

This lavish art deco-style 1931 movie house has been beautifully restored and now hosts music and theatrical presentations, some of which are appropriate for older children. If you're there when nothing is scheduled, ask to peek inside.

ASHLAND AREA ART GALLERY (ages 6 and up)

1516 Winchester Avenue, Ashland 41101; (606) 329-1826, www.aaag.net. Open Monday to Saturday from 10:00 A.M. to 4:00 P.M.; may stay open later on Saturdays in summer. **Free**.

The works of both regional artists and Kentuckians who have gained wider acclaim are on display here—a great way to inspire your older child who is a budding artist. Changing exhibits include works from a variety of media; you may see glass, pottery, paintings, and photography.

Where to Eat

Gattiland, *Midtown Shopping Center; Ashland; (606) 329-8381.* Game room and Italian buffet. $

J & J Family-Style Restaurant, *5260 Thirteenth Street, Ashland 41102; (606) 325-3817.* Home cooking, daily specials, and sandwiches. $

Rajah's, *US 60W, Meads; (606) 928-3382.* Despite the name, it's not an Indian restaurant; good home cooking.

Where to Stay

Ashland Plaza Hotel, *Fifteenth Street and Winchester Avenue, Ashland 41102; (606) 329-0055.* High-rise with river or skyline view. No pool. $$$

Hampton Inn, *1321 Cannonsburg Road, Ashland 41102; (606) 928-2888.*

Indoor pool, continental breakfast. $$-$$$

Holiday Inn Express, *4708 Winchester Avenue, Ashland 41102; (606) 325-8989.* Indoor pool, continental breakfast. $$-$$$

For More Information

Ashland Area Convention and Visitors Bureau, *1509 Winchester Avenue, Ashland 41105; (606) 329-1007 or*

(800) 377-6249, or www.visitashland ky.com.

Louisa

YATESVILLE LAKE STATE PARK (all ages)

KY 3 off US 25, near Louisa; (606) 673–1492; campground: (606) 673–1490. Open daily year-round. Admission Free*; camping $.*

Fishing for bluegill, bass, and crappie is the main activity at this 808-acre park. There are picnic areas, three hiking trails with lake views, and boat rentals. The campground is open April through October only.

Road Music KY 23, the main highway running from Ashland in northeastern Kentucky to the Virginia border in southeastern Kentucky—passing through Paintsville, Prestonsburg, and Pikeville along the way—has been named the "Country Music Highway." Signs along the route note the many country stars who are from this area of the state, including Loretta Lynn, Dwight Yoakam, The Judds, and Billy Ray Cyrus.

Paintsville Area

MOUNTAIN HOMEPLACE (all ages)

Off Highway 40 west of Paintsville; (606) 297–1850 or (800) 542–5790. Open Wednesday to Saturday from 9:00 A.M. to 5:00 P.M., Sunday from 1:00 to 5:00 P.M. Adults $$, children $.

Visiting this attraction is a little like dropping in on a nineteenth-century family. Costumed interpreters go about their lives and work as they might have done in the mid-1800s at a self-sufficient homestead, so what you'll see depends on the time of the year, from spinning to taking care of animals to making sorghum. The complex includes a blacksmith shop, grist mill, and schoolhouse in addition to the main house—it's enlightening to see how much hard work it took just to get through the day.

Fall Color Eastern Kentucky is a great place to catch color, and the state tracks the turning of the leaves to help visitors time their travels. ColorFall Kentucky reports are posted weekly at the www.kentucky tourism.com Web site from late September through the end of October.

LORETTA LYNN BIRTHPLACE (all ages)
Butcher Hollow, KY 302 southeast of Van Lear; (606) 789-3397. No set hours; tours generally available most days year-round. $

Country music fans will enjoy seeing the birthplace of singer Loretta Lynn of *Coal Miner's Daughter* fame. This board-and-batten cabin at her birthplace was rebuilt for the 1980 movie about Lynn's life. To take a tour, stop by Webb's Grocery nearby, owned by Lynn's brother Herman Webb.

 VAN LEAR HISTORICAL SOCIETY COAL MINER'S MUSEUM (all ages)
Highway 302, near Van Lear; (606) 789-0068. Open March through November, Monday to Saturday from 9:00 A.M. to 3:00 P.M. **Free.**

One of several attractions in eastern and southeastern Kentucky that cover the area's coal-mining industry and its history, this small museum includes a model of a typical early-twentieth-century company town. The museum is located in the former offices of Consolidated Coal Company.

Where to Stay

Paintsville Lake State Park Campground, *KY 40, off US 450, 4 miles west of Paintsville; (606) 297-8486.* Primitive and hookup camping, plus showers, laundry, and full-service marina.

Ramada Inn, *624 James Trimble Boulevard, Paintsville 41240; (606) 789-4242 or (800) 951-4242.* Indoor-outdoor pool, restaurant, game room. $$

For More Information

Paintsville Tourism Commission,
304 Main Street, Paintsville 41240; (800) 542-5790

Prestonsburg

 JENNY WILEY STATE RESORT PARK (all ages)
  75 Theatre Court, off US 23/460, Prestonsburg 41653; information: (606) 886-2711, reservations: (800) 325-0142. Open daily year-round. Many activities **Free.**

This very popular and scenic mountain resort park takes its name from a pioneer woman who was captured by Indians in 1789 and escaped eleven months later. (The summer theater at this park includes a production that tells her story.) Present-day Kentuckians escape to the park for outdoor fun—there are swimming, boating, and fishing in the

1,100-acre Dewey Lake, as well as hiking, miniature golf, a nine-hole regulation golf course, and a 3-mile mountain bike trail. Picnic areas and boat rentals are available. Daily mid-May through Labor Day and weekend through October, weather permitting, the Mountain Parkway Chair Lift will take you up 4,700 feet for hiking and scenic views atop Sugar Camp Mountain.

JENNY WILEY THEATRE (ages 6 and up)

Jenny Wiley State Resort Park Amphitheatre; (606) 886–9274 or (877) CALL–JWT. Evening and some matinee performances early June through mid-August; call for specific schedule. Adults $$$, under 21 $$.

Children old enough to sit still for a couple of hours will enjoy the music, bright costumes, and lively onstage action at the amphitheater at Jenny Wiley State Resort Park. The theater presents classic Broadway musicals and comedies, along with a historical drama about pioneer Jenny Wiley. The show goes on rain or shine—in bad weather, the performance moves indoors to the Wilkinson-Stumbo Convention Center next to the amphitheater. Ask about family night specials: On these occasional dates, two children are admitted free with the purchase of two adult tickets. Also, some hotels in the Prestonsburg and Paintsville area offer packages including accommodations and theater tickets.

The Real McCoys (and Hatfields) Pikeville, Kentucky, about 35 miles southeast of Jenny Wiley State Resort Park, was the site of the famous Hatfield–McCoy feud. Some of the McCoy family are buried in the city's Dils Cemetery. The families' modern-day members have made peace and gather each June in Pikeville for the Hatfield–McCoy Reunion Festival. (606) 432–5063.

KENTUCKY OPRY/MOUNTAIN ARTS CENTER (ages 5 and up)

Mountain Arts Center, 50 Hal Rogers Road, Prestonsburg 41653; (888) 622–2787. Performance dates vary; most Kentucky Opry performances are June through August and late November through mid-December. You can order advance tickets by phone. Ticket office open Monday to Friday from 9:00 A.M. to 6:00

P.M., Saturday from 10:00 A.M. to 4:00 P.M. Ask about one-price family admission. Tickets $$$. Self-guided tour Free.

The Kentucky Opry, a lively family showcase of country, bluegrass, gospel, oldies, and top 40s, is the house attraction in the modern, 1,050-seat performance hall locals refer to as "MAC." The show frequently features young performers. Other concerts with regional and national performers are scheduled from time to time. You can stop by during the day and walk through this 47,000-square-foot entertainment complex, which often has art exhibits.

Festive Places

A main attraction in some eastern Kentucky towns is the annual festival:

- **Pikeville** (about halfway between Jenny Wiley and Breaks Interstate Park)—Hillbilly Days, mid-April; (800) 844-7453

- **Hazard** (near Buckhorn Lake State Resort Park)—Black Gold Festival, late September (black gold is coal); (606) 436-0161

- **Harlan** (about halfway between Kingdom Come and Pine Mountain)—Poke Salad Festival, late May/early June (poke salad is a green that grows in the mountains); (606) 573-4717

- **Jackson** (southeast of Natural Bridge)—Breathitt County Honey Festival, Labor Day weekend; (606) 666-3800

- **Irvine** (southwest of Natural Bridge)—Mountain Mushroom Festival, late April; (606) 723-2450

- **Beattyville** (20 miles south of Natural Bridge)—Lee County Woolly Worm Festival, late October; (606) 464-2888

Where to Eat

Billy Ray's Restaurant, *101 North Front Street, Prestonsburg (606) 886–0001.* Home cooking. $

Jenny Wiley State Resort Park, *75 Theatre Court, off US 23/460, Prestonsburg*

41653; (606) 886-2711. Lodge restaurant overlooks Dewey Lake and serves Kentucky specialties and a daily buffet. Children's menu available. $

Where to Stay

Comfort Suites, *51 Hal Rogers Drive, Prestonsburg 41653; (606) 886–2555.* Indoor pool, free continental breakfast. $$–$$$

Holiday Inn, *1887 North US Highway 23, Prestonsburg 41653; (606) 886–0001 or (800) 466–5220.* $$$

Jenny Wiley State Resort Park, *75 Theatre Court, off US 23/460, Prestonsburg 41653; information: (606) 886–2711, reservations: (800) 325–0142.* Lodge rooms $–$$; cottages $$$–$$$$; camping $. Campground with rest rooms, showers; grocery open April through October 31.

Microtel Inn, *85 Hal Rogers Drive, Prestonsburg 41653, next to Mountain Arts Center; (606) 889–0331.* Exercise room, free continental breakfast. $$

For More Information

Prestonsburg Tourism Commission, *113 South Central Avenue, Prestonsburg 41653; (606) 886–1341 or (800) 844–4704, www.prestonsburgky.com.*

Elkhorn City

BREAKS INTERSTATE PARK (all ages)

KY 80 at the Kentucky–Virginia border; mailing address: P.O. Box 100, Breaks, VA 24607; (540) 865–4413 or (800) 982–5122. Open daily year-round. Many activities **Free**.

The huge 5-mile canyon within this park is sometimes called the "Grand Canyon of the South" for its 1,000-foot cliffs and breathtaking views. It's the largest canyon east of the Mississippi River. The park, jointly operated by Kentucky and Virginia, is popular with sightseers as well as hikers and experienced white-water rafters. Stop at the visitor center to view exhibits about the area's formation some 250 million years ago before heading to the four terrific scenic overlooks, or explore the area via hiking trails and trail rides on horseback. Pony rides offered for younger children.

ELKHORN CITY RAILROAD MUSEUM (all ages)

100 Pine Street, Elkhorn City 41522; (606) 432–1391. Open Tuesday and Friday from 9:00 A.M. to 4:00 P.M. or by appointment. **Free**; *donations accepted.*

For well into the twentieth century, roads in remote eastern Kentucky were few, and trains were the main transportation. This museum has a variety of equipment from the rail era, including a caboose, switch-stands, and a velocipede, on which workers rode to get to areas needing repair.

Where to Eat

Breaks Interstate Park, *KY 80 at the Kentucky–Virginia border; mailing address P.O. Box 100, Breaks, VA 24607; (540) 865-4413.* Restaurant overlooking scenic canyon. Regional specialties. $

Rusty Fork Cafe, *195 South Patty Loveless Drive, Elkhorn City; (606) 754-4494.* Home cooking. $

Where to Stay

Breaks Interstate Park, *KY 80 at the Kentucky–Virginia border; mailing address: Breaks, VA 24607; (540) 865-4413 or (800) 982-5122.* Lodge ($$), cottages ($$$), and campground ($) open April through October. Pool, showers, restaurant.

Whitesburg

 APPALSHOP (ages 5 and up)
91 Madison Avenue, Whitesburg 41858; (606) 633-0108, www.appalshop.org. Open Monday to Friday from 9:00 A.M. to 5:00 P.M. Reservations needed for guided tour. **Free.**

Appalshop is a not-for-profit community and media organization that produces documentary films about Appalachian culture, sponsors community events, concerts, and theater performances, and even has its own recording label and radio station. If you just stop by, you may be able to watch a video and see the art gallery and some activities, but if you want to be assured of a tour, make reservations. While you're there, ask about the nearby J. B. Caudill Store and History Center, which includes all kinds of artifacts. In June, Appalshop sponsors Seedtime on the Cumberland, with crafts, music, and food.

Nature Preserves In addition to the excellent state parks,

nature lovers can explore Kentucky's preserves. There are forty-one of these legally designated and protected areas in the state, twenty-one of which are open to the public from dawn to dusk daily.

Unlike the state parks, however, nature preserves are not operated mainly with visitation in mind. Just the opposite: The idea is to preserve these beautiful and important natural areas. Except for preserves located within state parks, there are no rest room facilities, and there may not be maps and guide information on site. They are for foot traffic only—no bikes or horses—and picnicking, camping, pets, and radio/tape decks are not allowed. Nature preserves open to the public in the area covered by this chapter are

- **Bat Cave/Cascade Cavern**—ask at Carter Caves Park for information and cave tours

- **Jesse Stuart**—W-Hollow Road off KY 1; includes land once owned by the famous author

- **Natural Bridge**—located in the park

- **Pilot Knob**—Brush Creek Road, off KY 15 in Powell County

- **Bad Branch**—off KY 932 near Whitesburg

- **Blanton Forest**—off KY 840 in Harlan County

- **Kingdom Come**—in state park

For more information on Kentucky's nature preserves, call (502) 573-2886, or visit www.kynaturepreserves.org.

Where to Eat

Courthouse Cafe, *127B Main Street, Whitesburg 41858; (606) 633–5859.*

Sandwiches, salads, and daily specials; local crafts on display.

Hindman

HINDMAN SETTLEMENT SCHOOL (all ages)

KY 160, off KY 80, northeast of Hazard; (606) 785-5475. Open from 8:00 A.M. to 5:00 P.M.; large groups should call first. **Free**.

The Hindman Settlement School was founded in 1902 and was the first rural social settlement school in the United States. The goal now, as it was then, is to provide educational opportunities and services with respect to the local heritage. Today this is a wonderful place to learn about Appalachian culture and folkways. If you stop by, you can watch a video about the school's history and get to see some of the buildings with their lovely handmade furniture and crafts. You'll also visit the Marie Stewart Craft Shop, which sells, quilts, pottery, baskets, and other items made by local craftspeople; children will love the wooden trucks and animals.

Some Things I've Learned (the Hard Way) about Family Hiking

Eastern Kentucky has hundreds and hundreds of miles of hiking trails, from very easy and accessible paths to extremely rugged and remote areas. The temptation is to get out there and explore. But first:

- Be sure everyone (including toddlers) is wearing athletic shoes or hiking boots with good traction. Not sandals!

- Take along (filled) water bottles, preferably one per person.

- Know how long the trail is and how difficult it is before you go; you should have a map. (What we assumed, mistakenly, was a short, easy walk along an unmarked trail turned out to be a tough 7-mile trek—and it was 90 degrees outside. Some of us thought we were going to die!)

- Don't be hard-headed—turn back if the trail is getting too long or difficult.

- If you have a toddler, strongly consider bringing a back or front carrier—you'll get awfully tired carrying him or her in your arms.

- With younger children, stick to the short and easy trails near facilities. There's no reason to push little ones. (Remember, their legs are shorter than yours.) You can always come back and hike the longer trails when they're older. (Believe me, before you know it, you'll be the one lagging behind!)

If you are serious hikers, get a hiking guide to the region, such as Globe Pequot Press's *Hiking Kentucky*.

Family Folk Week During the second week of June, the Hindman Settlement School offers a wonderful family vacation. Parents and children stay in the school dorms and attend all kinds of workshops on crafts, storytelling, music, and folk dancing. There are sessions for children ages four to twelve as well as for teens and adults, and all ages come together for some events. Each evening there are performances by the teachers (these are open to the public if you happen to be in the area). Many families return year after year for Family Folk Week, so make your reservations early. For information about tuition, call the school at (606) 785-5475.

 KENTUCKY APPALACHIAN ARTISAN CENTER (all ages)
16 West Main Street, Hindman 41822; (606) 785-9855. Open Monday to Friday from 10:00 A.M. to 6:00 P.M., Saturday from 10:00 A.M. to 2:00 P.M. Free.

Stop by this center in downtown Hindman to view changing arts and crafts exhibits. There's also a small sales shop.

Oh, Man! Bet you've never seen a 10-foot-plus gingerbread man! The world's largest gingerbread man is the star attraction of the annual **Gingerbread Festival** in Hindman. Why gingerbread? It's part of the area's political history; politicians used to give out gingerbread to woo voters. The festival starts the Thursday after Labor Day and continues through Sunday. For a taste of the gingerbread man, come on Saturday. (606) 785-5329.

Cumberland/Benham/Lynch

 KINGDOM COME STATE PARK (all ages)
502 Park Road, off US 119, Cumberland 40823; (606) 589-2479. Open daily year-round. Many activities Free.

 DO NOT FEED THE BEARS. You expect to see this warning posted in Yellowstone National Park in Wyoming, but in Kentucky? There were a lot of bears in eastern Kentucky a century ago, but they virtually disappeared because of logging and hunting. They're venturing back from Virginia and West Virginia. There's no guarantee that you'll see one, but they've become prevalent enough in Kingdom Come State Park that the park is bear-proofing its trash cans and warning campers not to leave any food in their tents. In case you don't see a bear, other things to do here include fishing, pedal boating, miniature golf, and hiking to Log Rock, a sandstone arch, and Raven Rock, a huge rock that reaches 250 feet in the air.

There are fourteen trails ranging in length from ⅛ to ⅞ mile. The park offers primitive camping only.

Amazing Kentucky Fact *The Little Shepherd of Kingdom Come,* the 1903 novel by Kentuckian John Fox Jr., was the first novel in America to sell more than a million copies.

 LILLY CORNETT WOODS (ages 6 and up)
KY 1103, off KY 7, north of Kingdom Come State Park, Allie 41821; (606) 633-5828. Open May 15 through August 15 from 9:00 A.M. to 5:00 P.M. daily; weekends only in April, May, September, and October. **Free**.

Your children need to be able to walk about 2 miles/two hours to take this guided hike through one of Kentucky's rare remaining areas of old-growth forest. Many of the trees are more than 200 years old.

 GODBEY APPALACHIAN CENTER (ages 6 and up)
700 College Road, Cumberland 40823; (606) 589-2145, ext. 2047.

Stop by this cultural center on the campus of Southeast Community College to view a collection of Appalachian photographs, crafts, and art.

 KENTUCKY COAL MINING MUSEUM (ages 4 and up)
Main Street (KY 160), Benham 40807; (606) 848-1530. Open Monday to Saturday from 10:00 A.M. to 5:00 P.M., Sunday from 1:00 to 4:00 P.M. $

When Benham was an International Harvester company town, this building was the commissary. Now it houses a variety of exhibits about mining and life in a mining camp. Children can climb onto a 1940s electric locomotive on the grounds and don hard hats and wiggle through a mock coal mine in the basement. Other exhibits include tools, mining equipment, and artifacts from the hospital and school. A collection of items relating to country singer Loretta Lynn is on the third floor.

PORTAL 31 MINE TOUR AND LAMPHOUSE MUSEUM (ages 4 and up)

KY 160, Lynch, southeast of Benham; (606) 848–1530 or www.portal31.org. Museum open Monday to Friday from 9:00 A.M. to 5:00 P.M. $

Just a couple miles from the Coal Mining Museum is the entrance to the old mine. Kentucky's first underground coal mine tours are scheduled to begin in 2003. Plans are that you'll don safety gear and ride a transport into the mine, where projected images

> ## **A**mazing Kentucky Fact About 96 percent of Kentucky's electricity is generated by coal, a nonrenewable fossil fuel. It takes about a pound of coal to power a 100-watt lightbulb for ten hours—so turn off those lights when you're not using them!

will give the impression of miners at work. In the meantime, you can see mining equipment and miners' hats on display at the 1920s lamphouse.

Where to Eat

Benham School House Inn, *100 Central Avenue, Benham 40807; (606) 848–3000.* Lunch and dinner. Fried chicken, catfish, sandwiches, daily special. $

Where to Stay

Benham School House Inn, *100 Central Avenue, Benham 40807; (606) 848–3000.* Rooms and suites in a school building built in 1926 for children of the coal-mining camp. $$$

Portal 31 RV Park, *Main Street, Lynch, right across from Portal 31; (606) 848–1530.* Open year-round. Primitive and hookup sites. $

Buckhorn

BUCKHORN LAKE STATE RESORT PARK (all ages)

4441 KY 1833, Buckhorn 41721; information: (606) 398–7510, reservations: (800) 325–0058. Many activities Free.

The 1,200-acre lake is the centerpiece of this mountain resort park. You can bring your own boat or rent one; pontoon sightseeing boats also available (rentals April through October only). The lodge dining room overlooks the lake. Work up your appetite with the 1½ mile easy walking trail or a round of miniature golf.

Amazing Kentucky Fact Black Mountain, on KY 160, off KY 38, is the highest point in Kentucky—4,145 feet.

There's a public beach, but the swimming pool is for lodge and cottage guests only. No campground.

Log Cathedral While in the Buckhorn area, take a short drive on KY 28 to Buckhorn, about 16 miles southeast of the state park, to see the Log Cathedral (606-398-7382; Free), a large, beautiful log church with amber stained-glass windows, a large bell tower, and a huge pipe organ inside. It was built in 1907 as part of a Christian school founded by New Yorker Harvey S. Murdoch.

Annual Events

Carter Caves Crawlathon, late January, Carter Caves State Resort Park; (606) 286-4411

Herpetology Weekend, late April, Natural Bridge State Resort Park; (800) 325-1710

Wildflower Weekend, early May, Natural Bridge State Resort Park; (800) 325-1710

Apple Blossom Festival, early May, Pikeville; (606) 754-5080

Seedtime on the Cumberland Festival of Mountain Arts, early June, Appalshop, Whitesburg; (606) 633-0108

Appalachian Celebration, late June, Morehead State University, Morehead; (606) 784-6221

Gingerbread Festival, September, Hindman; (606) 785-5881

Brenthitt County Honey Festival, Labor Day weekend, Jackson; (606) 666-3800

Harlan's Heritage Days, early September, Harlan; (606) 573-4156

Poppy Mountain Bluegrass Festival, late September, Morehead; (606) 784-2277

Black Gold Festival, late September, Hazard; (606) 436-0161

Kentucky Highland Folk Festival, late September, Prestonsburg; (800) 844-4704

Morgan County Sorghum Festival, late September, West Liberty; (606) 743-3330

Kentucky Apple Festival, early October, Paintsville; (800) 542-5790

Cumberland Mountain Fall Festival, early October, Middlesboro; (800) 988-1075

Levisa Cup Canoe Race, early October, Prestonsburg to Paintsville; (606) 886-1341

Court Days, weekend before and third Monday of October, Mount Sterling; (850) 498-8732

Jenny Wiley Pioneer Festival, mid-October, Prestonsburg; (606) 886-3876

Lee County Woolly Worm Festival, late October, Beattyville; (606) 464-2888

South-Central Kentucky

In this region you can explore Kentucky from just about every angle—the top of a mountain, on water, even deep beneath the surface of the earth. South-central Kentucky is really three vacation zones in one. The easternmost section features mountain scenery and traditional cultural attractions. Then you get to water world—fishing and boating enthusiasts flock to Laurel Lake, Cumberland Lake, Dale Hollow Lake, and Green River Lake. Heading east, the lakes give way to cave country. Mammoth Cave, the nation's longest cave system, and a bevy of other underground caverns offer natural air-conditioning and cool formations. At the western edge of the region is Bowling Green, Kentucky's fourth largest city. Throughout are an array of interesting and fun museums and attractions, relating to everything from coal to chicken to kangaroos.

Interstate access is good through much of this region: I-75 runs south from the Bluegrass; from there you can go west to Somerset and pick up the Louie B. Nunn Parkway (a toll road) that hooks into I-65 at Bowling Green. I-65 connects the cave area and Bowling Green with the Louisville area. Many chain hotels and restaurants are located along the interstate corridors.

Middlesboro

CUMBERLAND GAP NATIONAL HISTORICAL PARK (all ages)
US 25E South, P.O. Box 1848, Middlesboro 40965; (606) 248-2817. Open daily except Christmas. Admission and many activities $\mathbb{Free}$.

If you were doing a tour of Kentucky in chronological order, you'd start here, for this is where Daniel Boone and other early explorers and settlers first entered the state through a natural break in the Cumberland Mountains. Native tribes had used the gap, but their "Warriors' Path" to

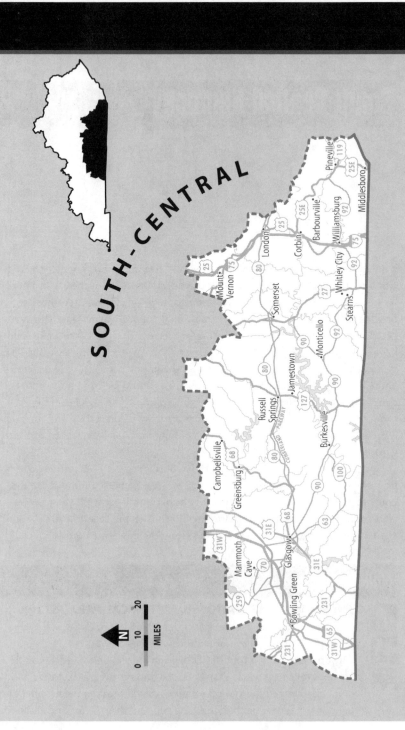

SOUTH-CENTRAL

Kentucky became known as the Wilderness Road as European settlers poured through in the late 1700s. The road was later paved, but after the modern tunnel through the adjacent mountain opened (see next entry), the old US 25 highway was removed, and the Wilderness Road path was restored in recent years. It's about ⁹⁄₁₀ mile long, a fairly easy hike from the parking lot off Pinnacle Road to the gap. You'll also want to drive up to Pinnacle Overlook to see three states (Kentucky, Tennessee, and Virginia). There are many ranger-guided activities in this 20,000-acre park, including two- to four-hour tours of Hensley Settlement and Cudjo's Cave (for a fee), as well as kids' hiking and history activities. (Did you know that Daniel Boone *didn't* wear a coonskin cap?)

CUMBERLAND GAP TUNNEL (all ages)

US 25E, Kentucky to Tennessee; (606) 248-2482. **Free**.

Leave and reenter Kentucky like a modern pioneer: Drive through the mountain via these ultramodern 4,600-foot twin portals under Cumberland Mountain. The project was completed in 1996 to make passage safer.

Teresa's Top Ten
Picks for South-Central Kentucky

1. Mammoth Cave National Park, (270) 758–2328
2. Kentucky Down Under, (800) 762–2869
3. Cumberland Gap National Historical Park, (606) 248–2817
4. Barren River Imaginative Museum of Science, (270) 843–9779
5. Lost River Cave and Valley, (866) 274–CAVE
6. Big South Fork Scenic Railway (and layovers Barthell Mining Camp, Blue Heron Mining Camp), (800) GO–ALONG
7. Kentucky Museum, (270) 745–2592
8. Wigwam Village 2, (270) 773–3381
9. Wolf Creek National Fish Hatchery, (270) 343–3797
10. Cumberland Falls State Resort Park, (606) 528–4121

COAL HOUSE AND MUSEUM (all ages)
106 North Twentieth Street, Middlesboro 40965; (606) 248–1075. Open Monday to Friday from 8:00 A.M. to 4:00 P.M. **Free**.

An entire house made of coal? Actually, this building housing the Bell County Chamber of Commerce is just faced with bituminous coal, but it's still a lot of coal—about 40 tons. The house was built in 1926. Next door is the Coal House Museum, which features various mining artifacts.

 LOST SQUADRON MUSEUM (ages 5 and up)
Middlesboro Airport, 1400 Dorchester Avenue, Middlesboro 40965; (606) 248–1149, www.thelostsquadron.com. Open daily from 8:00 A.M. to 5:00 P.M. **Free**.

When you visit this museum, you'll hear a remarkable story about the recovery and restoration of a World War II P-38 fighter plane. *Glacier Girl,* as the plane is called, was one of four P-38s that ran out of fuel and made forced landings on a remote Greenland glacier in 1942. There it stayed for fifty years, until a group of aviation enthusiasts organized an expedition to retrieve a plane. It took them three years to find the plane, then remove it part by part. They brought it to a hangar in Middlesboro and have been working on a meticulous restoration ever since. These days, *Glacier Girl* is looking good; stop by and see for yourself.

Amazing Kentucky Fact Middlesboro, Kentucky, is the only U.S. city known to be located within a meteor crater.

Where to Eat

J. Milton's Steak and Buffet, *Highway 25 E, Middlesboro 40965; (606) 248–0458.* Steaks, chicken, and seafood. $

J&L's Country Kitchen, *Village Square Mall, Middlesboro 40965; (606) 248–2854.* Real mashed potatoes and other home cooking. $

Webb's Country Kitchen, *602 Colwyn Avenue, Cumberland Gap 37724 (just over the state line in Tennessee); (423) 869–5877.* Country cooking with live music on Friday nights.

Where to Stay

Best Western Inn, *1623 Cumberland Avenue, Middlesboro 40965; (606) 248–5630 or www.bestwesternkentucky. com.* Complimentary breakfast, outdoor pool. $$

Days Inn and Suites, *1252 North Twelfth Street, Middlesboro 40965; (606) 248–1340.* Complimentary breakfast, outdoor pool. $$

Pineville

PINE MOUNTAIN STATE RESORT PARK (all ages)
1050 State Park Road (off US 25E, 1 mile south of Pineville), Pineville 40977; information: (606) 337–3066, reservations: (800) 325–1712. Open daily year-round. Many activities **Free**.

The beautiful tall trees and enchanted feel of this park attract bird-watchers and nature lovers along with golfers and would-be beauty queens (the park's main event is the crowning of the Mountain Laurel Queen each April at the natural amphitheater). The 8½ miles of hiking trails include a trek to Chained Rock (about ½ mile if you drive to the Chained Rock parking lot first; about 3 miles if you're hiking from the lodge). This giant rock is chained to the mountaintop to supposedly keep it from falling on the city of Pineville below (a 1920s publicity stunt). The park's challenging eighteen-hole championship course, Wasioto Winds, was designed by renowned golf course architect Michael Hurdzan. If you have a youngster who is interested in golf, check out the separate four-hole course; Pine Mountain is part of the World Golf Foundation's "First Tee" program for children ages seven to seventeen. (*Note:* The park swimming pool is for lodge and cottage guests only.)

HENDERSON SETTLEMENT SCHOOL AND LOG HOUSE CRAFT SHOP (all ages)
KY 190, 18 miles southwest of Pineville; Settlement School: (606) 337–3613, Log House Craft Shop: (606) 337–5823. Open Monday to Friday from 8:00 A.M. to 4:30 P.M. **Free**.

You're welcome to walk around this 1,300-acre United Methodist Church mission complex that includes orchards, gardens, and a community greenhouse. Handwoven items and other locally made crafts are sold at the crafts shop.

Where to Eat

Pine Mountain State Resort Park, *1050 State Park Road (off US 25E, 1 mile south of Pineville), Pineville 40977; (606)* *337–3066.* Kentucky specialties and buffet. Children's menu. $

Where to Stay

Pine Mountain State Resort Park, *1050 State Park Road (off US 25E, 1 mile south of Pineville), Pineville 40977; information: (606) 337–3066, reservations: (800)* *325–1712.* Lodge rooms ($–$$), cottages ($$$–$$$$), and primitive camping (April through October; $).

For More Information

Bell County Tourism Commission, *2215 Cumberland Avenue, Middlesboro* *40965; (606) 248–2482 or (800) 988–1075, www.mountaingateway.com.*

Barbourville

DR. THOMAS WALKER STATE HISTORIC SITE

KY 459, off US 25E, Barbourville 40906; (606) 546–4400. Grounds open daily year-round; facilities seasonal. 𝕱𝖗𝖊𝖊.

Though not as famous as Daniel Boone, Dr. Thomas Walker, a physician and surveyor, played an important role in opening Kentucky for settlement. He led the first expedition through the Cumberland Gap in 1750 and was the first settler from the east to build a log cabin in Kentucky. This was the place; the cabin is a replica. (Of course, there weren't picnic tables, miniature golf, a basketball court, playgrounds, and concession stands back then.)

BARBOURVILLE RECREATIONAL PARK/BRICKYARD WAVES WATERPARK (all ages)

Allison Avenue, Barbourville 40906; (606) 546–6197. Open daily; water park seasonal. Many activities 𝕱𝖗𝖊𝖊*; water park and BMX track $.*

Cool off or watch some hot BMX action in this activities-packed city park. Brickyard Waves Water Park has a wave pool, giant slide, lazy river, and kiddie pool. (Smile as you hit the water—sometimes the slide action is broadcast on the local access cable channel!) There are BMX bike races several times a month April through November at the ABA-sanctioned track, with practice sessions every Tuesday and Friday night. Other features include batting cages, pedal-boat rentals, miniature golf, and free fishing, picnic areas, and playgrounds. There's even an Olde Time General Store with fudge, snacks, and local crafts.

Just Ducky One of the special events for children at Barbourville Recreational Park is the KenDucky Derby, in early June, in which 3,000 plastic ducks race in the water park area. The park also has real ducks you can feed year-round.

Where to Eat

Vintage House Restaurant, *101 North Main Street, Barbourville 40906; (606) 546–5414.* Across from the courthouse. Lunch Wednesday through Friday (quiche and sandwiches; $); dinner Thursday through Saturday (prime rib, fresh fish; $$).

Where to Stay

Best Western Wilderness Trail, *1476 South US 25E, Barbourville 40906; (606)* 546–8500. Pool, restaurant, free continental breakfast. $–$$

For More Information

Barbourville Tourism and Recreation Commission, *P.O. Box 1300,* Barbourville 40906; (606) 546–6197, www.barbourville.com.

Williamsburg

 CUMBERLAND MUSEUM (all ages)
649 South Tenth Street, Williamsburg; (606) 539–4050. Open Monday to Saturday from 8:30 A.M. to 6:00 P.M. $

You don't expect to find a polar bear in Kentucky, but this eclectic museum operated by Cumberland College has not just one but two, along with hundreds of other preserved animals displayed in natural settings. And that's just the beginning. There's also a collection of 6,000 crosses, plus animated Christmas figures (Santa himself is around in December), and mountain crafts and artifacts.

HAL ROGERS FAMILY ENTERTAINMENT CENTER AND KENTUCKY SPLASH WATERPARK (all ages)

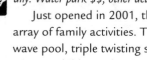
1050 Highway 92W, Williamsburg 40769; (606) 549-6065, www.kentucky splash.com. Water park seasonal; other attractions open year-round. Open Monday to Thursday from 11:00 A.M. to 9:00 P.M., Friday and Saturday from 11:00 A.M. to 11:00 P.M., and Sunday from 12:30 to 6:30 P.M. Hours may vary seasonally. Water park $$; other activities individual fees. All-day activity pass $$$$.

Just opened in 2001, this large family amusement center features an array of family activities. The water park includes an 18,000-square-foot wave pool, triple twisting slides, a drift pool, and Tad Pole Island for younger children. There's a go-cart track for older children, as well as a kiddie track, batting cages, and a big arcade. Snacks, burgers, and sandwiches are available.

Where to Eat

Athenaeum Restaurant, *Cumberland Inn, 649 South Tenth Street, Williamsburg 40769; (606) 539–4100.* Operated by Cumberland College. Breakfast, lunch, and dinner. Order from the menu, or try the extensive buffets. $

Where to Stay

Cumberland Inn, *649 South Tenth Street, Williamsburg 40769; (606) 539–4100.* Rooms and suites, plus sixty-bedroom log house. Indoor pool. Operated by Cumberland College as part of student work/study program. $$–$$$$

Days Inn, *US 25W and Highway 91, Williamsburg 40769; (606) 549–1500.* Free continental breakfast, outdoor pool. $

For More Information

Williamsburg Information Center, *exit 11 off I–75, Williamsburg 40769;* *(606) 549–0530 or (800) 552–0530, www.williamsburgky.com.*

Corbin

CUMBERLAND FALLS STATE RESORT PARK (all ages)

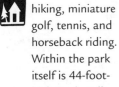
7351 Highway 90, near Corbin 40701; information: (606) 528–4121, reservations: (800) 325–0063. Open year-round. Many activities **Free**.

After you snap some family photos in front of the scenic falls (67 feet tall and 150 feet wide, the "Niagara of the South"), enjoy the swimming, hiking, miniature golf, tennis, and horseback riding. Within the park itself is 44-foot-high Eagle Falls, about a 1-mile hike from Cumberland Falls. The stone lodge built

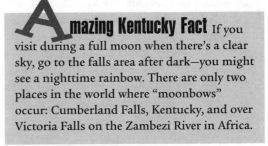
Amazing Kentucky Fact If you visit during a full moon when there's a clear sky, go to the falls area after dark—you might see a nighttime rainbow. There are only two places in the world where "moonbows" occur: Cumberland Falls, Kentucky, and over Victoria Falls on the Zambezi River in Africa.

in the 1930s includes a pleasant sitting room, game room, and exhibits relating to the local area. Pick up the visitor guide at the lodge for directions to other waterfalls and a scenic arch. In the summer, there are weekly square dances at the park pavilion.

SHELTOWEE TRACE OUTFITTERS (ages 7 and up)

Entry points vary depending on type of excursion; based in Whitley City 42653; (800) 541–RAFT. Mid-May through October; schedule and rates vary depending on activity.

This company offers water outings in the Cumberland Falls/Big South Fork area that range from mild to wild. At Cumberland Falls State Resort Park on weekends Memorial Day through Labor Day, you can take a Rainbow Mist Tour Ride to the bottom of the falls (children must weigh at least 25 pounds; trip dependent on water levels and weather; call the day before your planned visit). Lunch cruises are offered on Lake Cumberland aboard a 65-foot double-decker riverboat. Some of the more adventurous rafting, canoeing, and duckie boat outings are for ages thirteen and up only, but there are a few available for participants as young as seven.

Name Game Can you guess why Corbin calls its annual community festival the Nibroc Fun Festival? Study the name for a while, and it might come to you. Or just show up mid-August and ask while you enjoy street dances, a dog show, a parade, children's activities, and other events. (800) 528-7123.

FALLS MOUNTAIN CRAFT CENTER (all ages)

KY 90 west of Cumberland Falls State Resort Park; (606) 376-3463. Open daily except Wednesday from 10:00 A.M. to 6:00 P.M.

This shop, located in 1840s log buildings, carries a variety of arts and crafts produced locally—everything from painted gourds, ornaments, and candles to large cedar chests. It's operated by a nonprofit organization, and the selection changes often—whatever local craftspeople decide to make. The manager lives next door, so even if you come on a Wednesday, you may be able to visit the shop.

HARLAND SANDERS CAFE AND MUSEUM (all ages)

US 25E and 25W, Corbin 40701; (606) 528-2163. Open daily from 9:30 A.M. to 10:00 P.M. Admission **Free***; charge for food.*

The world's most famous chicken—and the "Colonel" who invented it—got their start here. Visit this restaurant/museum where, in 1940, Harland Sanders perfected his recipe of "secret herbs and spices" and began serving chicken so good that he decided to try to franchise it. The rest is finger lickin' history. There's memorabilia on display, and the place still serves KFC.

More Egg-citement! Corbin has the Colonel Sanders Cafe, but nearby London has the World Chicken Festival, each year in late September. See the World's Largest Stainless Steel Skillet!

Where to Eat

Cumberland Falls State Resort Park, *7351 Highway 90, near Corbin* — 40701; (606) 528-4121 Buffet, Kentucky specialties, kids' menu. $

Where to Stay

Comfort Suites, *I–75, exit 29, 47 Adams Road, Corbin 40701; (606) 526–6646. Indoor pool. Rooms and suites, free continental breakfast.* $$

Cumberland Falls, *7351 Highway 90, near Corbin 40701; information: (606) 528–4121, reservations: (800) 325–0063.*

Lodge rooms ($–$$), cottages ($$–$$$$), and camping (April through October only; $).

Holiday Inn Express, *I–75, exit 25, 1973 Cumberland Falls Parkway, Corbin 40701; (606) 523–4000.* $

For More Information

Corbin Tourist and Convention Commission, *101 North Depot Street,*

Corbin 40701; (606) 528–6390 or (800) 528–7123, www.corbinky.com.

London/Corbin Area Lakes

- **Laurel River Lake,** This 6,000-acre lake is located within Daniel Boone National Forest. There are two marinas and several Forest Service recreation areas. Stop at the ranger station on US 25 (606–864–4163) for maps and information. A state record smallmouth bass (8 pounds, 7 ounces) was caught here in 1998.

- **Wood Creek Lake,** KY 80 off I–75, exit 41, at the edge of Daniel Boone Forest, may be small—672 acres—but it has a big claim to fame. The state record largemouth bass—13 pounds, 10 ounces—was caught here on April 14, 1984.

London

LEVI JACKSON WILDERNESS ROAD STATE PARK (all ages)
998 Levi Jackson Mill Road, London 40744; (606) 878–8000. Park open year-round; museum open April through October. Many activities Free; *museum admission $.*

Pioneer artifacts are an added attraction at this 800-acre park. Two historic hiking trails, Wilderness Road and Boone's Trace, come through this park. At the Mountain Life Museum, a reproduction of a pioneer settlement, costumed guides tell about pioneer life, and you can see tools, household items, and other relics. One of the seven buildings is a reproduction of McHargue's Mill, with authentic interior works. The mill building is surrounded by a large collection of millstones. After all that history, you can have some modern fun at the park's miniature golf course, swimming pool, playgrounds, and picnic areas.

ast Action

- Near Levi Jackson Wilderness Road State Park on US 25 is the **London Go-Kart and Fun Park** (606–864–0761), with go-carts, miniature golf, and a game room.

- North of London, near I–75, exit 41, is **Daniel Boone Motocross Park** *(606) 877–1364 or www.mxaction.com)*, which features ATV, motocross, and mountain bike races. Schedule varies.

Mount Vernon

KENTUCKY MUSIC HALL OF FAME MUSEUM (ages 6 and up)
US 25 off I–75, exit 62, 2590 Richmond Road, Mount Vernon 40456; (606) 256–1000, www.kentuckymusicmuseum.com. Open Tuesday to Saturday 10:00 A.M. to 6:00 P.M., Sunday 9:00 A.M. to 5:00 P.M. $

"What's that song?" my daughter asked. "Bye, Bye Love," an old tune by the Everly Brothers, was being piped through the speakers as we toured this new museum (opened in 2002). While your children may not recognize all the stars whose music is played and costumes and artifacts displayed, young musicians will enjoy seeing the antique instruments and exploring pitch, rhythm, and timbre in the interactive area. The museum's recording studio wasn't finished when we visited.

RENFRO VALLEY (all ages)
US 25 off I–75, exit 62, Renfro Valley 40473; (800) 765–7464, www.renfro valley.com. Shows March through December; schedule and ticket prices vary. Shop hours also vary; most open Wednesday to Saturday from 10:00 A.M. to 9:00 P.M. spring through fall and during Christmas season. Motel $–$$, cabins $–$$, RV campground $.

Renfro Valley has been holding jamborees and barn dances since 1939. The schedule includes headliner concerts featuring well-known artists as well as a full array of performances featuring local and regional performers—up to a dozen shows a week in the summer. Regular features are the Saturday Barn Dance at 7:00 P.M. and Saturday Jamboree at 9:00 P.M. and the Sunday Gatherin' (gospel music) at 8:30 A.M. There's also a "village" of shops, including a cute gristmill general store, plus two restaurants, a motel, cabins, and RV campground.

For More Information

Renfro Valley Visitors Center, *I–75, exit 62, Renfro Valley 40456; (606) 256–2638 or (800) 765–7464.*

Mount Vernon/Rockcastle County Tourist Commission, *P.O. Box 1261, Mount Vernon 40456; (606) 256–9814 or (800) 252–6685.*

How 'Bout These Apples?

Follow your appetite to Liberty for the annual Casey County Apple Festival. Held the last week in September, this festival features a giant chocolate chip cookie on Wednesday, a giant pizza on Thursday, and the world's largest apple pie on Saturday (it takes a forklift to get it into the oven). If you happen to still be hungry, stop by Bread of Life Cafe, 5369 South Highway 127, for good home cooking.

Somerset/Monticello Area

1840s MILL SPRINGS MILL (all ages)

Highway 1275 off Highway 90, near Monticello; (606) 348-8189. Open daily May through the end of October from 9:00 A.M. to 5:00 P.M. **Free.**

Stop by to see this antique waterwheel—one of the largest overshot waterwheels in the world, at 40 feet, 10 inches in diameter. You can buy cornmeal ground at the mill in the gift shop; to see the grinding in

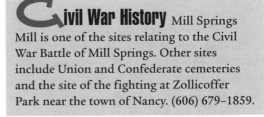

Civil War History

Mill Springs Mill is one of the sites relating to the Civil War Battle of Mill Springs. Other sites include Union and Confederate cemeteries and the site of the fighting at Zollicoffer Park near the town of Nancy. (606) 679-1859.

action, come by Saturday or Sunday at 2:00 P.M. Picnic areas available.

GENERAL BURNSIDE ISLAND STATE PARK (all ages)

8801 South Highway 27, Burnside 42519 (about 9 miles south of Somerset); (606) 561–4104 or (606) 561–4192. Some activities **Free***; Christmas Island $.*

We got a kick out of just driving over to this park since it's on an island. The golf course is a big attraction, but there are also picnic areas and fishing. Late November through December, the island becomes Christmas Island, a 3½-mile driving tour of 300 light displays (about a million lights are used), including a Santa Dragon and the Twelve Days of Christmas.

Amazing Kentucky Fact The term sideburns came from the hair and beard style of Union Civil War general A. E. Burnside, who had headquarters in this area.

Whitley City/Stearns

BIG SOUTH FORK SCENIC RAILWAY (all ages)

Board at 21 Henderson Street, Stearns 42647; (800) GO–ALONG or (606) 376–5330, www.bsfsry.com. Excursions mid-April through mid-November, weekends only April and November. May through September departs at 10:00 and 11:00 A.M. Wednesday to Friday, 10:00 and 11:00 A.M. and 2:30 P.M. Saturday, and 11:00 A.M. and 2:30 P.M. Sunday. In October, Tuesday excursions at 10:00 and 11:00 A.M. are added to this schedule, plus there are Halloween trains at 7:30 P.M. the last three Friday and Saturday nights. Runs rain or shine. Tickets sold first come, first served. Reservations taken only for groups of 15 or more. Adults $$$, children ages 3–12 $$.

This is really four attractions in one. Your ticket price includes admission to the Stearns Museum, with its exhibits about the town and the coal mining heritage of the area. Then you board an open-air train and ride to two layover stops. Blue Heron Mining Camp includes a coal tipple and innovative exhibits featuring oral histories of residents telling the story of life in the camp. Barthell Mining Camp is a rebuilt camp with shops, an antique car collection, and displays of artifacts in a village setting. You'll spend about forty-five to ninety minutes at each camp, then get back on the train to return to Stearns. With younger children in particular, keep in mind that it all takes three to four hours, depending on which departure time you choose. There are rest rooms and food at the two mining camps (as well as overnight lodging at Barthell), but no rest rooms on the train (about 30 minutes each way). Get there early to make sure you get a ticket, especially on Saturdays in October.

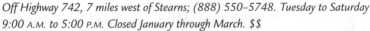

Spooky Railway The Big South Fork Scenic Railway offers Haunted Rides the last three weekends in October. These evening excursions depart Friday and Saturday at 7:00 P.M. and take you to Barthell Mining Camp for a Haunted House, storytelling, face painting, and other activities. Reservations (advised) are taken beginning October 1; call (800) GO-ALONG.

 ### BARTHELL MINING CAMP (all ages)
 Off Highway 742, 7 miles west of Stearns; (888) 550–5748. Tuesday to Saturday 9:00 A.M. to 5:00 P.M. Closed January through March. $$

This rebuilt mining camp is a stop on the Big South Fork Scenic Railway excursion, but you can also drive to it. However you get there, you'll enjoy meeting the Kogers, who spent five years rebuilding the mining camp and now offer guided tours as well as overnight lodging. The tour includes the Old Doctor's Office, a 1920s barber shop, bath house, one-room school, church, and mine openings. The Motor House includes a collection of 1909–1934 cars and trucks as well as mining equipment. The gift shops have some cute and inexpensive souvenirs for children, including handmade wooden train whistles and toys and corn husk flowers. You can get a sandwich or snack at the Coal Miner's Daughter restaurant.

 ### BLUE HERON MINING CAMP (all ages)
KY 742, off US 27, 9 miles southwest of Stearns; (606) 376–3008. Open daily 8:00 A.M. to 5:00 P.M. **Free.**

This is one of the stops on the Big South Fork Scenic Railway, or you can drive to it. A thriving mining camp from the late 1930s through the early 1960s, this camp now lives on as one of Kentucky's most intriguingly designed historic attractions. Unusual open-air "ghost structures" and life-size photographic figures suggest the buildings important in camp life—church, school, store, and homes—and, at the push of a button, you can hear the real voices of people who lived at Blue Heron tell their stories. Children may not have the patience to listen to all the recordings, but they will find the atmosphere interesting and enjoyable. The coal tipple and mine openings remain and are part of the tour. A hiking trail leads to a scenic overlook. In summer months, there's a concession stand.

***B*ig South Fork** The Barthell and Blue Heron Mining Camps are part of a 125,000-acre national recreational area that stretches into Tennessee, offering abundant hiking, sightseeing, and canoeing/rafting opportunities. The area has beautiful gorges, rock ledges, and waterfalls. The National Park Service Visitor Center in Stearns (Highway 92) is a good place to get a map, advice, and answers to any questions (606-376-5073). It's open daily April through October from 9:00 A.M. to 5:30 P.M.; hours vary from November through March.

 MCCREARY COUNTY MUSEUM AT STEARNS (all ages)
Stearns; (606) 376–5730. Open mid-April through October, Tuesday to Sunday 9:00 A.M. to 5:00 P.M. $

Learn about the area's coal-mining and other history in this museum located in the former Stearns Coal and Lumber office building near the train depot.

Where to Eat

Stearns Restaurant, *KY 1651, 14 Henderson Street, Stearns 42647, next to the depot; (606) 376–5354.* Good daily specials with vegetables, great cornbread, sandwiches, and homemade pies. Friendly service. Try a Coal Miner's Special (beans and cornbread). $

Where to Stay

Barthell Mining Camp, *off Highway 742, 7 miles west of Stearns; (888) 550–5748.* Secluded one- and two-bedroom cabins with full baths and kitchens, porch swings; linens supplied. Restaurant at the camp. Last night free if you stay a week. $$$–$$$$

Holiday Inn Express, *1116 Highway 27, Whitley City 42653; (606) 376–3780.* Outdoor pool, continental breakfast, laundry. $

A Day Family Adventure

A **Day Family Adventure** When we got down to Yahoo Falls, my daughter and I had a good laugh, wondering how many other people get here and say, "That's *it?*" Here's the story: Yahoo Falls is promoted as the state's tallest waterfall (about 130 feet), but it's a very thin stream of water. In summer (the time of our visit), it may even dry up completely. The good thing about Yahoo Falls is that it's very accessible—you can drive to the head of a ½-mile or so trail, and there are even rest rooms in the parking area. (For easier hiking, take the left part of the loop down—there are metal steps—and you'll hike up the easier, more gradual part of the loop.) Even though the falls was less than overwhelming—especially after seeing Cumberland Falls—we enjoyed the rock formations, the forest—and the toads—we saw along the way.

Jamestown/Russell Springs

LAKE CUMBERLAND STATE RESORT PARK (all ages)

5465 State Park Road, off US 27, Jamestown 42629; information: (270) 343–3111, reservations: (800) 325–1709. Open year-round. Many activities Free.

Both water lovers and landlubbers will find plenty to do at this 3,117-acre park. Rent a fishing boat and go after bass and crappie in one of the state's largest lakes, or rent a pontoon boat and spend the day just tooling around on the water. Ages six and up can take a trail ride from the park's horse stables. And then there's swimming (an outdoor pool open to day visitors as well as an indoor pool for lodge guests), miniature golf, a nine-hole regulation course, tennis, picnicking, and playgrounds.

Lake Cumberland

L **ake Cumberland** No wonder this is one of Kentucky's most popular fishing and boating spots. This lake is huge—more than 50,000 acres with 1,200 miles of shoreline extending into seven counties. The lake was created by the construction of a dam across the Cumberland River in 1950. Be sure to stop at the Wolf Creek Dam Powerhouse and Overlook off US 127 south.

Home Afloat

Home Afloat You can rent just about any kind of boat from pontoon to a luxurious floating home-away-from-home on Lake Cumberland. The lake's eleven marinas are the place to rent boats; some also feature restaurants, camping areas, and cabins for rent. Eight of the eleven marinas rent houseboats for floating vacations, including the state dock at Lake Cumberland State Resort Park (888–782–8336). Houseboat rental isn't cheap—you can pay up to $5,200 a week or so for the biggest, fanciest ones (and you still have to bring your own towels). For a "standard luxury" houseboat, expect to pay a couple of thousand dollars a week in summer, less in spring and fall. Weekend rentals are also available. Pontoon and fishing boats can be rented by the hour or by the day. For a listing of places that rent houseboats on Lake Cumberland and other Kentucky lakes, visit www.houseboat.net/ky.htm.

WOLF CREEK NATIONAL FISH HATCHERY (all ages)

50 Kendall Road, off US 127, 13 miles south of Wolf Creek Dam, Jamestown 42629; (270) 343–3797. Open daily from 7:00 A.M. to 3:30 P.M. **Free**.

This nursery for rainbow and brown trout definitely has kid appeal. For starters, there are seemingly millions of fish—from tiny, speck-sized ones inside to the growing youngsters getting exercise in the "raceways" outside. For a nickel you can buy fish food (bring a cup since it's more than you can hold in your hand) and feed the outdoor babies. The tanks are low enough so that kids can get a good view. There's fishing for all ages in the nearby fishing stream (over sixteen must have fishing license and trout stamp), and in early June there's a special fishing derby for youngsters with prizes in various age categories and a special kiddie fishing pool for ages one to four.

Where to Eat

Jamestown Cafe, *105 Jefferson Street, Jamestown 42629; (270) 343–5550.* Varied menu, music on weekend evenings. $

Lake Cumberland State Resort Park, *5465 State Park Road, off US 27, Jamestown 42629; (270) 343–3111.* Lodge dining room overlooks lake; regional specialties, buffet. Kids' menu. $

Little Chop Shop, *US 127 and Lakeway Drive, Russell Springs 42629; (270) 866–7711.* All kinds of smoked food, pork chops, steaks, hot dogs, and chicken. Homemade fudge. Carryout and picnic tables only. $

The Porch, *US 127 south of Highway 80, Russell Springs 42629; (270) 866–8988.* Home cooking, fresh salads, homemade pies (even the crust). $

Where to Stay

KOA Campground, *1440 Highway 1383, Russell Springs 42642; (270) 866–5616.* Open April through October. Primitive and full hookup sites. Snack bar, restaurant, tennis court, game room, miniature golf, bait store, and grocery. $

Lake Cumberland State Resort Park, *5465 State Park Road, off US 27, Jamestown 42629; information: (270) 343–3111; reservations: (800) 325–1709.* Two lodges ($-$$; the older, Pumpkin Lodge, offers more privacy), cottages ($$-$$$), and April through early November, primitive and full hookup camping ($).

Pinehurst Lodge, *1115 West Cumberland Avenue, Jamestown 42629; (877) 855–4143 or (270) 343–4143.* Z-shaped pool, family units with multiple beds as well as units with kitchens. Game room, basketball court. May require two-night minimum weekends in summer. $-$$

 icensed to Catch Remember: Anglers over age sixteen need a state fishing license ($$$), available at most lakes and bait shops. The one exception is the first weekend in June, Free Fishing Days in Kentucky.

Burkesville

 DALE HOLLOW LAKE STATE RESORT PARK (all ages)
6371 State Park Road (KY 1206 off KY 449 off KY 90), Burkesville 42717; information: (270) 433-7431, reservations: (800) 325-2282. Open year-round. Many activities **Free.**

Another popular spot for fishing (the lake is famous for smallmouth bass), this state park features full-service amenities for day or longer visitors. Along with hiking trails, there are bike and horse trails (but no stables or bike rentals). Boat rentals are available.

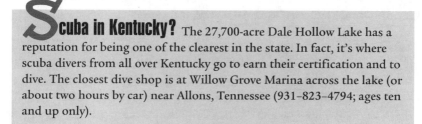 **cuba in Kentucky?** The 27,700-acre Dale Hollow Lake has a reputation for being one of the clearest in the state. In fact, it's where scuba divers from all over Kentucky go to earn their certification and to dive. The closest dive shop is at Willow Grove Marina across the lake (or about two hours by car) near Allons, Tennessee (931-823-4794; ages ten and up only).

Where to Eat

Dale Hollow Lake State Resort Park, *6371 State Park Road (KY 1206 off KY 449 off KY 90), Burkesville 42717; (270) 433–7431.* Dining room with scenic view. Kentucky specialties and kids' menu. $

Mike's Landing, *3498 Sulphur Creek Road, Sulphur Creek Resort, Burkesville 42717; (270) 433–7272.* Open April through October. Steaks, buffets, carry-out. Casual atmosphere. $

Where to Stay

Dale Hollow Lake State Resort Park, *6371 State Park Road (KY 1206 off KY 449 off KY 90), Burkesville 42717; information: (270) 433–7431, reservations:* *(800) 325–2282.* Lodge rooms ($–$$), year-round campground with showers ($), and grocery.

Amazing Kentucky Fact The first oil well in America was located near Burkesville (off KY 61 on Renox Creek).

Campbellsville

GREEN RIVER LAKE STATE PARK (all ages)
179 Park Office Road, KY 1061, off KY 55, Campbellsville 42718; (270) 465–8255. Open year-round. Many activities 𝕱𝕣𝕖𝕖.

A little bit more laid back than Lake Cumberland (but still crowded on a summer weekend), this 8,200-acre lake is a popular day and camping destination. The park includes a sandy beach on the lake, picnic and playground areas, miniature golf, and trails for horseback riding and biking (no rentals), as well as hiking.

U.S. ARMY CORPS OF ENGINEERS VISITOR CENTER/ATKINSON-GRIFFIN HOUSE MUSEUM (all ages)

Off KY 55; (270) 465–4463. 𝕱𝕣𝕖𝕖.

This is a good place to stop for information about the lake, as well as trail brochures and a Battle of Tebbs Bend Civil War driving tour. The visitor center also has exhibits, and you can pick up the keys to see the Atkinson-Griffin House Museum a short walk away. This 1840 log cabin served as a hospital and displays Civil War artifacts.

Where to Stay

Best Western Campbellsville Lodge, *1400 East Broadway, Campbellsville 42718; (270) 465-7001 or (800) 770-0430.* Outdoor pool. $$

Emerald Isle Marina and Resort, *Highway 372, Campbellsville 42719; (888) 815-2000 or (270) 465-3412.* Three-bedroom condominiums, restaurant, boat rentals. $$$$

Green River Lake State Park Campground, *179 Park Office Road, KY 1061, off KY 55, Campbellsville 42718; (270) 465-8255.* Year-round campground; both primitive and full hookups with boat ramp, marina, seasonal laundry, and grocery. $

For More Information

Taylor County Tourist Commission, *107 West Broadway, Campbellsville 42719; (270) 465-3786 or (800) 738-4719.*

Greensburg

GREENSBURG BOTTLING COMPANY (ages 10 and up)

108 South Depot Street, Greensburg 42743; (270) 932-5061, www.double colaski.com. Tours offered Monday to Friday from 8:00 to 3:00 P.M. **Free.**

Ever heard of Double Cola, Ski, or Cherry Ski? Unless you're from this part of Kentucky (or are fans of the music group Kentucky Headhunters, which mentioned Ski in a song), you probably haven't. These locally made soft drinks are sold only in about twenty south-central Kentucky counties (but are shipped to former south-central Kentuckians worldwide). And they're made only at this small, family-owned bottling operation that started in 1926. Come by for a tour to see the bottling process (it's one of only a couple of bottlers in Kentucky to still use returnable bottles), and try a free soft drink at the end to judge for yourself if Double Cola, as fans contend, is the best cola in the world.

Fancy Footwork When you're in Greensburg, try taking the 445-foot footbridge that leads from Courthouse Square to surrounding neighborhoods. Pop into the courthouse too—it's the oldest west of the Alleghenies.

For More Information

Greensburg/Green County Chamber of Commerce, *105 West Hod-* *genville Avenue, Greensburg 42743; (270) 932–4298, www.greensburgky.com.*

Glasgow Area

BARREN RIVER STATE RESORT PARK (all ages)

1149 State Park Road, Lucas 42156 (off US 31 E, 12 miles southwest of Glasgow); information: (270) 646–2151, reservations: (800) 325–0057. Open year-round. Many activities **Free**.

Another popular lake with Kentucky anglers, Barren River is known for its bass, bluegill, channel cats, and crappie. You can rent fishing boats, pontoon sightseeing boats, and houseboats for use on the 10,000 acres of water. On-land activities include trail rides (ages six and up), a beach for swimming (the pool is for lodge and cottage guests only), basketball and tennis courts, an eighteen-hole golf course, picnic areas, and playgrounds. There are 4 miles of nature trails.

*S*cotland in Kentucky Glasgow, Kentucky, was named after the city in Scotland, and every year, it celebrates Scottish heritage with a huge gathering of clans. The Glasgow Highland Games, held the weekend after Memorial Day, features bagpipe and harp competitions, concerts, and highland dancing, plus all kinds of athletic competitions (caber throwing, anyone?). There are numerous activities for children, including athletic competitions scaled to ages four to sixteen. Many events take place in Barren River State Resort Park; call (270) 651–3141, or visit www.glasgowhighlandgames.com for more information.

Where to Eat

Barren River State Resort Park, *1149 State Park Road, Lucas 42156 (off US 31 E, 12 miles southwest of Glasgow);* *(270) 646–2151.* Lodge dining room offers scenic views, Kentucky specialties, and children's menu. $

Where to Stay

Barren River State Resort Park, *1149 State Park Road, Lucas 42156 (off US 31 E, 12 miles southwest of Glasgow); information: (270) 646-2151, reservations: (800) 325-0057.* Lodge overlooks lake. Lodge rooms ($-$$), cottages ($$$$), campground open April through October with primitive and full hookup sites, showers ($).

Mammoth Cave Area (Cave City/Horse Cave/Brownsville)

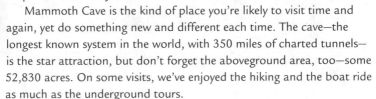

MAMMOTH CAVE NATIONAL PARK (all ages)
KY 70 from I-65, exit 48, or South Entrance Road from I-65, exit 53; follow signs. P.O. Box 7, Mammoth Cave 42250; information: (270) 758-2328, tour reservations (recommended): (800) 967-2283, reservations.nps.gov. Open daily except Christmas. Many activities Free*; cave tour admission varies $-$$$.*

Mammoth Cave is the kind of place you're likely to visit time and again, yet do something new and different each time. The cave—the longest known system in the world, with 350 miles of charted tunnels—is the star attraction, but don't forget the aboveground area, too—some 52,830 acres. On some visits, we've enjoyed the hiking and the boat ride as much as the underground tours.

Cave Tours. Tours ranging from one and a quarter to six and a half hours are offered, with up to forty cave tours per day in the busiest summer months. The Travertine is recommended for preschoolers (also a good option if the family group includes older folks who can't walk long distances). Part of the time is spent on a bus going over to the entrance. This tour has the fewest steps of any of the tours, but you can still see some interesting cave features. With older children who aren't afraid of heights (and can walk for two hours), you can take the Historic Tour, which includes areas used by Native Americans thousands of years ago, as well as saltpeter-mining areas; and the Frozen Niagara, an expanded Travertine Tour route, on which you see huge domes and many formations. The Trog Tour is a special tour for children eight to twelve (proof of age required) in which youngsters get to don helmets and lights and do some crawling as well as walking (parents go along for the first fifteen minutes of the two-and-a-half-hour adventure). Families with children ten to fifteen might also enjoy the Introduction to

Caving, a more adventurous three-and-a-half-hour excursion that includes crawling, climbing, and visits to passages not on the regular tour routes. Whatever tour you take, be sure children (and you) are wearing sturdy shoes, and take sweaters or jackets along; the temperature is in the 50s and 60s. Strollers are not allowed, and you're urged to use caution if you carry your child, since some ceiling areas of the cave are very low. In the summer season, tours sell out, so get advance tickets to be sure of getting the tour of your choice.

Trails. There are numerous hiking trails, including short and easy woodland trails that families can walk at a leisurely pace. The Heritage Trail is the easiest; it's paved, and you can take a stroller. More challenging trails are available for older hikers.

Mammoth Amusements Driving to Mammoth Cave from

the interstates is a little like running a gauntlet: If you stopped at every place that tempted your children, you'd never get there. Suffice to say that before or after your cave tour you'll find something to amuse the whole family. Some of the options:

- **Guntown Mountain,** Highway 70 at I-65, Cave City 42127; (270) 773-3530, GuntownMountain.com. Take the skylift or shuttle bus up to Wild West town with rides, games, shows, haunted house, and petting zoo. All-day pass available.

- **Kentucky Action Park/Jesse James Riding Stables,** 3057 Mammoth Cave Road, Cave City 42127; (800) 798-0560 or (270) 773-2560, www. mammothcave.com/kyaction.htm. The action here includes alpine slide, go-carts, bumper cars, miniature golf, old-time photos, and trail rides.

- **Hillbilly Hound Fun Park,** I-65, exit 53, Cave City; (270) 773-4644. Go-carts, mini golf, game room, with a cartoon theme.

- **Mammoth Cave Wax Museum,** I-65, exit 53, Cave City; (270) 773-3010. From Abe Lincoln to Marilyn Monroe, wax figures.

- **Mammoth Cave Wildlife Museum,** I-65, exit 53, Cave City; (270) 773-2255. Preserved animals from around the world.

- **Big Mike's Mystery House,** 566 Old Mammoth Cave Road, Cave City 42127; (270) 773-5144. Mirror and gravity illusions; gift shop includes many rocks and minerals.

Miss Green River II. We like to end the day with this leisurely and scenic boat ride; various departures daily April through October (adults $$, children $). You'll see deer and other animals and hear enjoyable stories about the area. This mellows everyone out for the long drive home. (270) 758-2243.

A **Day Family Adventure** Being the kind of traveler who likes to jump in the car on the spur of the moment and decide routes and lodging along the way, I've had to make some adjustments as a traveling parent. (It's no fun trying to find a hotel room with a screaming toddler—or cranky older child—in the car.) But old habits are hard to break. Pooh-poohing all the advice about advance reservations for Mammoth Cave tours in busy summer months, we headed out and arrived at the park mid-morning. I began to sweat as I saw all the SOLD OUT signs. I think we got the last four tickets for the last tour of the day. Next time I'll make reservations and avoid "Mammoth" anxiety!

KENTUCKY DOWN UNDER (all ages)
At I-65, exit 58, Horse Cave; (800) 762-2869, www.kdu.com. Open daily April through October from 8:00 A.M. to 5:00 P.M., November through March from 9:00 A.M. to 4:00 P.M. Closed Thanksgiving Day, Christmas Day, and New Year's Day. Adults $$$, children 5-11 $$. Children under 5 **Free**.

If you only have time to visit a few places in south-central Kentucky, make this Australian-themed animal attraction a priority. It's very well done and mixes education with fun. It begins with an Outback Walkabout, an area where children can see kangaroos and emus. In the Walk-in Flight Cave, brightly colored lorikeets will land on your head and eat from your hands. The tour also includes interesting presentations about aboriginal culture and the ecology of sheep farming. A forty-five-minute cave tour is included in the admission price, but the animal areas are the real highlight. There's also an Outback Cafe, open in summer, and a gift shop with a good selection of books for children about caving, Australia, and animals.

AMERICAN CAVE MUSEUM/HIDDEN RIVER CAVE (ages 4 and up)
119 East Main Street, Horse Cave; (270) 786-1466, www.cavern.org. Open daily year-round from 9:00 A.M. to 5:00 P.M. Monday through Friday; open until 7:00 P.M. on weekends. $$

Another attraction that effectively mixes education and fun, the museum combines exhibits about caves, karst, and groundwater with tours of Hidden River Cave. The tours emphasize the cave's remarkable story: Not too long ago, Hidden Cave was anything but hidden. All you had to do was follow your nose! Pollution made the cave smell so bad that it affected the entire downtown area. A dedicated group of citizens worked to reclaim the cave, and now it's a model of cave recovery and management.

Caves and More Caves Mammoth and Lost River aren't the only caves in the area. Here are some others open for touring:

- **Crystal Onyx Cave,** I-65, exit 53, at Cave City; (270) 773–2359. One-hour tours year-round. Includes many crystalline draperies and formations and working archeological site. $$

- **Onyx Cave,** I-65, exit 53, at Cave City; (270) 773–3530. Onyx waterfall and other formations. $$

- **Diamond Caverns,** Mammoth Cave Parkway, I-65, exit 48; (270) 749–2233 or www.diamondcaverns.com. Numerous formations and drapery deposits. $$

WIGWAM VILLAGE 2 (all ages)
601 North Dixie Highway (US 31W), Cave City 42127; (270) 773-3381. Open daily March through November.

Here you can "sleep in a wigwam," but even if you don't plan to stay here, drive by to see this wonderful world-famous motel. This complex of concrete teepees was built in the 1930s, before interstates with chain lodgings and restaurants homogenized American travel. At one time there were seven Wigwam Villages in the South and West; this is one of only two remaining. It's listed on the National Register of Historic Places. There's a huge gift shop.

Where to Eat

Mammoth Cave Hotel, *located in the national park; (270) 758–2225.* Restaurant and coffee shop serving breakfast, lunch, and dinner. Varied menu. $

Where to Stay

Mammoth Cave Hotel, *located in the national park; (270) 758–2225.* Motel rooms and cottages, tennis courts, laundry. $$

Mammoth Cave National Park Campground, *Four locations in park; make reservations through reservations.nps. gov or call (800) 365–CAMP.* No hookups. $

Wigwam Village 2, *601 North Dixie Highway (31W), Cave City 42127; (270) 773–3381.* Open March through November. Concrete teepees with 1930s cane and hickory furnishings. Center playground. $

For More Information

Edmonson County Tourism Commission, *P.O. Box 628, Brownsville 42210; (800) 624–8687, www.cavesand lakes.com.*

National Park Service, *www.nps. gov/maca/.*

Bowling Green

THE NATIONAL CORVETTE MUSEUM (all ages)

350 Corvette Drive (at I-65, exit 28), Bowling Green 42102; (270) 781-7973 or (800) 53–VETTE, www.corvettemuseum.com. Open daily from 8:00 A.M. to 5:00 P.M. except Thanksgiving Day, December 24, and December 25. Adults $$, children 6–16 $. Children under 5 **Free***. Family rate available.*

If you're driving on I-65, somebody in the car is likely to spot this museum and ask "What's that?" The building design is really unusual—a bright yellow cone-shaped structure with a red spire. Inside you'll find classic Corvettes going back to '53—the first year they were made—plus exhibits about how they're designed and experimental models—68,000 square feet in all.

CORVETTE ASSEMBLY PLANT TOURS (ages 7 and up)

At I-65, exit 28, adjacent to The National Corvette Museum; (270) 745-8419. Tours at 9:00 A.M. and 1:00 P.M. Monday to Friday except during plant shutdown periods. **Free***.*

Corvettes have been made in Bowling Green since 1981, and every Corvette made comes from this modern plant. The walking tour lasts about an hour and includes body weld and assembly areas as well as the "First Start" and line drive-off. If you've never been inside a modern automaking plant, it's quite an experience, from the robotic welders to the speed and efficiency with which vehicles come together. Children must be at least seven to take the tour. You must wear closed-toe shoes, and no cameras, purses, or backpacks are allowed. Plant shutdown times (no tours) vary but usually include the last week in December, the Friday and Monday of Labor Day weekend, and other holidays. Check the phone number for tour status, since business factors can also affect tours; reservations are for groups only.

 BARREN RIVER IMAGINATIVE MUSEUM OF SCIENCE (all ages)

1229 Center Street, Bowling Green 42101; (270) 843–9779. Open Thursday to Saturday from 10:00 A.M. to 3:00 P.M., Sunday from 1:00 to 4:00 P.M. $

Participation is the rule, not the exception, at this museum, where children can try all kinds of activities that illustrate principles of science— from mirror fun to generating electricity by pedaling a bicycle. The information arranged into "What to Do" and "What's Going On" makes getting the point easy.

More Unusual Buildings The National Corvette Museum
isn't the only unusual-looking building in south-central Kentucky. Check out the following:

- **John B. Begley Chapel,** on the Lindsey Wilson College campus in Columbia. (270) 384–8400. This interesting double-domed chapel was designed by one of the world's foremost chapel architects, E. Fay Jones. Other attractions in Columbia include the restored log home of Kentucky author Janice Holt Giles and a local historical museum in the 1820s Trabue-Russell House. Columbia is between Lake Cumberland and Green River Lake via the Louie B. Nunn Parkway or KY 55. (270) 384–6020.

- **Octagonal Hall,** 6040 Bowling Green Road, Franklin. This is an eight-sided brick building. While in Franklin, also learn about local African-American history at the African-American Heritage Center, 501 Jefferson Street, and see life-size drawings made on the walls of the Old Jail by Civil War soldiers. (270) 586–3040.

*B*ookworms Take Note! At the annual Southern Kentucky Festival of Books in Bowling Green, children (and adults) can meet authors and celebrate the fun of reading. Children's authors who have attended in the past include R. L. Stine, who writes the popular *Goose-bumps* horror series. There are many children's activities during the two-day event, including music and drama and hands-on creative fun, along with author signings. It's held in mid-April at the Sloan Convention Center, and admission is free. Call (270) 745–5263, or visit www.soky bookfest.com for the latest news about which authors are coming.

KENTUCKY MUSEUM (ages 5 and up)

Kentucky Building, Western Kentucky University, Bowling Green; (270) 745–2592. Open Tuesday to Saturday from 9:30 A.M. to 4:30 P.M., Sunday from 1:00 to 4:00 P.M. $

What was it like to be a child in the mid-1800s? What toys would you have played with? What kinds of clothes would you have worn? What would have been expected of you? Your children can learn the answers at this museum's "Growing Up Victorian" display, just one of the fascinating exhibits at this gem of a museum tucked away on the Western Kentucky University campus. Budding archaeologists can see arrowheads and other early artifacts at "Taking the Mystery Out of Pre-history." Other exhibits relate to early downtown Bowling Green (fun to compare with a modern-day walk) and Kentucky guitar maker Hascal Haile. Next to the main museum building is the Felts House, an authentic 1815 cabin that was moved to the campus and contains reproduction early-nineteenth-century tools and household items. Ask about the family activities guide for the Victorian exhibit, and check out the teachers' guides and other books in the gift store.

LOST RIVER CAVE AND VALLEY (all ages)

2818 Nashville Road, Bowling Green 42101; (866) 274-CAVE or (270) 393–0077, www.lostrivercave.com. Tour offered daily year-round; schedule varies, so call for times. Adults $$, children 6–17 $. Children under 5 **Free**.

Now, here's something different and fun: a boat cave tour. Some time ago, Mammoth Cave used to offer them, but it hasn't for years (in fact, the boats used at Mammoth are now here at Lost River). A forty-five-minute tour begins with a twenty-minute guided walk along the river and the twenty-five-minute boat tour inside this cave. The cave has a huge opening and short but deep river. It was used by Native Americans 11,000 years ago and may have been a hiding place for the Jesse James gang; it even has a nightclub that was popular from the 1930s through the 1960s (it's been recently renovated). You're also welcome to walk the easy trails near the cave opening, which includes "Blue Holes," where the river rises to the surface before becoming "lost" again under the city of Bowling Green.

$tar Watch While on the Western Kentucky University campus, see if any shows are scheduled at the college's Hardin Planetarium. **Free**.

BEECH BEND RACEWAY PARK (all ages)

798 Beech Bend Road, Bowling Green 42101; (270) 781-7634, www.beech bend.com. Drag races March through October, Saturday at 5:00 P.M., Sunday at 11:00 A.M. Adults $$. Children under 12 **Free** *with adult. Amusement park and water park open weekends May and September, daily Memorial Day through Labor Day, from 10:00 A.M. to 6:00 P.M. Admission $ includes water park; pay for individual rides.*

Older children may enjoy the drag races, but the main attraction for families here is the amusement park, which includes a large swimming pool and water slides, a Looping Star rollercoaster and dozens of other rides for kiddies and older, and arcade games. There's an on-site campground.

RACE WORLD (ages 6 and up)

255 Cumberland Trace (I-65, exit 22), Bowling Green 42101; (270) 781-RACE. Open daily March through October, noon to midnight. Open Friday to Sunday, November and December, weather permitting, from noon to 11:00 P.M. Closed when it rains. Pay by attraction.

Older children and adults can get into racing action themselves at this park, which has two tracks, racing displays, and an arcade. One track is for ages sixteen and over only. A smaller "Naskart" track is for younger children; they must be 53 inches tall to

$ace Days Bowling Green is race car crazy year-round but especially so in April, when the Junior Achievement Mini Corvette Challenge is held. Mini-Corvettes race Grand Prix–style on the streets of downtown. (270) 782-0280.

compete in the nightly races. Displays include a car belonging to NASCAR great Dale Earnhardt. There's food on site and a seasonal Halloween House geared toward older children, teens, and adults.

 RIVERVIEW AT HOBSON'S BEND (ages 6 and up)
End of Main Street at Hobson Grove Park, Bowling Green 42101; (270) 843-5565. Open Tuesday to Saturday from 10:00 A.M. to 4:00 P.M., Sunday from 1:00 to 4:00 P.M. $; children under 6 **Free***.*

Historic house fans will enjoy seeing this elegant Italianate building and learning about the Hobson family, who owned it from 1857 to 1952. Particularly interesting are the interpretive tours given the third Saturday of each month at 10:00 A.M. on various topics ranging from holiday celebrations to servant life. The house is located in a park, so if everybody isn't into old houses, one parent can entertain them outside while the other parent tours.

Other Things to See and Do

Capitol Arts Center *(877) 694–ARTS*

Civil War Driving Tour *(800) 326–7465*

Flea Land of Bowling Green, *weekends indoor/outdoor; (270) 843–1978*

Fountain Square Park *downtown Bowling Green; (800) 326–7465*

Phoenix Theatre *(270) 781–6233*

Russell Sims Aquatic Center, *pool, slides and play areas; (270) 393–3271*

Where to Eat

Brickyard Cafe, *1026 Chestnut Street, Bowling Green 42101; (270) 843–6431.* Brick-oven pizza and pastas, homemade breads, and desserts. Located in historic house, but casual. Kids will love the Bambino Pizza for lunch. Lunch and dinner. $

Mariah's, *801 State Street, Bowling Green 42101; (270) 842–6878.* Casual atmosphere in a restored historic house. Steaks, sandwiches, seafood. $$

The Parakeet and The Fletcher House, *1129 College Street, Bowling Green 42101; (270) 781–1538.* Two restaurants in one. Best for families is The Parakeet on the first floor, which is casual with outdoor dining; $$. (The Fletcher House upstairs offers elegant dining.) $-$$$

Teresa's Restaurant, *509 Gordon Avenue, Bowling Green 42101; (270) 782–6540.* Home cooking in a friendly atmosphere. Breakfast and lunch only. $

West Kentucky Barbecue, *430 US 31W Bypass, Bowling Green 42101; (270) 781–5719.* Closed Sunday and Monday. Good barbecued ribs, chicken, pork, and mutton with sides and desserts. $

Where to Stay

Beech Bend Campground, *798 Beech Bend Road, Bowling Green 42101; (270) 781-7634.* Open year-round. Full hookups (including some sites with modem hookups), bathhouses. $

Bowling Green KOA, *1960 Three Springs Road, Bowling Green 42101; (270) 843–1919.* Pool, game room playground. $

Courtyard by Marriott, *1010 Wilkenson Trace, Bowling Green 42101; (270) 783-8569.* Indoor pool. $$

Hampton Inn, *233 Three Springs Road, Bowling Green 42101; (800) HAMPTON.* Outdoor pool, continental breakfast. $$

University Plaza Hotel, *1021 Wilkenson Trace, Bowling Green 42101; (800) 801–1777.* High-rise hotel, indoor pool, restaurant. $$$–$$$$

For More Information

Bowling Green Area Convention and Visitors Bureau, *352 Three Springs Road, Bowling Green 42101; (800) 326–7465 or (270) 782–0800.*

Amazing Kentucky Fact South-central Kentucky gave America cake and coffee: Duncan Hines was from Bowling Green (in June, at the Duncan Hines Festival, the town bakes a 950-pound brownie in his honor), and Joel Owsley Creek of Burkesville developed Maxwell House coffee.

Annual Events

Native American Weekend, late January, Lake Cumberland State Resort Park, Jamestown; (270) 343-3111

Eagle Watch, late January, Dale Hollow State Resort Park; (800) 255–PARK

Family Fishing Fun Weekend, late March, Dale Hollow State Resort Park; (800) 255–PARK

Southern Kentucky Festival of Books, late April (during National Library Week), Bowling Green; (270) 745-5263 or www.sokybookfest.org

Springfest, late April, Mammoth Cave National Park; (270) 758-2254

Junior Achievement Mini Corvette Challenge, late April, Bowling Green; (270) 782-0280

Mountain Laurel Festival, late May, Pine Mountain State Resort Park; (606) 337-3066

Glasgow Highland Games, late May/early June, Glasgow; (270) 651-3141

Catch a Rainbow Kids Fishing Derby, early June, Wolf Creek National Fish Hatchery, Jamestown; (270) 866-4333

Wayne County Fair, late June/early July, Monticello; (606) 348-3064

Lakefest, early July, Jamestown; (270) 343-4594

Old Joe Clark Bluegrass Festival, early July, Renfro Valley; (800) 252-6685

Laurel County Fair, mid-July, London; (800) 348-0095

Master Musicians Festival, mid-July, Somerset; (606) 678-2225

Russell County Fair, late July, Russell Springs (near Jamestown); (270) 343-3191

Cave City's Floyd Collins Good Old Days, second week of August, Cave City; (800) 346-8908

NIBROC Festival, mid-August, Corbin; (606) 528-2163

Monroe County Watermelon Festival, early September, Tompkinsville; (270) 487-5504

Cow Days, late September, Greensburg; (270) 932-4298

Cumberland Mountain Fall Festival and Air Show, late September/early October, Middlesboro; (606) 246-2482

Casey County Apple Festival, late September, Liberty; (606) 787-6747

World Chicken Festival, late September, London; (606) 878-6900

Aussie Fest, early October, Kentucky Down Under; (800) 762-2869

Colonial Trade Fair, late September/early October, Cumberland Gap National Historic Park; (606) 248-2817

Cumberland Mountain Fall Festival, early October, Middlesboro; (800) 988-1075

Colorfall, mid-to-late October, Mammoth Cave National Park; (270) 758-2254

Heritage Day at Blue Heron Mining Camp, mid-October, Blue Heron Mining Camp near Stearns; (606) 376-5073

Winter Lights, late November through December, Bowling Green; (270) 782-3660

Christmas Island, late November through December, General Burnside State Resort Park; (800) 642-6287

Western Kentucky

Most people think of water when they think of western Kentucky. Kentucky's largest lakes, Lake Barkley and Kentucky Lake, and the wild area they border, known as the "Land Between the Lakes," are great places to enjoy the great outdoors, from fishing to seeing elk and American bald eagles. There are four state resort parks in the region, three of them along the lakes, as well as dozens of privately operated marinas and resorts. But as vast as the lake region is, it's just the beginning. At area museums, attractions, and events, tap your foot to the sound of bluegrass and blues, learn about Native American heritage, view fine art, and discover the unexpected. This region gets my vote for the most unusual attractions—and in Kentucky, that's an accomplishment! Paintings by a World War II prisoner of war, a giant chain and anchor once stretched across the Mississippi River, an eighteen-statue memorial, a replica of King Arthur's Round Table—you'll find all this and more in western Kentucky. And don't forget to try the region's food specialty: barbecue. One thing is certain: Once you experience western Kentucky, you'll want to come back for more.

Attractions are listed beginning with the southern part of the region, moving west from Bowling Green, then circling northeast to end in Kentucky's third largest city, Owensboro. Travel is a combination of interstates, limited access parkways, and generally good two- to four-lane U.S. highways. *FYI:* This part of the state is in the central time zone. Times listed are local times.

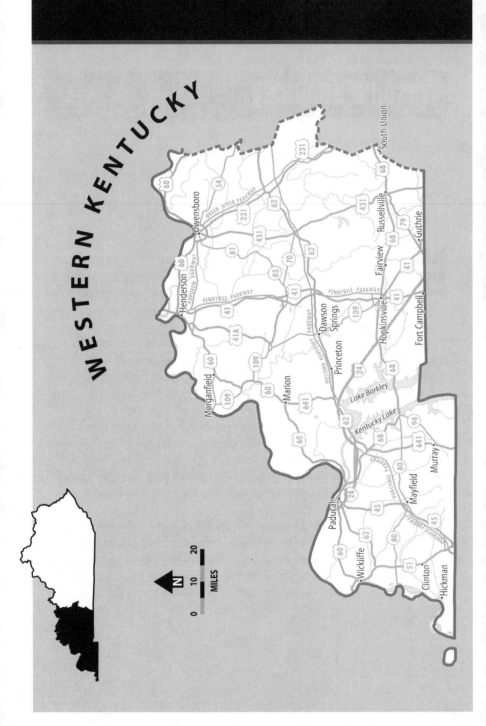

WESTERN KENTUCKY

Teresa's Top Ten
Picks for Western Kentucky

1. Land Between the Lakes National Recreation Area, (800) LBL-7077
2. Trail of Tears Commemorative Park, (270) 886-8033
3. John James Audubon State Park, (270) 826-2247
4. Adsmore, (270) 365-3114
5. Noble Park, Paducah, (800) PADUCAH
6. Columbus Belmont State Park, (270) 677-2327
7. Owensboro Museum of Science and History, (270) 687-2732
8. Pennyroyal Area Museum, (270) 887-4270
9. Round Table Literary Park, (270) 886-3921
10. James D. Veatch Camp Breckinridge Museum and Arts Center, (270) 389-4420

South Union

 SOUTH UNION SHAKER VILLAGE (ages 6 and up)

Off US 68, South Union 42283, 10 miles west of Bowling Green; (800) 811–8379. Open March through November, Monday to Friday from 9:00 A.M. to 4:00 P.M.; open until 5:00 P.M. May through October. $; children under 6 **Free**.

The Shakers, a religious community, lived here from 1807 to 1922. As you tour the 44-room main building and outbuildings, including the smokehouse and milk house, you'll learn about the community's many industries—it sold products ranging from seeds to silk handkerchiefs—as well as Shaker religious beliefs. The numerous artifacts and large collection of furniture are all authentic. An especially enjoyable time for families to visit is during the special events such as the Shaker Summer Nights music entertainment in mid-July, the Civil War encampment in August, Shaker Farm Day in early October, and Christmas at Shakertown, late November through December.

Russellville Area

LAKE MALONE STATE PARK (all ages)

KY 973 off U.S. 431, Dunsmore 42339; (270) 657–2111. Free.

Centered around a 788-acre lake whose shorelines range from sandy beach to 200-foot rock cliffs, Lake Malone State Park is a lovely spot for a day of picnicking and fishing. Boats are available in summer, and you can swim at the beach. Hike along 1.5-mile Laurel Trail.

1817 SADDLE FACTORY MUSEUM (ages 5 and up)

East Fourth Street, Russellville 42276; (270) 772–1560. Tours by appointment. Free.

Exhibits of an early saddle-making operation and other area industries.

DOGWOOD LAKE FUN PARK (all ages)

7777 State Road 973, Russellville; (270) 657–8380. Open Memorial Day through Labor Day, Monday to Friday from 10:00 A.M. to 5:00 P.M., Saturday and Sunday from 9:00 A.M. to 6:00 P.M. $

The swimming pool at this family amusement center near Lake Malone State Park is a sandy-bottom lake (chlorine-treated) with water slides. There are also go-carts and arcade games. A restaurant is open on weekends.

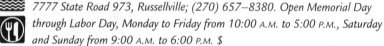

Outlaws While in Russellville, drive by the old Southern Deposit Bank building at the corner of Main and Sixth. This was the scene of the city's most famous crime: On May 20, 1868, Jesse James and his gang dropped by and made an unauthorized withdrawal, getting away with $9,000.

Guthrie

GUTHRIE RAILROAD MUSEUM (all ages}

Third and Kendall Streets (across from courthouse), Guthrie 42234; (270) 483–2683. Open by appointment only. Free.

This red caboose is filled with items of interest to train buffs, from photos and lanterns to model trains (not running) relating to the L&N railroad.

ROBERT PENN WARREN BIRTHPLACE (ages 8 and up)
Third and Cherry Streets, Guthrie 42234; (270) 483–2683. Open Tuesday to Saturday from 11:30 A.M. to 3:30 P.M. **Free**.

You can introduce older children to the works of one of America's greatest literary figures at this modest cottage. Robert Penn Warren was born here in 1905 and went on to become one of America's most distinguished writers and the nation's first poet laureate. His most famous work is probably *All the King's Men*, but he wrote many volumes of beautiful poems, as well as a couple of children's books, *Remember the Alamo* and *Gods of Mount Olympus* (you may be able to find them at your local library). Children will enjoy seeing the childhood pictures and other mementos, and if your child likes to read or listen to you read poetry, pick up one of the volumes of poetry at the house's gift shop.

Where to Eat

American Cafe, *306 North Ewing Street, Guthrie 42234; (270) 483–2288.* Popular local spot for plate lunches and burgers seven days a week. $

Hopkinsville

 PENNYROYAL AREA MUSEUM (ages 4 and up)
217 East Ninth Street, Hopkinsville 42241; (270) 887–4270. Open Monday to Friday from 8:30 A.M. to 4:30 P.M. $

All kinds of interesting things relating to local history are on display in this former post office building. Adults will enjoy the exhibits about the "Tobacco Wars" of 1914 and clairvoyant Edgar Cayce (who lived in Hopkinsville), while youngsters will be drawn to the antique toys, carriage, and 1924 Ford "Skeeter" automobile that was made in Owensboro.

 TRAIL OF TEARS COMMEMORATIVE PARK (all ages)
Pembroke Road (Highway 41), Hopkinsville 42241; (270) 886–8033, www.trailoftears.com. Park open daily year-round. **Free**. *Museum open Monday to Saturday from 10:00 A.M. to 4:00 P.M.; closes at 2:00 P.M. and on Mondays November through March.* **Free** *(donations accepted).*

Kentucky has many sites and activities that celebrate pioneer bravery and the settlement of America, but everyone should also learn the rest of the story. This park commemorating the "Trail of Tears," the forced removal of the Cherokee people from North Carolina to western reservations, is an informative and moving experience. The site is documented as a real encampment spot along the trail as it passed through Kentucky, and two chiefs, Fly Smith and White Path, are buried here. Large statues commemorate the chiefs, and a log cabin Heritage Center contains exhibits from seven Cherokee clans. Ask at the center about the historic driving tour; this is a national route with many stops in western Kentucky.

ribal Gathering The first full week of September, Native American clans gather in Hopkinsville for an **Intertribal PowWow.** Some 16,000 people come each year to participate in and watch drum contents, dances, storytelling, crafts, and other activities celebrating Native American heritage. There are many special activities for children. (270) 886–8033.

ROUND TABLE LITERARY PARK (all ages)

720 North Drive, Hopkinsville Community College campus, Hopkinsville 42240; (270) 886–3921. Open daily. **Free**.

Read the King Arthur legend or watch *The Sword in the Stone,* then bring a picnic and come see a 22,000-pound replica of King Arthur's Round Table. There are a host of other literary-inspired structures in this campus park, including a Greco-Roman-style amphitheater and a statue of the Muse of Tragedy—it's all the legacy of HCC literature professor Francis Thomas and her students.

FERRELL'S SNAPPY SERVICE (all ages)

1001 South Main Street, Hopkinsville 42240; (270) 886–1445. Open Monday to Saturday.

It isn't a visit to Hopkinsville without a stop (or at least driving by to see) this tiny eight-stool diner. Ferrell's has been dishing out burgers and chili since 1936 and is now a Kentucky landmark.

COPPER CANYON RANCH (all ages)

14750 Ovil Road, Hopkinsville 42240 (north of Hopkinsville, off Highway 189); (270) 269–2416. Open by appointment. $$; children under 5 **Free**.

Tim Emery loved westerns when he was a kid, and as an adult he has spent nearly two decades building his own Old West town—complete with livery stable, general store, saloon, a Punch-and-Judy puppet show, and something the Old West didn't have, Hillbilly Putt-Putt. The Emerys stage reenactments of gunslinger and action events such a bank robbery and shootouts for youth groups, but they are also interested in entertaining families and smaller groups. So if your posse is searchin' for Wild West fun, give Tim a call.

Where to Eat

J's on Main, *1004 South Main Street, Hopkinsville 42240; (270) 885–2896.* Chops, steaks, pasta, burgers, and daily specials. $

Horseshoe Steak House, *2112 Fort Campbell Road, Hopkinsville 42240; (270) 886–7734.* Good burgers and steaks. $

Knockum Hill BBQ, *KY 107 south, near Herndon 42236; (270) 271–2947.* A local favorite for barbecued chicken, ribs, and pork. $

Where to Stay

Best Western, *4101 Fort Campbell Boulevard, Hopkinsville 42240; (270) 886–9000. $$*

Fairfield Inn and Suites, *345 Griffin Bell Drive, Hopkinsville 42240; (270) 886–5151. $$*

For More Information

Hopkinsville/Christian County Convention and Visitors Bureau, *2800*

Fort Campbell Road, Hopkinsville 42241; (800) 842–9959

Fort Campbell

DON F. PRATT MEMORIAL MUSEUM (ages 4 and up)

Building 5702, Tennessee Avenue, Fort Campbell Military Base, 18 miles southwest of Hopkinsville via US 41; (270) 798–3215. Open daily from 9:30 A.M. to 4:30 P.M. except Christmas and New Year's Day. Free.

Fort Campbell Military Reservation, which straddles the Kentucky-Tennessee border south of Hopkinsville, has been home to the

"Screaming Eagles" 101st Airborne Division since the base was founded in World War II. The Division was at D-Day and participated in Desert Storm, as well as recent military actions in Afghanistan. Uniforms, World War II memorabilia, photos, and a restored World War II glider plane are among the indoor-outdoor exhibits. Enter the base through Gate 4 off Highway 41A, where you'll be issued a visitor pass.

Fairview

 ### JEFFERSON DAVIS MONUMENT STATE HISTORIC SITE (all ages)

US 68, Fairview 42221 (10 miles east of Hopkinsville); (270) 886–1765. Open daily from 9:00 A.M. to 5:00 P.M. $

The presidents of both the Union and the Confederacy during the Civil War were born in Kentucky. Jefferson Davis, president of the Confederacy, was born near Fairview in 1808. The monument is a 351-foot-tall obelisk that offers a panoramic view of the surrounding countryside (closed for renovation in 2002; scheduled to reopen in 2003). The visitor center features exhibits about Davis and Kentucky during the Civil War.

Dawson Springs

 ### PENNYRILE FOREST STATE RESORT PARK (all ages)

 20781 Pennyrile Lodge Road, Dawson Springs 42408; information: (270) 797–3421, reservations: (800) 325–1711. Open year-round. Many activities Free.

 Surrounded by 15,000 acres of forest, this park offers a lovely setting for a day of picnicking or hiking or a longer stay. Play tennis or miniature golf, rent a pedal boat or rowboat, play regular golf on the nine-hole course, or explore the 5 miles of hiking trails. There are also mountain bike trails outside the park area.

Where to Eat

Pennyrile Forest State Resort Park, *20781 Pennyrile Lodge Road, Dawson Springs 42408; information: (270) 797–* 3421. Dining room in rustic stone lodge feature Kentucky specialties, children's menu. $

Where to Stay

Pennyrile Forest State Resort Park, *20781 Pennyrile Lodge Road, Dawson Springs 42408; information: (270) 797–3421, reservations: (800) 325–1711.* Lodge rooms ($-$$), one- and two-bedroom cottages ($$-$$$$), and seasonal campground (April through October; $).

Princeton

 ADSMORE (ages 6 and up)

304 North Jefferson Street, Princeton 42445; (270) 365–3114. Open Tuesday to Saturday from 11:00 A.M. to 4:00 P.M., Sunday from 1:00 to 4:00 P.M. $

Come "meet" a family from the early 1900s and learn about their daily life at this house museum. Engaging tours change monthly and relate to real events in the life of the Garrett family. Katharine Garrett lived here all her life, and before she died in the 1980s, she set up a foundation so the house could be preserved and operated as a museum. Because there are so many well-preserved items—from furniture to clothing to photographs and letters—tours are set up to offer a very in-depth, detailed, and changing look at life in the household. Each month's tour is set up around a different event—a wedding, a wake, holidays, Katharine's birthday in the spring, and so on—with appropriate items displayed. Children will especially enjoy Katharine's childhood room, with toys and child's clothing and pictures of her dog, Trouble. The Ratliff 1840s Gunshop, housed in a cabin near the mansion, is a tour option that some children will enjoy.

Princeton Picnic Pick up a delicious barbecued ham sandwich at **Newsome's Old Mill Store,** 208 East Main Street, Princeton (270-365-2482), and head a block over to **Big Springs Park** for an enjoyable lunch. Although the store is famous for its country ham, children will like the barbecued ham better because it's tender and sweet. They'll also like the genuine country store atmosphere, with produce on the sidewalk and baskets of goods sitting and hanging inside. The park was a stopping point on the Trail of Tears march.

CALDWELL COUNTY HISTORICAL RAILROAD MUSEUM (all ages)

116 Edwards Street, across from Big Springs Park, downtown Princeton; (270) 365–0582. Open Wednesday to Sunday from 1:00 to 4:00 P.M. **Free***; donations accepted.*

Train enthusiasts will want to stop by to see the model trains, railroad nails, photos, signals, and renovated caboose.

Where to Eat

Majestic House, *208 Highway 62, Princeton 42445; (270) 365–3009.* Daily specials, varied menu. $

Pagliai's Pizza, *Highway 62W, Princeton Plaza, Princeton 42445; (270) 365–2323.* Pizza, spaghetti, Italian sandwiches. $

Where to Stay

Stratton Inn, *534 Marion Road (Western Kentucky Parkway at Highway 91N), Princeton 42445; (270) 365–2828.* Rooms with refrigerators and microwaves available. $

For More Information

Princeton/Caldwell County Chamber of Commerce, *110 West Washing-ton Street, Princeton 42445; (270) 365–5393.*

Lake Barkley/Kentucky Lake Area

There are all kinds of marinas, recreation centers, restaurants, campgrounds, and lodging in the area right around Kentucky's two biggest lakes, Lake Barkley and Kentucky Lake. At the center of the lakes is the Land Between the Lakes National Recreation Area. We've combined attractions in Grand Rivers, Cadiz, Benton, Eddyville, and other towns close to the lakes, since any would be within easy access if you're in the area.

 LAND BETWEEN THE LAKES NATIONAL RECREATION AREA (all ages)

 US 68/KY 80 between Kentucky Lake and Lake Barkley (access off I–24 through Grand Rivers); (800) LBL–7077. Open year-round; some attractions seasonal.

 Nature activities, an 1850s homestead, and the sheer wilderness feel of it all will make you want to return again and again to this 140,000-

acre outdoor playground flanked by Lake Barkley on the east and Kentucky Lake on the west. LBL extends into Tennessee, and it's about 40 miles from one end to the other.

There are over 200 miles of trails for hiking and biking (bike rentals available in summer), as well as sixteen lake access areas along the 300 miles of shoreline. Whether you come for a day or a week, you'll find something interesting to do. If entering from KY 453, stop at the North Welcome Station (open March through November from 9:00 A.M. to 5:00 P.M. daily); if entering from US 68, stop at the Golden Pond visitor center (open year-round from 9:00 A.M. to 5:00 P.M. daily) to get started. Special attractions include:

The Nature Station. Northern end of LBL, between Honker and Hematite Lakes. Open March through November. This is a very child-oriented center for viewing animals (the backyard exhibit includes owls, coyotes, and a red wolf). There are also guided nature hikes and numerous special events, from guided owl walks to a "Howl-o-Ween" celebration. Open daily from 9:00 A.M. to 5:00 P.M. April through October; open Wednesday to Sunday in March and November ($). You can rent canoes here summer through fall ($ per hour). (270) 924–2000.

Elk and Bison Prairie. Near the center of LBL, this is an auto path through a habitat restoration area that's home to buffalo and elk. We didn't see any elk, but we enjoyed looking. Open year-round, dawn to dusk daily. (270) 924–2000. $

Golden Pond Planetarium and Observatory. Just south of the elk and bison area at the Golden Pond Visitor Center. General astronomy shows in an eighty-one-seat planetarium, plus occasional outdoor "Star Parties." Open March through December. Several shows daily in summer. (800) 455–5897. $

The Homeplace 1850. South of Golden Pond (actually, just over the Tennessee line). We walked into the log house just as the family was sitting down to lunch. "Come on in and look around," the mother said (although we weren't invited to eat). Children love seeing the feather beds, the giant Percheron draft horses, and other animals when you drop in on an 1850s family as they go about their daily work and lives. Open March through November. Variety of special events include sheep shearing in the spring and harvest festivities in the fall. $

Hiking and Biking Trails. The trails range from ¾₀ mile to the 69-mile North/South Trail and come in all difficulty levels. Several easy trails start at the Nature Center. Pick up maps and information about where to rent bikes at the welcome centers.

Horseback Riding. If you don't bring your own horse, you can take a guided trail ride (ages six and up) or pony ride at J Bar J Riding Stables at Wranglers Campground. ($$$ trail ride; $ pony ride). Open Tuesday to Sunday April through October; November through March by reservation. (270) 832–6513.

Camping. There are several camping areas. A good option for families are the shelters offered at Piney and Wranglers campgrounds. These are one-room buildings with one double bed and one or three bunk beds, plus porch and electricity. Open March through November. (270) 924–2044. $

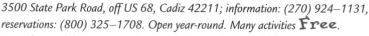

Amazing Kentucky Fact Kentucky's "big lakes" are actually big and bigger—Lake Barkley, is about 58,000 acres, and Kentucky Lake is about 160,000 acres. Kentucky Lake and Lake Barkley have more combined shoreline than Lake Superior.

LAKE BARKLEY STATE RESORT PARK (all ages)

3500 State Park Road, off US 68, Cadiz 42211; information: (270) 924–1131, reservations: (800) 325–1708. Open year-round. Many activities **Free**.

A beautiful post-and-beam lodge overlooks the lake at this popular state resort park. The park features indoor and outdoor pools, an eighteen-hole golf course, guided horseback rides (ages six and up), miniature golf, and tennis courts. Several trails begin near the lodge; despite the name, "Wilderness Trail" is probably the easiest. You can rent anything from a fishing boat to a big sightseeing pontoon at the marina.

BARKLEY DAM AND U.S. CORPS OF ENGINEERS VISITOR CENTER (all ages)

Dam located off KY 453 near Grand Rivers; Corps visitor center on US 62, northwest of the dam; (270) 362–4235. Open daily. **Free**.

It's fascinating to watch barges come through the locks at this 10,180-foot-long and 157-foot-high dam with locks. At the U.S. Corps of Engineers visitor center there are displays on the dam as well as about steamboat days on the Cumberland River.

KENTUCKY DAM VILLAGE STATE RESORT PARK (all ages)

Off US 62/641, near Gilbertsville 42044; information: (270) 362–4271, reservations: (800) 325–0146. Open year-round. Many activities Free.

Another waterside playground for day, weekend, and extended visits, Kentucky Dam Village offers picnic areas, marina with boat rental, swimming, trails, and an eighteen-hole golf course.

KENLAKE STATE RESORT PARK (all ages)

KY 94, south of US 68, between Aurora and Hardin (mailing address: 542 Kenlake Road, Hardin 42048); information: (270) 474–2211, reservations: (800) 325–0143. Open year-round; some activities seasonal. Many activities Free.

Located on the western shore of Kentucky Lake, this is the only state resort park with indoor tennis courts. The Tennis Center offers temperature-controlled courts and racquet rental for day visitors as well as overnight guests. Other park features are picnic areas, playgrounds, a nine-hole golf-course, and boat rentals.

PATTI'S 1880S RESTAURANT AND SETTLEMENT (all ages)

1793 J. H. O'Bryan Avenue, Grand Rivers 42045; (888) 736–2515, www.pattissettlement.com. Open daily from 10:30 A.M. to 8:00 P.M. $

If you haven't been here before and think you're just going out to eat, you may wonder where the restaurant is as you follow the path through the settlement, past the miniature golf course, playground, animal area, gardens, and shops. Eventually you get there and join the throngs waiting for a table. Read about the family who turned a twenty-seat burger joint (Hamburger Patti's) into an entertainment empire. Patti's has been featured in many national publications and is a must-see family stop for food and fun in the lake area. (And, hey, the food's even good—try the 2-inch pork chops and "mile-high" meringue pies. Years after we visited my daughter still talks about the flowerpot bread.)

VENTURE RIVER WATER PARK (all ages)

280 Park Place, Eddyville 42038 (I–24, exit 40 at Eddyville); (270) 388–7999. Open in summer Monday to Saturday from 10:00 A.M. to 7:00 P.M., Sunday from 11:00 A.M. to 7:00 P.M. $$$

As if 180,000 acres of lakes weren't enough water! But the big attraction here are the five big slides and the wave pool. There's a kiddie pool and other areas for little ones, plus floating pools for the less adventurous.

MAGGIE'S JUNGLE GOLF AND JUNGLE RUN (all ages)
US 641, near Gilbertsville. Open Memorial Day through Labor Day, Monday to Friday from 10:00 A.M. to 9:00 P.M., Saturday and Sunday from 10:00 A.M. to 10:00 P.M. Golf $, animal area $; $$ with cart.

Another lake-area classic, this mini-golf course features a large elephant statue and water stream, plus a camel, emu, and other creatures in the Jungle Run. You can walk it or rent an open-air Safari Car that seats two adults and three small children.

Lake Break Some nonwatery things to do:

- Visit the **Janice Mason Art Museum** in the old post office building at 71 Main Street in Cadiz; (270) 522–9056. Kid-friendly art space with changing local exhibits. Closed Wednesdays. Free.

- Hear some toe-tapping music in a family atmosphere at **Lakeland Jamboree,** 61 Jefferson Street, Cadiz; (270) 522–0086. Saturday nights at 7:00. $

- Explore local history at the **Lyon County Museum,** KY 730, Eddyville 42038 (270) 288–9986, includes a working model of an iron furnace and exhibits relating to the "Eddyville Castle" (Kentucky State Penitentiary). Open May 15 through October 15, Wednesday to Sunday from 1:00 to 4:00 P.M. and by appointment.

- Visit **Drury's Candyland,** 734 US 62, Lake City; (270) 362–8067. See how they've been making old-fashioned taffy, peanut brittle, and 150 other kinds of sweets for forty years.

- Hop over to Hardin (about 9 miles west of Aurora on Highway 80) and take a two-hour train excursion in 1940s Pullman cars (and a twelve-seater caboose) on the **Hardin Southern Railroad,** Railroad Avenue and Second Street, Hardin 42048; (270) 437–4555, www.hsrr. com. Runs Saturdays and Sundays Memorial Day through Labor Day, plus Santa excursions in December. $$

Where to Eat

Country Cupboard, *Highway 62 west, Eddyville 42038; (270) 388–5178.* Huge home cooking buffets for three meals daily, with dessert buffet. $

Countryside Family Restaurant, *1842 Canton Road, Cadiz 42211; (270) 522–5859.* Order from buffet or sandwiches and specials on regular menu. $

Kenlake State Resort Park, *KY 94, south of US 68, between Aurora and Hardin (mailing address: Hardin 42048); (270) 474–2211.* Lodge dining room with Kentucky favorites and children's menu. $

Kentucky Dam Village State Resort Park, *off US 62/641, near Gilbertsville 42044; (270) 362–4271.* Lodge dining room with varied menu, kids' menu. $

Lake Barkley State Resort Park, *3500 State Park Road, off US 68, Cadiz 42211; information: (270) 924–1131.* Lodge dining room features Kentucky specialties and children's menu. $

Patti's 1880s Settlement, *1793 J. H. O'Bryan Avenue, Grand Rivers 42045; (888) 736–2515 or www.pattis-settlement. com.* Pork chops, hamburgers, sandwiches, meringue pies, and flowerpot bread. $

Where to Stay

Kenlake State Resort Park, *KY 94, south of US 68, between Aurora and Hardin (mailing address: Hardin 42048); information: (270) 474–2211, reservations: (800) 325–0143.* Lodge rooms ($), one-bedroom cottages ($$), and two- and three-bedroom cottages ($$$–$$$$), plus seasonal campground (open April through October; $)

Kentucky Dam Village State Resort Park, *off US 62/641, near Gilbertsville 42044; information: (270) 362–4271, reservations: (800) 325–0146.* Lodge rooms ($–$$), one-bedroom cottages ($$), and two- and three-bedroom cottages and villas ($$$$), plus year-round campground with showers, laundry, and grocery ($).

Lake Barkley State Resort Park, *3500 State Park Road, off US 68, Cadiz 42211; information: (270) 924–1131, reservations: (800) 325–1708.* Lodge rooms ($–$$), lodge suites ($$$$), cottages ($$$$), and log cabins ($$$$), plus year-round campground with showers, laundry, and grocery ($).

For More Information

Cadiz/Trigg County Visitor Information Center, *Main Street (P.O. Box 735), Cadiz 42211; (270) 522–3892.*

Lyon County Tourist Commission, *P.O. Box 1030, Eddyville 42038; (800) 355–3885, www.lakebarkley.org.*

Grand Rivers Chamber of Commerce, *P.O. Box 181, Grand Rivers 42045; (888) 493–0152.*

Marshall County Tourist Commission, *P.O. Box 129, Gilbertsville 42022; (800) 467–7145.*

Murray

WRATHER–WESTERN KENTUCKY MUSEUM (ages 5 and up)

University Avenue (off Sixteenth Street), Murray State University Campus, Murray 42071; (270) 762–4771. Open Monday to Friday from 8:30 A.M. to 4:00 P.M., Saturday from 10:00 A.M. to 1:00 P.M. **Free**.

The soapbox derby cars and antique radio exhibit are highlights for children at this regional history museum. There are all kinds of cool things, from Civil War artifacts to old tools, nicely arranged.

PLAYHOUSE IN THE PARK (ages 6 and up)

Performances at Murray City Park, Gil Hopson Drive, Murray 42071; (270) 759–1752. Several productions annually; schedule varies. $$

This community theater group performs family-oriented musicals, comedies, and mysteries; call to see what's coming up.

*S***oapbox Speeders** Homemade soapbox race cars take over the streets of Murray in late May. The Soapbox Derby is part of the city's Freedom Fest activities. Area businesses sponsor cars, and there are heats for adults and children. The main action is on Main, Sixteenth, and Chestnut Streets. This is a preliminary to the International Soapbox Derby in Akron, Ohio. (800) 651–1603.

Where to Eat

15th and Olive Delicatessen, *216 North Fifteenth Street, Murray 42071; (270) 753–1551.* Near Murray State University campus, a great spot to pick up sandwiches and fresh baked goods for lunch or enjoy pasta and steaks for dinner. $$

Log Cabin Restaurant, *505 South Twelfth Street, Murray 42071; (270) 753–8080.* Country cooking and barbecue. $

Matt B's Pizza, *1411 Main Street, Murray 42071; (270) 759–1234.* Pizza and Italian favorites. $

Mayfield

 WEST KENTUCKY MUSEUM (ages 5 and up)
120 North Eighth Street, Mayfield 42066; (270) 247–6971. Open Tuesday to Friday from 10:00 A.M. to 4:30 P.M., Saturday from 10:00 A.M. to 1:00 P.M. Free.

A potpourri of items relating to local agriculture and industry, including the first General Tire ever made.

WOOLRIDGE MONUMENTS (all ages)

Maplewood Cemetery, Highway 45 and North Seventh Street. Open daily. Free.

This is just something that children and adults will find curious—eighteen sandstone and marble figures erected in the late 1890s by a man named Henry G. Wooldridge as his grave monument. Known as the "strange procession that never moves," it includes statues of Wooldridge on his famous horse, hounds, a fox, a deer, and various family members. Guess Mr. Wooldridge didn't want to face eternity alone!

Where to Eat

Carr's Barn, *216 West Broadway, Mayfield 42066; (270) 247–8959.* A tiny place (just sit on stools at the counter) with great barbecue. $$

Hill's Barbecue, *2001 Cuba Road, Mayfield 42066; (270) 247–9121.* Western Kentucky–style barbecue. $$

Hickman

 WARREN THOMAS BLACK HISTORY MUSEUM (ages 8 and up)
603 Moulton Avenue, Hickman 42050; (270) 236–2423. Open by appointment. Free.

Exhibits on local African-American history include a display about the Tuskeegee Airmen (a local man was a member). The museum building itself is the largest artifact; it was a church built in 1890 by former slaves, and pews still remain.

Clinton

COLUMBUS BELMONT STATE PARK (all ages)

350 Park Road, off KY 123, west of Clinton; (270) 677–2327. Open year-round; some activities and museum open April through October from 9:00 A.M. to 5:00 P.M. Many activities Free*; museum $.*

OK, if you were Confederate troops and your job was to stop Union boats from coming up the Mississippi River to Paducah and other cities, how would you do it? Bet nobody in your family came up with the idea of a giant chain across the river. Well, the Confederates did, and you can see part of the chain and its huge anchor, along with cannons and other Civil War artifacts, at this scenic riverside park. There are also earthen-wall fortifications that you can walk amid.

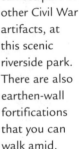

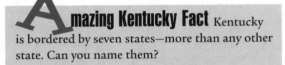

Amazing Kentucky Fact Kentucky is bordered by seven states—more than any other state. Can you name them?

(Missouri, Illinois, Indiana, Ohio, West Virginia, Virginia, Tennessee)

Your kids will love the anchor even if they aren't interested in Civil War history. And everybody will enjoy the miniature golf, play areas, and great view overlooking the river. There's a small museum of Civil War artifacts in a building used as a hospital during the conflict.

Wickliffe

WICKLIFFE MOUNDS RESEARCH CENTER AND ARCHAEOLOGICAL SITE (ages 6 and up)

94 Green Street (Hwy. 51/60/62 West), Wickliffe; (270) 335–3681. Open daily March 1 through November 30; closed weekends December through February. Hours are 9:30 A.M. to 4:30 P.M. $

If there are any budding archaeologists in the family, stop by this attraction southwest of Paducah. Not only will they get to see a real excavation site, but they'll also get words of encouragement from the on-site archaeologist. This is a preserved excavation of a 3,000-year-old mound village, with pottery and other artifacts on display and information about how early inhabitants lived. (The skeletal remains of adults and infants are replicas, by the way.) The gift shop includes some educational posters and materials as well as inexpensive reproductions of early pottery figures.

A Day Family Adventure

This is a little silly, but we did it accidentally (couldn't get off the highway before the bridge) and got a kick out of it once we realized what was going on. From Wickliffe Mounds, turn right onto Highway 51/60/62 combined and take the bridge across the river. Once across, bear left onto Highway 60/62 and cross another bridge. Turn around and come back. Congratulations! You've just visited three states—Kentucky, Illinois, and Missouri—in ten minutes!

Paducah

THE MARKET HOUSE MUSEUM (ages 5 and up)

121 Market House Square, Paducah 42002; (270) 443–7759. Open March through December, Tuesday to Saturday from 10:00 A.M. to 4:00 P.M. Closed January and February, and Monday and major holidays year-round. $; children 5 and under **Free**.

An entire 1870s drugstore, complete with glass counters, old patent medicine bottles, and elaborately carved Victorian woodwork, is housed within Paducah's 1905 market house building. Along with the drugstore items, there are all kinds of other curiosities—something for just about every interest, from history to fine glassware to folk art. Children will especially enjoy the 1913 LaFrance Fire Engine, the hand-carved statue of Henry Clay (once they learn it was carved by a twelve-year-old boy), and the Civil War spurs and sabers. (My son was also impressed by the huge punch bowl from the USS *Paducah*—it includes 700 ounces of silver.) The guides are very friendly and knowledgeable about local history. They also gave us a vivid accounting of the exciting annual Battle of Paducah Celebration in the city in late March, which involved lots of civilian Civil War reenactments around downtown as well as a battle reenactment.

PADUCAH WALL-TO-WALL (all ages)

100 Broadway, Paducah; (800) PADUCAH; Open daily year-round. **Free**.

Take time to stroll by these large, colorful murals recounting scenes from Paducah history. Paducah is located right on the river, and this is a decorative floodwall. (Plus it's a good stroll: There are more than thirty murals.) The murals were done by artist Robert Dafford (who also did the murals in Maysville in northern Kentucky) and capture scenes ranging from the Civil War Battle of Paducah to scenes from Paducah Summer Fest to a panel re-creating a 1948 Harley-Davidson magazine cover featuring local motorcycle riders posing with the statue of Chief Paduke that stands in the city's Noble Park. Cool.

 ### YEISER ART CENTER (ages 4 and up)
200 Broadway, Paducah 42001; (270) 442–2453. Open Tuesday through Saturday from 10:00 A.M. to 4:00 P.M. $

This fine arts museum, located at the other end of the Market House from the general history museum, features changing exhibits of fiber and other visual arts. It's a kid-friendly place that offers some quality educational programs for schools. (The education department was in the process of being revamped at press time, but ask if there are handouts or materials

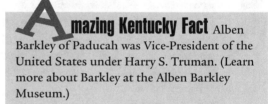

Amazing Kentucky Fact Alben Barkley of Paducah was Vice-President of the United States under Harry S. Truman. (Learn more about Barkley at the Alben Barkley Museum.)

your children might be able to use.) Older children will be interested in the annual exhibit of area student artwork.

 ### MARKET HOUSE THEATRE (ages 6 and up)
Performances at historic Market House Theatre, 132 Market House Square, Paducah 42001; (270) 444–6828 or (888) MHT–PLAY, www.mhtplay.com. Schedule varies; call or check Web site for current offerings. $$

In addition to its mainstage season, this theater company offers several Youth Theater productions each year.

 ### PADUCAH SYMPHONY ORCHESTRA (ages 6 and up)
Performances are at Tilghman Auditorium, 2500 Washington Street, Paducah 42003; (270) 444–0065 or (800) 738–3727. Concert dates vary. $$

Performances of interest to children include the Children's Chorus performances and annual Christmas concerts. At the March symphony performance, winners of the year's Young Artist Competition perform with the symphony.

RIVER HERITAGE MUSEUM (ages 5 and up)
117 South Water Street, Paducah 42001; (270) 575–9958. **Free***.*

Open but still in development, this museum shows the importance of the river to area history and commerce. Right now, the displays most interesting to children are the steamboat models. Older children will also be interested in the observation area of navigation simulation activities at the Seaman's Center for Maritime Education next door. The center trains riverboat captains.

NOBLE PARK (all ages)
Twenty-eighth Street and Park Avenue, Paducah; (800) PADUCAH. Open daily

year-round. **Free***.*

Take a picnic lunch to this 150-acre park and spend a morning or afternoon walking the nature trail, exploring the Civil War redoubt (small earthen fort), enjoying the playgrounds, or fishing in the small lake. Your

children will probably want to take a picture of the huge statue of Wacinton. This statue of a Chickasaw Indian was carved from a 56,000-pound red oak by Hungarian-born sculptor Peter Toth, who has carved and donated a giant sculpture to each state to honor Native Americans.

TILGHMAN HERITAGE CENTER AND CIVIL WAR INTERPRETIVE CENTER (ages 6 and up)
631 Kentucky Avenue, Paducah 42003; (270) 575–1870. Open Friday and Saturday from 10:00 A.M. to 4:00 P.M. or by appointment.

Children interested in the Civil War will enjoy seeing the artifacts and learning about the 1864 Battle of Paducah. (Don't be surprised if their favorite part is hearing how Confederate colonel A. P. Thompson was decapitated by a Union cannonball just 2 blocks from his home.) The museum is housed in the former home of Confederate general Lloyd Tilghman, who was killed at Vicksburg.

ALBEN W. BARKLEY MUSEUM (ages 7 and up)
533 Madison Street, Paducah; (207) 443–0512. Open April to September, Saturday and Sunday from 1:00 P.M. to 5:00 P.M. $

Learn about a Western Kentucky boy who grew up to be Vice-President. Alben W. Barkley was born near Mayfield, Kentucky, and started his political career as McCracken County attorney. He was a U.S. Senator when Harry S. Truman tapped him to be Vice-President. This museum, located in one of Paducah's oldest standing houses (built in 1852), includes photographs, clothing, furniture, and other memorabilia from Barkley's life.

PADUCAH RAILROAD MUSEUM (ages 6 and up)

300 South Third Street, Paducah; (270) 442–4032. Open Saturday from 10:00 A.M. to 4:00 P.M. **Free**.

Located in the upper floor of the old N.C. & St. L. freight offices, this museum features a model train, lanterns, and other local railroad exhibits. If your family is interested in trains, also drive down to Kentucky and South Water Streets near the river to take a peek at the restored Steam Locomotive No. 1518, the last "Iron Horse" owned by Illinois Central Railroad.

MUSEUM OF THE AMERICAN QUILTER'S SOCIETY (ages 8 and up)

215 Jefferson Street, Paducah 42001; (270) 442–8856, www.quiltmuseum. org. Open year-round Monday to Saturday from 10:00 A.M. to 5:00 P.M., Sunday from 1:00 to 5:00 P.M. $

This museum displays some incredible quilts, both traditional and contemporary designs, and sponsors a show every April that draws quilt enthusiasts from around the world. If you love quilts, ask your spouse to take the children for a walk along the nearby Riverwall Murals so you'll have time to fully take these in—only children with a serious interest in quilting or sewing will want to spend much time here. The museum's annual Arts Festival on the grounds in late October offers activities for all ages.

Sweets and Treats Treat the family to ice cream at **Alberti's**, 130 South Third Street, Paducah, located in a historic building. (270) 442-0055.

Kirchhoff's Bakery, at 118 South Second Street, Paducah, is a great place to pick up cookies, pastries, sandwiches and calzones. It's been in business since 1873. (270) 442-7117.

ANNIE'S HORSEDRAWN CARRIAGES (all ages)

Depart from Carriage Corner, Second and Broadway, Paducah. Adults $$, children $; short tour ($) also available.

The whole family will enjoy a horse-drawn carriage ride through Paducah's pretty downtown area.

After Dinner Fun

After Dinner Fun Every Saturday evening from early May through mid-October, downtown Paducah features outdoor entertainment (from music to strolling clowns) and activities for all ages. Shops stay open late, too, for After Dinner Downtown. (800) PADUCAH.

Where to Eat

C.C. Cohen, *103 Broadway, near Market House Square, Paducah 42001; (270) 442–6391.* Steaks, burgers, and sandwiches. Lunch $; dinner $$. Ask about the resident ghost!

Kirchhoff's Bakery and Deli, *118 South Second Street, Paducah 42001; (270) 442–7117.* Deli sandwiches and calzones. $

Max's Brick Oven Cafe, *112 Market House Square, Paducah 42001; (270)* *575–3472.* Casual dining in a restored building; outdoor dining area seasonally. Brick-oven pizza and pasta. $

The Pork Peddler, *Park Avenue at Eighth Street, Paducah 42001; (270) 442–7414.* Terrific barbecue and homemade desserts. $

Whaler's Catch, *123 North Second Street, Paducah 42001; (270) 444–7701.* Indoor-outdoor dining. Seafood is the specialty. $$

Where to Stay

Executive Inn Riverfront, *1 Executive Boulevard, Paducah 42001; (800) 866–3636 or (270) 443–8000, or www.jrs executiveinn.com.* Huge hotel complex (434 rooms) with its own shopping arcade, plus indoor pool and game room. Get a river view for a little extra, and watch boats and barges from your balcony. $$–$$$

Trinity Hills Farm Bed and Breakfast, *10455 Old Lovelaceville Road, Paducah 42001; (888) 488–3998.* A 17-acre farm 12 miles from Paducah. Children welcome in two-bedroom Grand Suite. $$$$

For More Information

Paducah/McCracken County Convention and Visitors Bureau, *128 Broadway, P. O. Box 890, Paducah 42002;* *(800) PADUCAH or www.paducah-tourism.org.*

ADay Family Adventure While you're traveling in Kentucky, just reading the map can be entertaining—there are so many unusual and funny place names. You may even find a town with your family name. My daughter and I happened upon Daysville during a trip to western Kentucky (on US 68 not far from Elkton). To be honest, there wasn't much to it, but I did enjoy snapping a picture of her in front of the sign to commemorate our day in Daysville. Interesting town names to look for on your map in western Kentucky: Hardmoney, Neosheo, and one of our favorites, Monkey's Eyebrow.

Marion

BEN E. CLEMENT MINERAL MUSEUM (ages 4 and up)

205 North Walker Street, Marion 42064; (270) 965–4263. Open Tuesday to Saturday from 10:00 A.M. to 3:00 P.M. $

Fluorite crystals discovered in local mines are the "rock stars" here—the museum has some 30,000 native mineral specimens and a cool blacklight area.

BOB WHEELER HISTORICAL MUSEUM (ages 4 and up)

222 West Carlisle Street, Marion 42064; (270) 965–9257. Open April through October, Tuesday to Saturday from 10:00 A.M. to 4:00 P.M. Free.

A huge 200-year-old loom and military artifacts are among the local history items on display in this 1880s cabin.

Amish Ways The Marion-area Amish community offers baked goods and other products for sale at shops and stands in the KY 91, US 60, and Ford's Ferry Road area.

For More Information

Crittenden County Chamber of Commerce, *113 Carlisle Street, Marion* *42064; (270) 965–5015 or (800) 755–0361.*

Morganfield

JAMES D. VEATCH CAMP BRECKINRIDGE MUSEUM AND ARTS CENTER (ages 7 and up)

1116 North Village Road, Morganfield 42437; (270) 389–4420. Open Tuesday to Friday from 10:00 A.M. to 3:00 P.M., Saturday from 10:00 A.M. to 4:00 P.M., and Sunday from 1:00 to 5:00 P.M. $

In addition to uniforms, medals, pictures, and other World War II artifacts, this former military camp officer's club building features some unusual sights that put a human face on the complex issues of war. Painted on the walls are beautiful murals of the Black Forest and other German scenes created by a German prisoner of war, Daniel Mayer, who was imprisoned here from 1943 until 1945. He painted the scenes from memory and from postcards sent by his wife. Mayer's own story has a sad ending: He died at Camp Breckinridge in 1945 and is one of four German prisoners of war buried at Fort Knox. The building also houses Unicorn Players, a community theater group that does several productions a year, some of which may be of interest to older children. (270) 389-9121.

Where to Eat

Brandon's Restaurant, *531 US Highway 60 E, Morganfield 42437; (270) 389–0500.* Home cooking. $

Feed Mill, *3541 US Highway 60E, Morganfield 42437; (270) 389–0047.* Cajun food. $

Henderson

JOHN JAMES AUDUBON STATE PARK (all ages)

3100 Highway 41N, Henderson 42419; (270) 826–2247. Open year-round. Many activities **Free***. Museum admission $.*

Children can climb into a giant bird's nest, learn how birds are able to fly, and see a red-tailed hawk up close at this nature center and art museum. Older visitors will enjoy the extensive collection of huge folio nature prints by the famous artist and exhibits about his work and his time in the Henderson area. From the viewing area you and your children can look through binoculars to spot live birds. More birds and wildflowers are among the things you'll see along the park's easy nature trails. You can rent a pedal boat or fish from the short at the small fishing lake (it's quiet—no motorized boats allowed). The park also includes tennis courts, a nine-hole golf course, picnic areas, and playgrounds.

RIVER WALK (all ages)

Atkinson Park, Riverfront off Merrit Drive, Henderson; (270) 827–0016. Open daily year-round. **Free**.

This 1-mile paved walking trail along the river features scenic overlooks and fountains.

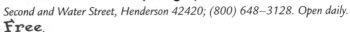

Hot Event Henderson's biggest event is the annual **W. C. Handy Blues and Barbecue Festival**, held mid-June in downtown Henderson. Honoring the "Father of the Blues," William Christopher Handy—who lived in Henderson around the turn of the century—this festival sponsored by the Henderson Music Preservation Society brings in great regional and national blues, zydeco, and gospel acts for **Free** concerts. In addition to the official Kentucky State Barbecue Championship, there are barbecue dinners and bake sales sponsored by local churches, plus an array of children's games and activities. (800) 648–3128, www.handyblues.org.

AUDUBON MILL PARK (all ages)

Second and Water Street, Henderson 42420; (800) 648–3128. Open daily. **Free**.

Another great riverfront park for family fun. Watch the boats dock, play or have a picnic, and see the millstone used when John James Audubon operated a grist mill at this site. Check the local calendar for special concerts and events.

HENDERSON FINE ARTS CENTER

Henderson Community College campus, 2660 South Green Street, Henderson 42420; (270) 850–5324. Various performances and ticket prices.

This 1,000-seat auditorium boasts a 4,000-square-foot stage with state-of-the-art light and sound systems. It's host to a variety of concerts and drama performances, some of which are appropriate for children.

Where to Eat

Downtown Diner, *122 First Street, Henderson 42420; (270) 827–9671. Breakfast and lunch, daily specials. $*

Ralph's Hickory Pit, *739 North Green Street, Henderson 42420; (270) 826–5656. Barbecue and daily specials. $*

Wolf's, *31 North Green Street, Henderson 42420; (270) 826–5221. Famous for its bean soup and open-faced Hot Brown sandwich. $*

Where to Stay

John James Audubon State Park, *3100 Highway 41N, Henderson 42419; (270) 826–2247. One- and two-bedroom cottages ($$–$$$$) and year-round camping with primitive and hookup sites, showers, laundry ($).*

Holiday Inn Express, *2826 Highway 41 North, Henderson 42420; (270) 869–0533. Indoor pool, free breakfast bar. $$*

Owensboro

 INTERNATIONAL BLUEGRASS MUSIC MUSEUM (all ages)
114 Daviess Street, Owensboro 42303; (270) 926–7891. Open Tuesday to Saturday from 10:00 A.M. to 5:00 P.M., Saturday and Sunday from 1:00 to 5:00 P.M. Adults $$, ages 7 to 16 $, children 6 and under Free.

Bluegrass music originated in Kentucky, and western Kentucky was the home of "the Father of Bluegrass Music," Bill Monroe. This museum, which reopened in April 2002 after extensive renovations, features exhibits on bluegrass, its roots and its stars. Kids will love the brightly colored giant lawn chairs in the exhibit areas during festivals.

 OWENSBORO MUSEUM OF SCIENCE AND HISTORY (all ages)
220 Daviess Street, Owensboro 42303; (270) 687–2732. Open Tuesday to Saturday from 10:00 A.M. to 5:00 P.M. and Sunday from 1:00 to 5:00 P.M. $, entire family admission $$.

From giant mammoth bones to real birds and reptiles, this museum lets children explore science and natural history. There's a special area for toddlers, plus an Encounter interactive area on the second floor. The newest exhibit is a NASCAR-auto race area, the "Speedzeum," with race cars and exhibits about NASCAR drivers from the Owensboro area such as Jeff Green.

SASSAFRAS TREE (all ages)

Corner of Frederica and Maple Avenues, Owensboro. **Free**.

This isn't just any old tree. According to the American Forestry Association, it's the *world's largest* sassafras tree—about 100 feet tall and 21 feet in diameter. And it is old—about 300 years.

 ### MOONLIGHT BAR-B-Q INN (all ages)

2840 West Parrish Avenue, Owensboro 42301; (270) 684–8143. Lunch and dinner buffets daily. $$

In much the same way that the sassafras tree is not just any old tree, this is not just any old restaurant. Moonlight is an internationally known institution of smoked meats, and as you dine at the buffet, you may find yourself elbow to elbow with visitors from around the world. It's also a great family success story. Several generations of the Bosley family work here, and since the 1960s, they have turned a little barbecue joint into a world-famous restaurant. (They've also made about eighteen additions to the building—this place is huge!) You can order off the menu, but most people go for the lavish buffet. A separate roomful of food, the buffet features ribs, beef, pork, chicken, and lamb, plus veggies and a salad bar.

 ### RIVERPARK CENTER (ages 6 and up)

101 Daviess Street, next to the Bluegrass Music Museum, Owensboro; information: (270) 687–2770, tickets: (270) 687–ARTS, www.riverparkcenter.org. Schedule and ticket prices vary.

This modern complex on the river reminds you that you're in Kentucky's third largest city. Check the schedules of concerts and theater for performances appropriate for families. The center hosts children's theater performances and sponsors a summer arts camp for kids.

 ### OWENSBORO SYMPHONY ORCHESTRA (ages 6 and up)

Performances at RiverPark Center; office at 122 East Eighteenth Street, Owensboro 42303; (270) 684–0661, www.owensborosymphony.org. Schedule and ticket prices vary.

This professional orchestra's season usually includes at least one family concert. Older children may also enjoy the pops concerts and occasional special concerts combining bluegrass and classical music. The Youth Orchestra, made up of local student musicians, gives concerts in November and April. The OSO has a great section on its Web site, OSO for Kids, that features information about instruments and music and includes puzzles and activities.

Owensboro in Bloom Late April and May are scenic times to visit Owensboro. A 25-block area around Griffith Avenue is called the "Dogwood Azalea Trail" for its beautiful spring blooms.

OWENSBORO MUSEUM OF FINE ART (ages 6 and up)

901 Frederica Street, Owensboro 42303; (270) 685–3181. Open Tuesday to Friday from 10:00 A.M. to 4:00 P.M., Saturday and Sunday from 1:00 to 4:00 P.M. Free.

This museum's diverse collection includes European and American art, an Atrium Sculpture Court, a collection of beautiful German stained glass, and even children's art (in the Young at Art gallery).

GOLDIE'S BEST LITTLE OPRYHOUSE IN KENTUCKY (ages 6 and up)

418 Frederica Street, Owensboro 42301; (270) 926–0254, www.goldiesopry house.com. Open Friday and Saturday at 8 P.M. year-round. Reservations recommended. $$

This place has been crankin' out good old bluegrass, country, and gospel sounds for family audiences for two decades. Its annual talent contest (eight weeks beginning in early September) offers a $1,000 prize (ages thirteen and older can enter, so start the kids practicing now so they'll be ready).

WESTERN KENTUCKY BOTANICAL GARDEN (all ages)

Thompson-Berry Complex, US 60N near Owensboro; (270) 993–1234. Open spring and summer daily from dawn to dusk, October daily from 10:00 A.M to 2:00 P.M. Free.

This ever-growing (no pun intended!) botanical garden is a good place for an education walk. Six of twenty-three planned gardens are complete, including the Fruit and Berry Garden, Herb Garden, Rose Garden, Daylily and Iris Garden, and the family favorite, the Children's Butterfly Garden. Numerous events and demonstrations are offered for children, from learning to ID trees to making a "pizza garden."

Natural Attractions Two good nature areas in the Owensboro area are

- **Panther Creek Park,** 5160 Wayne Bridge Road, off Highway 81, about 5 miles southwest of Owensboro. Picnic areas, six-acre lake, nature center, paved pathways with activities. Trail of Dreams leads to lookout tower. Interesting solar fountain. Facilities available. Nature center closes at dusk. (270) 281–5346.

- **Yellow Creek Park,** 5710 Highway 144, east of Owensboro. Easy to moderate hiking trails, playgrounds, picnic areas, and ball fields. Open daily year-round. (270) 281–5346.

Where to Eat

Briarpatch Restaurant, 2750 Veach Road, Owensboro 42301; (270) 685–3329. Home cooking and daily specials. $

Old Hickory Bar-B-Q, 338 Washington Avenue (Twenty-fifth and Frederica, Owensboro 42301; (270) 926–9000. Moonlight gets all the fame, but many locals think this restaurant also serves world-class barbecue. $

Where to Stay

Best Western Owensboro Inn, 3220 West Parrish, Owensboro 42301; (270) 685–2433. Outdoor pool, free continental breakfast, free cookies and popcorn. $$

Executive Inn Rivermont, One Executive Boulevard, Owensboro 42301; (270) 926–8000. High-rise near the River-Center. Indoor and outdoor swimming pools, game room. $$–$$$$

Sleep Inn, 51 Bon Harbor Hills Drive, Owensboro 42301; (270) 691–6200. Newer hotel with indoor pool and complimentary continental breakfast. $$

Windy Hollow Campground and Recreation Center, 5141 Windy Hollow Road, Owensboro 42301; (270) 785–4150. Open April through October. Tent and hookup camping, with fishing, beach, miniature golf, picnic areas (many area residents come here as a day destination).

For More Information

Owensboro Visitor Information Center, 215 East Second Street, Owensboro 42303; (800) 489–1131 or (270) 926–1100, www.visitowensboro.com.

Annual Events

Visit with the Eagles Weekend, late January, Gilbertsville; (270) 362-0146

Trigg County Civil War Days, mid-March, Cadiz; (270) 552-6167

Last Chance Eagle Viewing, late March, Land Between the Lakes; (800) LBL-7077

Battle of Paducah Celebration, late March, Paducah; (800) PADUCAH

Dogwood Trail Celebration, mid-April, Paducah; (800) PADUCAH

Benton Tater Days, late March, early April, Benton; (270) 527-3128

International Bar-B-Que Festival, early May, Owensboro; (800) 489-1131

W. C. Handy Blues and Barbecue Festival, mid-June, Henderson; (800) 648-3128

McCracken County Fair, late June, Paducah; (800) PADUCAH

Henderson County Fair, mid-July, Henderson; (800) 648-3128

Children's Nature Fest, Woodlands Nature Center, Land Between the Lakes; (800) LBL-7077

Paducah Summer Festival, late July, Paducah; (800) PADUCAH

Western Kentucky State Fair, early August, Hopkinsville; (270) 885-5237

Bluegrass in the Park, mid-August, Henderson; (800) 648-3128

Kenlake Hot August Blues Festival, late August, Aurora; (800) 325-0143

Labor Day Celebration, Labor Day weekend, Paducah; (800) PADUCAH

Trail of Tears Intertribal Powwow, early September, Hopkinsville; (270) 886-8033

Hopkinsville Salutes Fort Campbell Week, early September, Hopkinsville; (270) 885-1499

Western Kentucky Highland Festival, mid-September, Paducah; (800) PADUCAH

Kentucky Celtic Festival, late September, Hopkinsville; (800) 842-9959

Barbecue on the River and Old Market Days, late September, Paducah; (800) PADUCAH

Arts in Action Festival, early October, Paducah; (800) PADUCAH

Shaker Farm Day, early October, South Union; (800) 811-8379

Trigg County Ham Festival, early October, Cadiz; (270) 522-3892

D

About the Author

A nearly lifelong Kentuckian, Teresa Day writes scripts for educational television programs and documentary videos. She began her writing career as a feature writer and newspaper editor. Previous travel credits include editing three editions of the Globe Pequot guidebook *Kentucky Off the Beaten Path*. Teresa lives near Georgetown, Kentucky, with her husband, Charlie, and their three children.